WRITING WITH PASSION

The Ponds

Every year
the lilies
are so perfect
I can hardly believe

their lapped light crowding
the black,
mid-summer ponds.
Nobody could count all of them—

the muskrats swimming
among the pads and the grasses
can reach out
their muscular arms and touch

only so many, they are that
rife and wild.
But what in this world
is perfect?

I bend closer and see
how this one is clearly lopsided—
and that one wears an orange blight—
and this one is a glossy cheek

half nibbled away—
and that one is a slumped purse
full of its own
unstoppable decay.

Still, what I want in my life
is to be willing
to be dazzled—
to cast aside the weight of facts

and maybe even
to float a little
above this difficult world.
I want to believe I am looking

into the white fire of a great mystery.
I want to believe that the imperfections are nothing—
that the light is everything—that it is more than the sum
of each flawed blossom rising and fading. And I do.

Mary Oliver

WRITING WITH PASSION

Life Stories, Multiple Genres

TOM ROMANO
Miami University

Boynton/Cook
HEINEMANN
Portsmouth, New Hampshire

Boynton/Cook Publishers
A subsidiary of Reed Elsevier Inc.
361 Hanover Street
Portsmouth, NH 03801-3912

Offices and agents throughout the world

Library of Congress Cataloging-in-Publication Data

Romano, Tom.
    Writing with passion : life stories, multiple genres / Tom Romano.
      p. cm.
    Includes bibliographical references.
    ISBN 0-86709-362-5
    1. English language—Rhetoric—Study and teaching. 2. English language—Rhetoric—Psychological aspects. 3. Interdisciplinary approach in education. 4. Autobiography—Authorship. 5. Report writing. I. Title.
    PE1404.R64   1995
    428'.007—dc20   95-8647
                                    CIP

Acquisitions Editor: Toby Gordon
Copy Editor: Alan Huisman
Production Editor: Renée M. Nicholls
Interior Designer: Joni Doherty
Cover Designer: Judy Arisman

Front Cover Photo Subjects (l. to r.): Felice Romano, Giuseppe Romano, and Antonio Romano

Printed in the United States of America on acid-free paper
99 98   DO   3 4 5 6

*F*or

MARK HAYES
who understands workmanlike
progress

JOHN GAUGHAN
who knows where the expressivists
and the socially constructed
meet

DON MURRAY
who has made so many things
possible

PHILIP ROMANO (1905–1964)
who came to America in 1914 and
made his way ❧

CONTENTS

PROLOG ix

Chapter One. 1
TRUTH THROUGH NARRATIVE

JENNIFER. 13

Chapter Two 14
TRUTH, RISK, AND PASSION

THINE, WINE, AND PINE. 27

Chapter Three. 30
FAITH AND FEARLESSNESS

WHY, INDEED. 54

Chapter Four 55
FURTHER WAYS OF KNOWING:
DIALOG, POETRY, AND SONG

FIRST DAY OF SCHOOL 73

Chapter Five. 74
BREAKING THE RULES IN STYLE

BEYOND BOUNDARIES. 91

Chapter Six 93
EVOLVING VOICE THROUGH THE ALTERNATE STYLE

CLEARING THE WAY 105

Chapter Seven 109
THE MULTIGENRE RESEARCH PAPER:
MELDING FACT, INTERPRETATION, AND IMAGINATION

THE SILENCE OF LOSS 131

Chapter Eight 133
PROBLEMS, ISSUES, DILEMMAS OF
THE MULTIGENRE RESEARCH PAPER

RELATIONSHIPS WITH LITERATURE 148

Chapter Nine 154
READING FOR THE REAL WORLD

AN *I* ONLY WITH OTHERS 173

Chapter Ten 174
AN ALLY IN OTHERS

DIANE 188

Chapter Eleven 190
BLISSFULLY LOST IN LITERACY

EPILOG 199

APPENDIX A 207
"Decision" by Robin Back Fakes

APPENDIX B 213
"Masquerade" by Jennifer Steele Christensen

APPENDIX C 217
"The Wooden Pony" by Mariana Romano

APPENDIX D 221
"My Quest" by Mariana Romano

APPENDIX E 225
Birth Certificate of Felice Romano

WORKS CITED 227

ACKNOWLEDGMENTS 233

CREDITS 237

PROLOG

I AM OF OLD AND YOUNG, OF THE FOOLISH AS
    MUCH AS THE WISE,
REGARDLESS OF OTHERS, EVER REGARDFUL OF
    OTHERS,
MATERNAL AS WELL AS PATERNAL, A CHILD AS
    WELL AS A MAN,
STUFF'D WITH THE STUFF THAT IS COARSE AND
    STUFF'D WITH THE STUFF THAT
    IS FINE.

Walt Whitman

*S*ince I wrote my first book, *Clearing the Way*, much has happened: so much teaching, learning, reading, and writing. I taught two more good years at Edgewood High School in Trenton, Ohio. I wrote articles, stories, and poems. I went back to graduate school at the University of New Hampshire—after quitting four years earlier—and earned a doctorate in reading and writing instruction. I wrote a young adult novel and a dissertation, both of which have gone unpublished. I accepted a teaching job at Utah State University, where one quarter I supervise student teachers and the other two teach courses in writing and English methods.

    Writing with Passion evolves from those experiences and more. Its subtitle is *Life Stories, Multiple Genres*. Let me explain. I have long been interested in telling stories. My primary way of knowing the world comes through narrative thinking, through fragmented tableaus, images in motion, and interconnected, often ironic, events.

    Writing with Passion embodies my interest in stories, particularly those from our lives. Although a large part of the text is exposition—me hopped up about something, seeking to persuade you to look at reading, writing, teaching, and learning as I do—another substantial portion consists of stories. They are woven through my arguments, persuasion, and analysis. Stories teach me abstractions, help me explain what I mean, provide flesh and specificity to concepts.

Each chapter of *Writing with Passion* (other than the first) is preceded by an interchapter—often a story of one kind or another. The interchapter is a prelude to the chapter that follows. It sets the tone, provides pertinent information, and sometimes contains examples I later refer to. Although the interchapters foreground some of the meaning conveyed in their companion chapters, I also intend each interchapter to stand alone, to work as an entity in itself, *implicitly* making meaning I hope is unmistakable.

All through the book you'll read my personal stories—of teaching, surely, but also of my experience as a reader, writer, and learner, as a father, son, and friend. Literacy is one with my life, not apart from it, not an adjunct. The way I am literate today is because of things that have happened. Events and relationships shape my life; they are responsible for who and why and what and how I teach, read, write, and learn. My father—one of the people to whom I dedicate this book—figures throughout the text. His death when I was fifteen left an indelible mark on me. His name was Felice. In the cover photograph circa 1915—probably taken just after the family arrived in America—he stands on the left. Beside him are his older brother, Giuseppe, and younger brother, Antonio. A younger sister, Filomena, is not pictured. These four children were born in Italy. Five more children were born in America. I've included Felice's birth certificate in Appendix E.

I hadn't taught too many years before an observer in my classroom remarked about the passion I exhibited, the excitement I generated about reading, writing, and learning. This was news to me. I was merely working hard to bring all of myself to teaching English without pretense and without, I admit, much decorum.

Passion, yes—that's at the core of my living and my literacy. As soon as that observer mentioned the word, I knew that passion was my strength. I feel deeply about things—reading and writing, courage and empathy, death and sensuality, relatives, teaching, and friends, people expressing in fiction, nonfiction, poetry, drama, and film some private, universal feeling we know in our bones, some idea or circumstance that heightens our consciousness. I become passionate about what moves me. Sometimes I am moved and delighted, sometimes sobered, sometimes outraged, sometimes touched, sometimes sorrowed. Often I am surprised. My eyes blink open at what I hadn't imagined.

Maybe this passion is what has made me so in tune with Walt Whitman. I didn't know that such a person had walked the earth until I was nineteen years old and encountered "Song of Myself" in an American Literature survey class at Miami University. I resonated to Whitman's language and vision—the importance of our sensuous experience, the worthiness and equality of all humanity—of all living things—the idea of continuance amid life and death: "All goes onward and outward," Whitman wrote. "Nothing collapses."

At nineteen I needed to hear that. My father had been killed less than four years earlier. Through Whitman I came to a spirituality that made sense. His words have sustained me for more than twenty-five years now. So I honor dear Walt with a quotation from *Leaves of Grass* at the beginning of each chapter of *Writing with Passion*.

You may have noticed that the back cover of this book features a photograph of me and a young woman in her early twenties. That young woman is my daughter, Mariana. She appears all through *Writing with Passion*: a short story, essay, and letter she wrote, accounts of my interaction with her over the years, her conversations with me, her influence everywhere. She has hastened my seeing. She was an important child in my life and is now an important adult.

I dedicate this book to four men. My first book is dedicated to three women: my daughter, my wife, and my mother. Women have been vital to my emotional and physical happiness, professional fulfillment, and intellectual growth. Most of the friends I've made through English education have been women. Two thirds of the students whose writing appears in this book are women. When I began to contact former students to ask for permission to publish their writing, I discovered that women can disappear. They marry, assume their husbands' last names, forgo their own, relocate. Friends and family move. Suddenly phone books and long-distance information don't help.

Through networks of friends and former students, and finally through newspaper personal ads, I was able to contact each of my female former students. In tribute to who they were as well as who they have become—and with their consent—I've listed both their married and original last names after their writing. No one should disappear. It should be a law.

Four chapters of *Writing with Passion* explain and discuss the "alternate style" and the "multigenre research paper," two big ideas for me and my students during the last eight years. The alternate style asks students to purposefully break standard rules of written English as a way of communicating powerfully. The multigenre research paper asks students to research a topic well and then to report what they know by composing a paper that combines many genres—poetry, stories, songs, exposition, news writing, dialog, what have you. The hard part—and the most satisfying—is getting such a multigenre paper to hang together as a unified whole.

As in my first book, students' voices are the heart of this one. And since *Writing with Passion* comes out of my teaching experience both in high school and college, the students' voices I've chosen reflect a wide range of maturity, development, and education. At one end of the continuum is Cal, fifteen years old and experiencing a writing workshop for the first time as a midyear transfer student. At the other end is Linda, a middle-aged teacher at a community college. Between them are Tari, Mark, Aimee, Ted, Jennifer, Jayne . . . so many distinctive voices. I'm happy I met them all and thankful they've given me permission to publish their writing.

By way of invitation, I'll quote Whitman again, exclamation points and all:

Allons! whoever you are come travel with me!
Traveling with me you find what never tires.

Chapter One

Truth Through Narrative

Logic and sermons never convince,
The damp of the night drives deeper into
my soul.

Walt Whitman

W e sat around the kitchen table at my aunt and uncle's house on a Saturday morning. Aunt Filimon had set out a bottle of homemade white wine and a plate of biscotti. A tape recorder stood ready. My daughter, Mariana, ten years old, sat in a straight-backed chair, alert and eager, on her lap a notepad filled with questions about Italian food, weather, education, and customs.

We had made this visit so Mariana could gather information for her social studies "country report." She had chosen to investigate Italy. From the day she announced her topic, she knew where she could get colorful, firsthand information: from her eighty-six-year-old great-uncle, Luigi Chiavari, the old man with a head of thick white hair, a large hooked nose, a lush garden, and a penchant for romping on the floor with toddlers. Three generations knew him as Uncle Gigi. He had been born in Caprarola, near Rome, in 1895 and had emigrated in 1913 to work in the brickyards of northeastern Ohio.

Uncle Gigi leaned forward in his chair. Mariana pressed *record*. As she began her first question, the tiny door of the clock on the wall flipped open; out shot a strident miniature cuckoo.

Uncle Gigi wheeled around in his chair. "Cuckoo yourself!" he said. "Every damn day, 'Cuckoo, cuckoo.' What the hell's a matter with you?"

We all laughed. The interview began on just the right note. The cuckoo's 9:00 A.M. announcement marked a wonderful, rambling conversation with Uncle Gigi featuring his thick Italian accent, animated face, and ceaseless humor that had won over scores of nieces, nephews, and grandchildren. When Mariana ran out of questions, I got into the conversation with some of my own. I asked Uncle Gigi what had made him come to the United States:

> A man I work with once ask me three, four times the same thing you ask me. He say, "Gigi, what make you come to this country?"
>
> I say, "Wait a minute. You ain't red in the face."
>
> He say, "What do you mean?"
>
> I say, "You're not an Indian. What make you people come to this country?"
>
> He say, "My daddy was born here."
>
> "Oh, your daddy was born here? How 'bout your grandpa?"
>
> "Oh, I don't know, he come 'cross."
>
> "Same thing I come 'cross," I say. "You make a better living, a better home, a better life."

To help us understand his reasons for coming to the United States nearly seventy years earlier, Uncle Gigi told a story, one he'd told countless times since 1913. It contained characters, dialog, a distinctive narrative voice, suspense, tension, and resolution. He re-created a lived-through experience that had enabled him to understand why he had left his mother, father, and brothers in Caprarola. The narrative revealed his knowledge of the settlement of America, his resentment of Americans who conveniently forgot their old-country roots, and the slight umbrage he took at being reminded that he was an immigrant—after all, he had citizenship papers and had lived in the United States sixty-eight years. No matter how thick his accent, he was American.

Uncle Gigi had analyzed his actions, too. He knew why he had "come 'cross" the Atlantic Ocean: to "make a better living, a better home, a better life." That last line was all he had needed to say to answer my question. But jumping to an analytical answer was not Uncle Gigi's style, not his primary way of knowing. Story was. Through story he saw and communicated. Through story he entertained himself and his listeners. Uncle Gigi lived particular stories again and again if he needed to. That's how he came to understand their significance.

"By telling stories," writes Tim O'Brien in *The Things They Carried*, "you objectify your own experience. You separate it from yourself" (179).

A maxim writing teachers have been fond of for years holds true: how can I know what I think until I see what I say? And I would add this: how can I know *what I think about what I think* until I tell a story about it?

In universities and a great many secondary schools, teachers must battle to make a place for story. Narrative thinking—*rendering* experience as opposed to explaining it, abstracting it, or summing it up—is an orphan child in academia. In *What Is English?* Peter Elbow laments that one of the ruling assumptions of our profession has been that "expository writing that explains and argues is more important and more mature than narrative or imaginative writing that renders experience" (189).

This assumption, this stranglehold, really, that exposition exerts on the way writing is used in every subject area has tyrannized students and narrowly defined the nature of acceptable academic writing. Many teachers view nonexpository writing as frivolous and softheaded. "Real" writing, they maintain, is cognitively rigorous. "Real" writing emphasizes analysis and argumentation. That cuddly kind of writing—often pejoratively referred to as "creative" writing—might be suitable for clever flights of fancy in some English classes, but it is *not* suitable for serious thinking in academic subjects.

When I taught creative writing in high school, one guidance counselor sent me two kinds of students: the linguistically gifted and the academically alienated. "In creative writing," I heard him say once, "you can write anything. *Anything.*" In creative writing the linguistically gifted could do what the counselor was never comfortable doing—write poems, stories, and dramatic dialogs. And the academically alienated would be sure to pass the class as long as they wrote something. "After all," he said, "how can you grade creativity?"

In the minds of many, creative writing equals no discipline, no rigor, no craft, no skills, no thinking. Just spewing, gushing, spilling, and, if the writing works in some surprising way, mere cleverness. Nothing of depth, nothing of substance, nothing of weight.

In that high school creative writing class we did pour forth language, using it to explore inner and outer worlds. We cultivated a writerly stance of boldly launching a line of language. We worked hard to objectify experience, to dramatize scenes and characters, not just explain or describe them. We sought truths about what we experienced and what we imagined. We tried to avoid stereotypes and clichés. And students *could* write "anything." They could roam over any of their world: loves, hates, complaints, powerful memories of angels that danced at the heart of happiness and demons that hid in the shadows of regret. It wasn't long before I changed the name of the course from Creative Writing to simply Writing I.

"Discourse that renders is also thinking," writes Elbow. "It is nonanalytic, nondiscursive, nonlogical, but it is thinking or cognitive nevertheless—however heavy an affective load it carries" (1990, 191).

Part of me applauds when I read that. Another part bristles. I have no argument with "discourse that renders is also thinking." I believe that. But I further believe that discourse that renders can be analytic and logical, too, just as expository essays can. Moreover, writing that renders can be pointed and compelling. It can, as Whitman tells us, drive deep into the soul, like the damp of night.

Consider the following piece of fiction by a high school senior:

FIRST DAY

I felt myself being moved along in the mass. I frantically checked my schedule: Room 315. I wondered where it was. I bumped into a tall nice-looking boy.

"Uh, where's room 315?" I tried to sound nonchalant.

"Go back down the hall and it's the last door."

I backtracked, thinking how sweet and cute that boy was. I found the door. Room 111.

My face felt hot as I started back the other way. I was halfway down the 300 hall when the bell rang. I skidded to a halt at the door and tried to compose myself. Opening the door, I walked in. Thirty faces looked up.

"You're late," the teacher announced.

"Uh, I couldn't find the room," I mumbled. I heard a few snickers and felt myself shrinking so I sat down in the nearest chair.

"What's your name? No, never mind. What's your student number?"

I looked down at my schedule taped to my folder.

"000274."

"What was that?"

"000274," I said a little louder. Stuttering on the 0's, I shrank two more inches.

"What are you?"

I couldn't understand this question and looked up beseechingly.

"Sophomore, senior, what?"

"Uh, f-freshman." I lost five more inches.

"Well, you'll have to go over there. You're in the senior group."

I shrank over to the far table, climbed into a chair, and disappeared.

Julie Taylor Sandlin, Senior, Edgewood High School

Julie demonstrates her understanding of a complex societal system, one organized for efficiency but insensitive to human needs. To convey her understanding, she had to analyze her world then argue persuasively, through fiction, that her conception was valid. Nonanalytic? Nonlogical? Give me a room full of such nonanalytic, nonlogical students.

The mode of Julie's discourse, however, is not expository. It is not like my previous paragraph, in which I explain what I see Julie doing and suggest with one-word rhetorical questions the absurdity of maintaining that the story does not demonstrate first-rate cognition. "First Day" is narrative. It renders emotional experience. It is logical in its ordering of events and in its satisfying, vanishing denouement. Julie used analytical skills, even though she didn't write a discursive essay that analyzes the dehumanizing nature of the monolithic public school system. In addition to being logical and analytic, "First Day" is also dramatic, metaphorical, lively with active verbs, respectful of a reader's ability to make meaning, and poignant.

ANALYSIS AND SYNTHESIS: EVER THE TWAIN SHALL MEET

Why this dichotomy between *analysis*, breaking something down into its parts and making clear distinctions among them, and *synthesis*, what David Johnson defines as "connecting parts into wholes, . . . relating wholes to other wholes and discovering overall unity" (1990, 1)? Analysis and synthesis might seem opposite operations, but they are not mutually exclusive. Analysis and synthesis complement each other.

When I write a poem or a story—when I am synthesizing, some would say—I do a lot of analysis in the process. I pay fierce attention to the words I choose, the images I conjure, the sounds I create. I weigh. I compare. I evaluate both my sentences and my sense. I do this even as I am drafting and trying not to be too hard on myself so I can get plenty of language on the page. My ongoing analysis leads to more synthesis. Analysis helps me generate new images, connections, and echoes of language.

When I write an article or book review, however—when I am primarily concerned with analyzing, some would say—I also do a lot of synthesizing. I work hard to forge ideas into a fluid whole that carries readers inevitably along. I try to connect what I know to what other writers in the field have written. And I hope to strike on rhythmical language, indelible images, and vivid narrative examples as well as convincing lines of argument. Synthesis enables me to report my analysis.

Indeed, synthesis often *leads* to analysis. I see such movement at work in my students when they first start to write fiction. They often write unbroken fictional dreams with no exposition or authorial interpretation—until the last paragraph. At that point, the expository-thinking gears grind into action. After rendering imagined experience for pages, they tack on an analytical paragraph explaining the meaning of what they've written. Doing so is irresistible. They are like Uncle Gigi telling why he immigrated to America. The experience of telling the story—living through it, objectifying it—teaches these novice fiction writers what their fiction means. I know from writing fiction myself that composing that final, unnecessary paragraph is a joyous moment for students. The characters, images, and plot have coalesced in their minds. Their story, they see, has unity and meaning. It adds up. And they write the sum down. That final expository paragraph, of course, ruins the fiction.

I see no dichotomy between analysis and synthesis. They are Fred and Ginger. Poncho and Cisco. Thelma and Louise. Yin and yang. Neither is as effective separately as it is when partnered with the other. Good writing, regardless of the mode of discourse, causes writers to think. That thinking involves a productive dialectic between analysis and synthesis.

RENDERING EXPERIENCE FOR ITS OWN SAKE

I've argued that writing that renders experience can be analytical and logical. Julie's "First Day" surely demonstrates that. But suppose the writing that renders is not so explicit about the analysis and logic at work—what then? In such cases is writing that renders of less import, value, sophistication?

It is "deeply practical," writes Elbow, "to teach students to write discourse that gives others a sense of their experience—or, indeed, that gives them back a sense of their own experience with a little perspective" (1990, 192).

Writing that renders experience is valid and useful in its own right. Modes of writing that render help us understand both past and imagined experience. They help us look closely and see life more specifically. Following a thread of narrative, for example, enables us to call up detail we have forgotten.

Let's look at another example of rendering, one in which the analysis and point are not so obvious as they are in "First Day." Below is a narrative written by Jayne, a high school senior, nearly a year after her parents died in the Beverly Hills Supper Club fire in Southgate, Kentucky:

HUNTING

I opened the front door to a middle-aged man. His hair, thin on top, was graying around his temples and sideburns. His stubble of a few days was gray, also. He wore a soiled T-shirt under a faded gray flannel shirt. His gut bulged through the material, making it impossible to button. His baggy pants were buckled way below his beer belly. He shifted his weight as he began to talk.

He told me he had known my father for a long time. Dad had told him to come hunting. Then he lowered his head and said something almost inaudible about the fire.

"Yeah, that's right. Dad was in the fire," I said, trying to ease his discomfort.

"I didn't know. They told me he was, but I didn't know if they were joking or not."

I shook my head yes. This time my eyes dodged his.

"I don't want ya to get upset, ma'am, but he was a helluva man."

No pain, no feeling at all.

"I work for the county," he went on. "That's how I got to know your father. You had to get up early to beat him."

"I know." I proudly smiled at the man.

"He just was a helluva man. Excuse my bad language. Well, it's not really bad. But he was just a nice guy. I don't want to upset you, now."

"Oh, you're not. It's OK."

He kept turning toward his truck in the driveway as he talked. "Well, me and the boys just thought we'd come hunting. We probably won't get nothing but we wanted to let ya know we're hunting."

He started backing away, and he stopped for a moment, searching for something to say. I watched. He shifted his weight again but found no suitable words. Then he uttered a good-bye, turned, and slowly walked to his truck.

Jayne Koontz Prushing, Senior, Edgewood High School

An important piece of writing for Jayne. She dramatizes a significant moment in her world. She objectifies her experience. Writing this scene enabled her to see the stranger's awkwardness as greater than her own. And thus she could measure the degree of her recovery from irrevocable loss.

As a reader I get a strong sense of Jayne's experience. I come to understand her process of recovery, the chance meetings that can help heal us.

It is easy for me to empathize with Jayne. My father, too, died a senseless death when I was a teenager. I remember the awkwardness and throat-tightening tension I felt when anyone mentioned his name. I remember my own hunt for succor in a world suddenly chaotic and unforgiving.

USING STORY TO SYNTHESIZE AND EMBED LEARNING

Although I want there always to be room in academia for expository modes of writing, I want equal room made at all levels of school for writing that renders experience. On more occasions than we might admit, students can use story to deepen and communicate their learning.

By creating fictional dreams peopled with fully realized characters driven by tension amid enough detail of setting to create atmosphere, students can create truths that show what they know. In *The Grapes of Wrath* Steinbeck created truths about the effects of the Depression on Oklahomans fleeing poverty and encountering capitalism at its worst. Octavia Butler created truths in *Kindred* about the effects of oppression on African American slaves and their Caucasian owners in Maryland in the early nineteenth century. Students, too, can go beyond explaining concepts, conditions, and strategies, can go beyond exposition. As Julie did in "First Day," students can render experience with such detail that readers don't merely understand their meaning. They live it.

My most compelling encounter with story as a way of knowing and communicating involved my daughter during her senior year of high school. Late one evening Mariana stepped into the room where I sat writing.

"Will you listen to my story?" she asked.

I turned my head to her but kept my fingers at the keyboard. I was pursuing a hot topic and the deadline was near. Mariana wore sweats. Her blonde hair was clipped back from her forehead. Her contact lenses were soaking in a heat sterilizer for the night. Her glasses had slid halfway down her nose; she pushed them into place with a forefinger. She looked weary. Track practice had been longer than usual.

Mariana held a dozen ragged-edged sheets of the notebook paper she liked to write on with soft-leaded pencils. I knew those pages were the draft of her final paper for senior English. She had been thinking about this assignment for months, researching here and there, gathering information and impressions, asking me questions about my family. Since a late supper of microwaved leftovers, she had been lying on her bed, filling pages of a notebook with her looping handwriting.

Mariana's English teacher had asked students to research a particular year and then—instead of composing a traditional research paper—to write a short piece of fiction that incorporated details from their research. They would do just what novelists like E. L. Doctorow, Barbara Kingsolver, and Michael Ondaatje did. As she had done since grade school whenever confronted with a major project, Mariana had made the assignment her own, had chosen to research Ellis Island and 1914, the year my father, then a boy of nine, immigrated to the United States from Italy.

Mariana dropped to the floor and sat cross-legged to read me her story. I removed my fingers from the keyboard and swiveled to face her. She began reading, turning the pages sideways at times to read words written in the margins, looking closely other times to make out words squeezed between lines.

"Felice felt he was drowning in the ocean of people," she read. "He closed his eyes and tried to breathe. He could feel the small wooden pony against his heart and remembered Luca. Tears welled in his eyes but he swallowed them this time. Giuseppe would call him *bambino* again and hit him. Felice wanted to be strong too, and he wanted to be able to stand up to Papa like Giuseppe said he was going to."

Elbows on my knees, chin resting in my hands, I gazed down at my daughter, then let my eyelids close. I entered the fictional dream Mariana had woven of my father, his two brothers, sister, and mother as they shuffled along in a crowd, moving off the ship that had brought them across the Atlantic Ocean. Filomena, the youngest child, slept in her mother's arms. Antonio, the youngest boy, whimpered and held his mother's skirt with both hands. Giuseppe, the oldest child, carried himself bravely, almost disdainfully, as he moved toward American soil. Felice, my father, was between his brothers, but closer to Antonio's tears than Giuseppe's defiance. The wooden pony Felice kept in his shirt pocket had been carved and given to him by his friend Luca before the family left their village near Naples.

In her short story Mariana explored a mystery she'd been aware of for years—the great influence on our lives of my father, he dead then twenty-five years, the mythlike story of his family's immigration to an America decades away from designer jeans, fast-food restaurants, and alternative rock music. She conjectured in her fiction, too, inventing detail, action, and characterizations that had not been documented in family stories but that carried the illusion of reality nevertheless.

Mariana's research in books had not been extensive. A half-dozen times, however, she had watched the opening of a cinematic story—the scenes in Francis Ford Coppola's *The Godfather Part 2* when the Italian immigrants enter New York harbor, are awestruck by the Statue of Liberty, and disembark at Ellis Island. These images had shown Mariana early-twentieth-century America and the look of frightened, hopeful immigrants. The images spurred her imagination, bringing new vividness to the stories told and retold by members of our family, stories I'd heard my father and aunts and uncles tell when I was a boy sitting at the dining room table after a traditional Italian Christmas Eve supper, stories that rolled from their tongues in the quiet fullness after the meal, stories that sparked further stories and drew my beloved relatives into debates about events, people, and memories.

During those fleeting hours of storytelling, I had sat transfixed, asking questions that prompted an uncle or aunt to retell some incident or maybe, just maybe, reveal some bit of information I'd never heard before. And when my uncles and aunts and father slipped into the assured rhythms of reminiscence, I hoped that the telephone would not ring and that no one would knock at the door. Carefully, quietly, I refilled the small glasses with the dry red wine my uncle Joe made each year. I wanted nothing—not an empty glass, not an unexpected call, not a glance at the clock—to break the spell of telling.

Mariana leaned forward, reading slowly, treating her language with great respect, adopting a colloquial tone when she read dialog. Her sincere, urgent voice rolled up to me from the floor and entered my bones. I'd never imagined my father as a boy at the moment he arrived in America, never imagined that he may have left a best friend in Italy, that his sister may have slept and his younger brother may have cried. Because of "The Wooden Pony," Mariana's fictional dream woven of image and story, language and imagination, I would never think of my father in the same way again. Mariana read the final lines:

> Felice looked past Mama and met the gaze of Giuseppe. He watched two tears roll out of his older brother's eyes and make their varied path down his face.
> The two brothers stared at each other, expressionless.
> Felice grinned. "*Bambino*," he whispered.
> They laughed silently together. Felice patted his heart and thought about the future.

She looked up at me and saw my eyes filled with tears.

A day or two after that evening I thought of buying Mariana a carved wooden pony for high school graduation. I had no luck finding one in area stores. I remained optimistic, though, since I was traveling a lot. On trips to Calgary, Toronto, Montana, and New York, I found wooden bears, raccoons, wolves, seals, whales, moose, but no wooden ponies. Not even wooden horses.

My mother-in-law saved the day. She knew a wood carver, a longtime friend, who agreed to whittle a wooden pony for me. I sent him a copy of Mariana's short story so he could generate his own vision. Before he began his woodworking, however, he had a heart attack and underwent triple-bypass surgery.

Two months later I learned that he still wanted to carve the pony, that he and his wife thought the work would be good therapy for him. By this time it was midsummer.

"Are you getting me something for graduation or not?" Mariana asked.

"Be patient," I told her.

The following year, ten months after she had written "The Wooden

Pony," Mariana was home from college for spring break. The day before she headed back to school she and her mother went shopping. While they were gone, a small package arrived in the mail. I opened it and pulled out an object wrapped in tissue paper: a stiff-legged, blockish wooden pony. I turned it over in my hands, touching the ears, running my finger along the smooth back. I stood the pony on the kitchen counter. I was disappointed; it looked amateurish.

I found a note from the wood-carver's wife. "Merle wasn't happy with the way this turned out," she wrote, "but our ten-year-old grandson loves it and wanted to take it home. We thought it might be just the thing Luca would have carved for Felice."

Precisely.

Mariana arrived home in a flurry, dropping plastic bags to the floor and plopping down to open them. I sat reading in a chair.

"Open the package," I said to her.

Mariana was busy removing skirt, sweater, and shoes from the bags.

"What's in it?" She laid the sweater against the skirt on the floor and eyed the combination.

"Just open it. Please."

"I will in a minute," she said, her voice colored with annoyance. Mariana spent a moment or two more with her new clothes, then walked to the refrigerator and opened a can of soda. Finally, she turned to the package. Her eyebrows were pursed, troubled, as I had often seen my father's. She lifted the object. The tissue paper fell away. She held the wooden pony in both hands, her eyebrows raised in startled surprise. She glanced across the room to me. And this time it was her eyes that filled with tears.

Learning discovered and expressed through story—through narrative thinking—can be compelling. In "The Wooden Pony" (the entire story is reprinted in Appendix C) Mariana had written truth through fiction she shaped from imagination and fact. Felice, his siblings, and mother actually had joined my grandfather in the United States after he had worked in a brickyard in northeastern Ohio for two years. And my Grandfather Romano had been a brutal man at times, his sons standing up to him in later years when he was abusive. But was Filomena sleeping in her mother's arms? Was Antonio whimpering? Was Giuseppe disdainful? Did Felice leave an artistic friend named Luca behind in Italy?

That's conjecture, that's fiction, that's part of Mariana's narrative thinking. The action of the children and the history of Felice are inventions in Mariana's learning that took me to a place I'd never been before. I'd never imagined my father as a nine-year-old boy, wearing a *berretto*, leaving behind his best friend, contending with the fear and anxiety of starting a new life.

I doubt whether a discursive essay about immigrants and Ellis Island would have moved me and commanded my attention the way "The Wooden Pony" did. *Doubt,* I say. It certainly *can.* An expository essay doesn't have to be dry, dusty, and lifeless.

But Mariana wrote fiction. Her fictional dream went far beyond the class- room, much farther than her teacher could have imagined. Mariana's uncles, aunts, and cousins, great-uncles, great-aunts, and grandmother, read the story and talked about it and read it again. The story triggered further stories. In a small town in northeastern Ohio, a retiree recovering from open-heart surgery used the images he envisioned from reading "The Wooden Pony" to guide his hand, eye, and brain in shaping his own creative response.

Mariana's fiction reached back seventy-five years, took readers to a mo- ment when an immigrant child stepped ashore at Ellis Island. America and his life lay ahead of him. And years later, one of his granddaughters, a girl born seven years after his death, thought long about this grandfather she knew only through family stories and photographs, wondered further about a magical day in 1914 that her relatives had talked about ever since she could remember.

It wasn't lines of argument that assembled in Mariana's mind. It was images that took shape. It was the detail of narrative that unreeled as she reached for language to tell her story and relate emotions. The ship, the crowd, Felice's memories of Luca, the *statua di liberta* standing in the harbor—all became real. Characters spoke, moved, and felt. Mariana wrote a fictional dream. And we who entered that dream were never the same.

Writing that renders—call it creative, narrative, or imaginative, cast it in modes of poetry, dialog, personal essay, or fiction—is a respectable sibling of expository writing. Through writing that renders, many of us can learn and communicate things we cannot come to know through expository writing. And as with Uncle Gigi and Mariana, telling stories can lead to powerful knowing.

❧
JENNIFER

Jennifer was a sophomore enrolled in Beginning Fiction Writing at Utah State University. An excellent writer and student, she brought all her intellect and emotion to the job of learning to write uninterrupted fictional dreams. She diligently read and connected with essays about writing fiction, worked productively in small groups, wrote fiction, and conferred with me each week. At term's end she compiled a portfolio that documented her learning. In her cover letter she wrote:

> *You told me once, "Write about what you care about." I did that, and it taught me that good stories have to be honest, writers must be brave, and there has to be passion.*

Chapter Two

TRUTH, RISK, AND PASSION

GIVE ME THE DRENCH OF MY PASSIONS.

Walt Whitman

Cal was an affable, freckled, slightly built transfer student from another state. When he joined my sophomore reading and writing workshop one week before Christmas break, I asked two students to explain to Cal how the workshop operated. Although he began reading a young adult novel, he did no writing before vacation.

I talked to him when we returned to school in January.

"You like to write, Cal?"

"It's OK."

"In here you can write anything you want: poems, stories, letters, essays."

Cal smiled.

"Ask Les to show you his writing folder," I said. "That might give you some ideas."

Cal smiled again, nodded, went back to his seat, wrote nothing. He seemed bemused by what the other students were doing in writing workshop. I guessed that his previous experience had been in classrooms that featured little personal writing. He had probably spent the bulk of his time receiving the thinking of teachers and authors. Here I was asking him to look at his life, pick out what mattered, and commit his thinking about it to paper—to become an originator of knowledge. No wonder he was baffled, maybe even a little frightened. At the end of each period when the students and I met on the rug in the helping circle and students read their writing aloud, Cal sat, polite and mute, listening, weighing, watching.

With a week left in the semester, Cal brought in the piece shown in Figure 2–1. Since I might never see Cal again after the semester ended, I decided to prompt him to take a monumental leap.

"How about reading this to the class?"

He agreed.

On the rug at the end of class, Cal gulped mightily. He began to read, his voice quavering. He never raised his eyes from the paper. Later, he told me it was the first time he had ever read his words to his peers. When Cal finished reading, class members—quite experienced conferencers after four months—began to comment, resonating Cal's thinking. They told him what they understood. They asked questions. Students who had seen the same movie brought up other scenes they remembered. Cal was an expert. He revealed more information about character and plot.

The next day Cal drew a caret in the margin by the information about Brad's Jewish schooling. On another sheet of paper (see Figure 2–2) he wrote a paragraph he intended to add—the first time, he said, he had ever "messed" with something he'd written.

Barb Rindflesh showed up at my evening extension class in Salt Lake City, accompanied by her friend and colleague, Charlene. Both taught at an elementary school in the city. Neither was enrolled in our masters degree program in the theory and practice of writing at Utah State University. They simply wanted to write. I had conducted a writing workshop at their school two months earlier and mentioned the extension class I would teach in the spring: Creative Writing in the Classroom.

The core of the course was the students' weekly writing. I asked each student to choose a topic she cared deeply about and to shape the entire term's writing into a multigenre paper. Barb had two daughters—one eighteen, one fifteen. She chose to write about motherhood and titled her multigenre paper "Sketchbook: Scenes from a Mother's Life."

Barb had been immersed in motherhood for years. Now she immersed herself in reflecting and writing about it. She took deep trips into all aspects

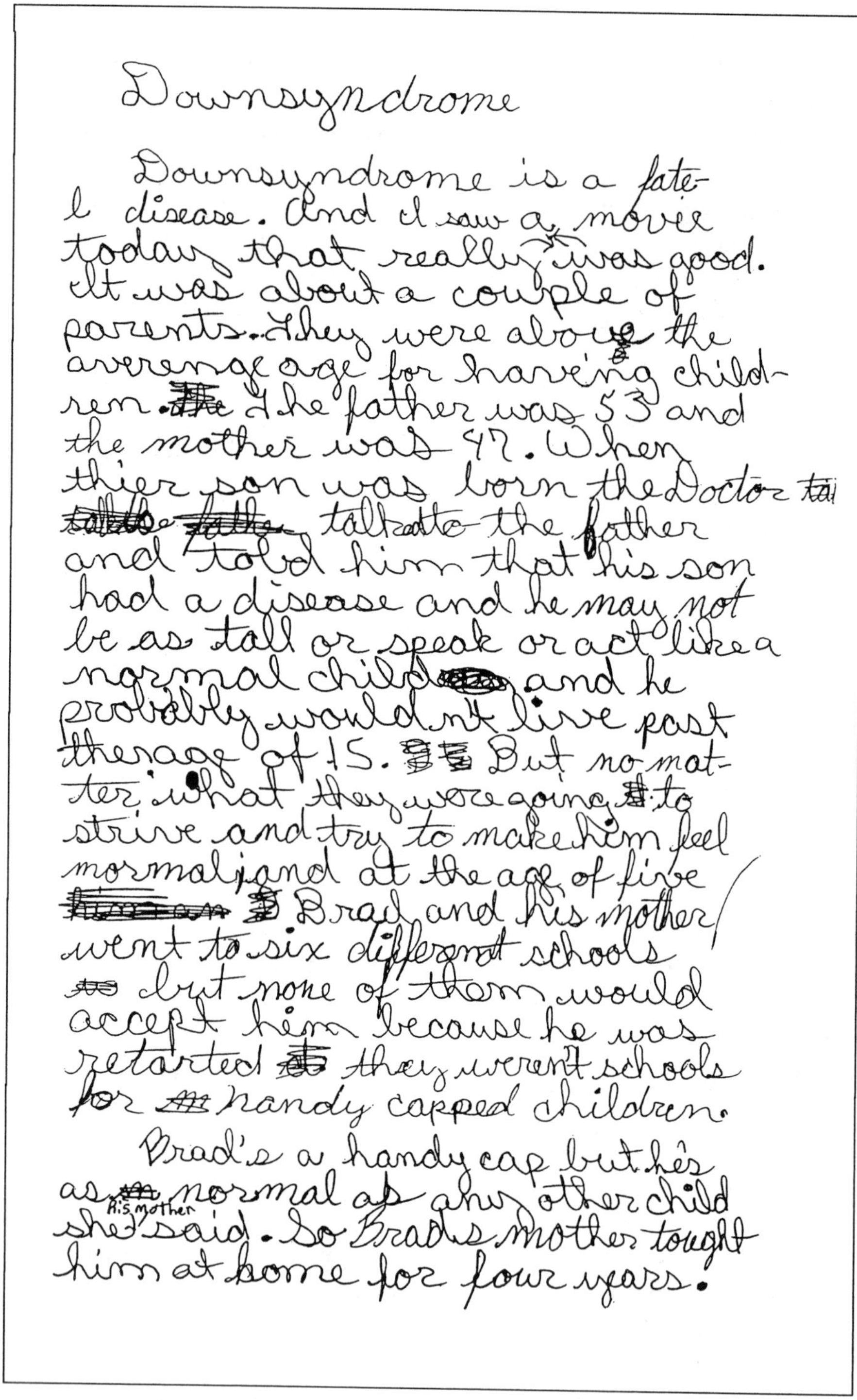

Downsyndrome

Downsyndrome is a fatel disease. And I saw a movie today that really was good. It was about a couple of parents. They were above the averenge age for haveing children. The father was 53 and the mother was 47. When thier son was born the Doctor talke to the father and told him that his son had a disease and he may not be as tall or speak or act like a normal child and he probably wouldn't live past the age of 15. But no matter what they were going to strive and try to make him feel normal and at the age of five Brad and his mother went to six different schools but none of them would accept him because he was retarted they werent schools for handy capped children.

Brad's a handy cap but he's as normal as any other child his mother she said. So Brad's mother tought him at home for four years.

FIGURE 2—1

16

Truth, Risk, and Passion

At the age of nine his mother signed him up for baseball camp and he went and while there other kids would pick on him and call him names and he made a really great friend his name was Coach Blake and if it wasn't for him he never would have made it through camp. Two years went by & 12 more schools wouldn't accept him. Brad and his mother went to a jewish school and they accepted him. And he studied the jewish poems + prayers + he became jewish at the age of thirteen. And as he grew older he acted more normal. At the age of 15 he went to High school and found all kinds of new friends some were even jewish like him.

After he got out of High school Brad got a job at the age of 23 and made it big in the world as a normal person in his own way.

THE END

P.S. You have got to see this movie it is great

FIGURE 2—1 CONTINUED

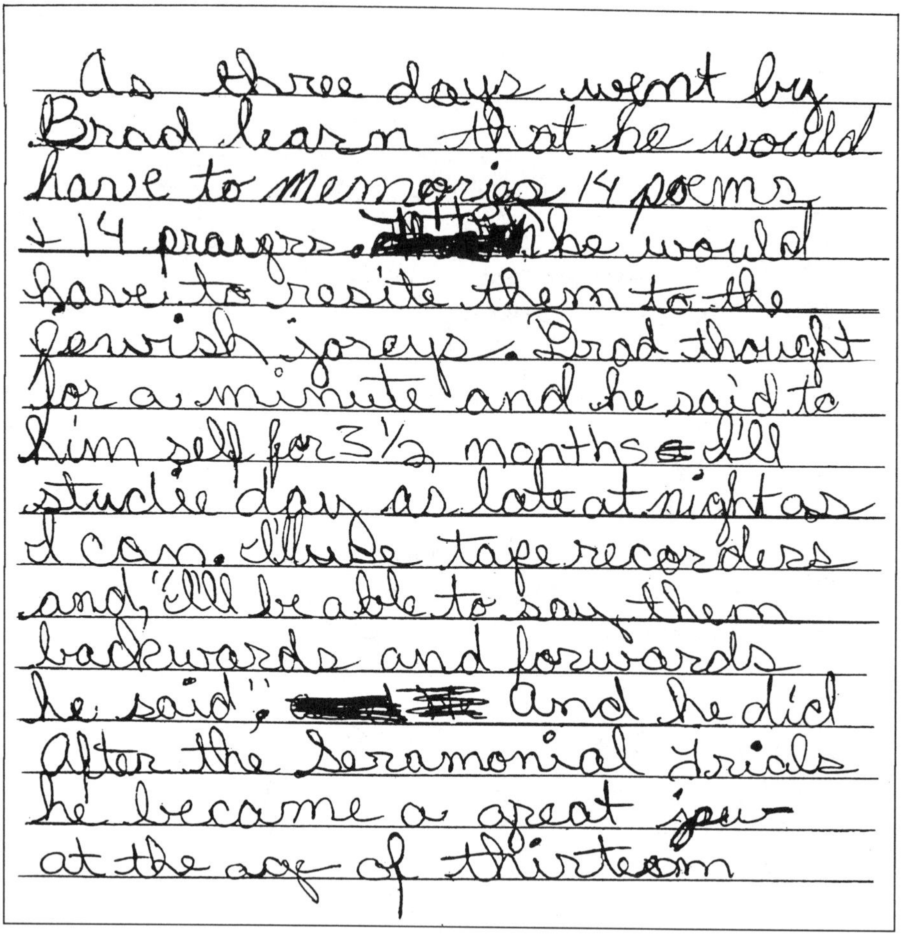

FIGURE 2—2

of motherhood. She wrote about the bright side:

LULLABY

Sleep, my little one
my darling buttercup dandelion
butterfly flutterby baby
blue-eyed
wonderfulmiraculous
love of my life.
Sleep.

Sleep, my wee one
little bird
dear heart

sweetprecious star child
summerflower angel
punkinpie
honey bunny.
Sleep.

Pledges I sing to you
the promises a mother makes:
all is well
I'll keep you safe
no harm will come
the world is dark
but I am here
have no fear
dry your tears.
And sleep.

And she wrote about the dark side:

CONFESSION

There is a dark side to motherhood which no one speaks of and no one tells you about but it is there and I know because I remember as if it were yesterday the night when, in my exhaustion and frustration that you wouldn't nurse and wouldn't stop crying and I'd done everything I knew how to do and I'd been days without sleep, I threw your small body down on the soft blankets of my bed and wept like a mad woman because I had just had a vision of myself throwing you across the room where you broke against the wall and with your blood came blessed silence and I was grateful.

Barb Rindflesh, Teacher, Beacon Heights Elementary, Salt Lake City, Utah

Barb's multigenre paper consisted of poems of many kinds, a help-wanted advertisement, letters to her mother, reflective narratives, found poems shaped from her students' remarks about motherhood, a fable, a news story, and third-person narratives that gave her needed distance.

As her writing increased over the quarter and she ranged over her maternal experience, examining each part closely and bravely, Barb's confidence grew. The writing was generative. The more she wrote, the more she wrote. Instead of exhausting her subject matter in a few weeks, Barb found that she had ever more she wanted to say about the experience of mothering two daughters.

When the course ended, she turned in a superbly written, expansive multigenre paper. On yellow sticky notes attached to some pages, Barb explained future plans for that piece. And in a memo that accompanied the paper, Barb told me about other areas of motherhood she intended to write about that summer.

Mark was my student the third year I taught. He remains one of the best students of literature I encountered in seventeen years as a high school teacher. He also smoked dope, drank beer, skipped school, and played a mean trumpet in the high school band.

Mark was a fast, perceptive reader. I sometimes gave in-class writing assignments on short stories, assignments designed to make students read closely, practice putting together ideas, and—not unimportant to a young teacher—keep busy the entire period. Mark completed these writing assignments with dispatch, then used his incisive paper to negotiate a pass to the band room, where, I later learned, he kicked back, socialized, and sneaked outside to smoke joints with his friends.

Mark liked talking about fictional characters and the meanings he made from their actions. "Seymour was too sensitive for this world," he said about Salinger's protagonist in "A Perfect Day for Bananafish." "That's why he killed himself. He wasn't going to hurt anyone. Look how well he related to that little girl. He wasn't going to molest her. His gossipy mother-in-law and bitchy wife were the villains. They made us *think* he was dangerous."

Mark loved words. I remember him pursuing a line of argument when speaking about a Faulkner short story. His reasoning came down to the definition of a single word—*gingerly*. I wasn't sure what the word meant and told the class so—a remarkable move for me, since I had learned implicitly all through my schooling that the proper stance for a teacher was omniscience. I took that ill-conceived notion further: when I didn't know something, I feigned that I did.

So why did I admit to students I didn't know the meaning of *gingerly*? Because Mark sat in class, that's why.

You couldn't bullshit Mark.

I didn't want to be a fool in his eyes.

Mark didn't put much stock in grades. In my department chair's modern-novel class, he missed a test covering *A Farewell to Arms*. On the following day, when he made no move to make up the test, my colleague reminded him of it.

"What's my grade if I take an F on the test?" Mark asked.

"C," said my colleague.

"That's good enough."

Without any prompting from me, Mark became a producer of literary artifacts as well as a consumer of them. In January he missed a week of school to accompany his parents to Florida. During the vacation, he read Hemingway's *Nick Adams Stories*, which he found in a bookstore. When Mark returned, he gave me the book to read and presented me with a matter-of-fact, understated, unsentimental story about a retarded black man he'd met on the trip. I could see Hemingway's good influence in Mark's sentence rhythms, tone, and choice of subject. As a young man Hemingway wrote "Up in Michigan." Mark's story could have been titled "Down in Florida."

Mark got caught skipping school when he was a senior. Maddening enough, the punishment for school-skippers was a three-day suspension.

When Mark returned to school, I asked him how his vacation had been.

He brushed aside my immature barb. "You know how Salinger has that book of short stories?"

"*Nine Stories.*"

"He published a lot more than nine."

"Yes," I said, "I remember a professor reading us what he said was Salinger's first published short story, 'This Sandwich Has No Mayonnaise.'"

"I spent the day at Miami's library," Mark said. "I found a ton of Salinger's stories in old magazines."

"You learned more yesterday than you would have in school!"

Mark raised his eyebrows to acknowledge the obvious.

Before he left for his next class, Mark gave me a fat manilla envelope. It was full of photocopies of Salinger's uncollected stories.

Some years ago I was involved in organizing activities for our high school's celebration of Right-to-Read-Week. I'd been planning special events, writing skits for an assembly, and rehearsing at six-thirty each morning. Late one afternoon I dragged myself to the faculty lounge. A math teacher–football coach reclined on the couch.

"Right-to-Read-Week," he said, yawning. "What a pain in the ass."

Weeks of overwork, frustration, and stress manifested themselves in a reflex action: I shot my indolent colleague the bird.

My department chair, who had been working equally long hours, thought my gesture of disapproval definitive and most appropriate. But I agonized over it, felt ignominious about my impulsive reaction. I—an English teacher, a believer in the power of language—should have been able to generate a more reasoned, though no less passionate, response to that antiprint literacy blackguard.

The idea ate at me. Two days later I came home from school, went straight to my desk, and drafted a piece about teaching reading. I broke to make supper, then revised throughout the evening. At nine o'clock I bathed my daughter, read her a story, and put her to bed. Then I typed a final copy. A day later I read the piece at a faculty meeting. The following week, just in time for the Right-to-Read-Week celebration, a local newspaper published it.

At a conference at Miami University in 1983 I heard keynote addresses by Don Murray, Peter Elbow, and Bill Strong. I became so fired about teaching, learning, and writing that after the conference I did the damnedest thing: I wrote a letter of inquiry to someone I'd never met, someone I'd heard was starting a doctoral program in reading and writing instruction. Here is the conclusion of my letter:

> Until three weeks ago I considered my life settled and my niche at Edgewood High School secure. I was content. Now I'm afire. Uproot, let go, voyage out, reach for something I'm not sure I can grasp. My feelings are akin to the thrill and fear I felt as a boy when we ventured from our warm houses on Halloween night. In our paper bags was plenty of shucked corn, in our pockets were thick bars of Ivory soap, in our hearts was the sweet anxiety of great expectation.

I put myself on the line in that letter to Don Graves, letting him know where I hoped to go professionally and what I valued and feared. It was voice that did that—my individual, passionate, risk-taking voice that sprang into Graves's mind from black symbols on paper.

Sometimes my passionate writing voice has gotten me into trouble—like the time I published my first piece in *English Journal.* I had come home from school one unsettling day and furiously written several pages in my journal about the emotional roller coaster I had ridden. I wrote madly in both senses of the word. Just hours before, an administrator at the county vocational school had moved to censor our creative arts anthology.

"Either delete all four-letter words and these two stories," he said, "or we won't print the magazine."

I was proud enough of the students' work and artistic integrity that I stood up to the administrator's soft-spoken, fascist ideas of control. I refused to alter the anthology, gathered the negatives that had been shot by the graphic arts students, and walked out of his office.

My principal helped me find Mr. Bruck, community member and printer by trade, a gentle man whose bright, witty daughter Vicky—my former student—was dying of cancer. In the living room I spread the negatives on the floor and discussed with Mr. Bruck what needed to be done. All the while Vicky dozed feverishly on the couch. By working nights and one weekend, Mr. Bruck rescued our publication.

A few months later I shaped my inflamed journal entry into a case history of the incident, including both the attempted censorship and the subsequent triumph. I sent "Censorship and the Student Voice" to *English Journal*. Editor Stephen Tchudi accepted it.

Months later when the article appeared, I was giddy with pride at being published in a national journal. I shared the article with my colleagues. The next day, amid my euphoria, I was summoned by my superintendent. The meeting featured considerable browbeating and was not about the deathless quality of my prose.

The only required course in the doctoral program in reading and writing instruction at the University of New Hampshire is a seminar offered every two years in—what else—reading and writing instruction. The year I took the seminar Don Graves taught it.

The learning environment couldn't have been more supportive and encouraging. Each Monday morning we met at Graves's house just off a back road in New Hampshire woods. All the students were bright, eager professionals who—if they were anything—were passionate about reading, writing, learning, and education. We all knew that in the atmosphere of the class everyone was rooting for everyone else. And yet, the anxiety many of us periodically felt ran deep.

Early in the first semester, one of my fellow students said to me, "Sometimes I feel like crying in the middle of class." Not because the class was bad or tedious or lacking substance. We represented a diversity of experience, learning, and vision. Sometimes in many of us the intellectual pressure mounted and our passion seemed insignificant, even misdirected, in the face of everyone else's passion and knowledge. Graves exhorted us to "disagree with glee."

Still, some of us sometimes felt empty, lost, and powerless.

The final year I was in graduate school, I received a letter from John Gaughan, a good friend of mine in Ohio. He taught in a small high school just north of Cincinnati. He met with seven classes each day, five preparations. To supplement his income and further stimulate his intellect, he also taught an overload class of freshman English at nearby Miami University. In his letter John included an essay by one of his high school seniors.

The essay—part satire, part hard-driving argument—was about homework. The concluding lines read,

> Teachers test us with their assignments, searching for a fine line between the amount of work we'll complete and the amount of work we'll refuse to do. In this ongoing search, they inevitably overstep the barrier, and burnout results, which they often mistake for apathy in students.
>
> *Steve Schwettman, Senior, Lockland High School, Lockland, OH*

John was disheartened. "Here I am trying to give them 'real' writing experiences as opposed to the grammar, usage, and punctuation drills they're used to," he wrote, "and they still resist."

I felt for my friend. I've been to the land of despair, disillusioned when students thwarted my best efforts. I knew John's agony and I knew how hard he worked. I wrote him back right away because I thought he should take heart. I thought he had a success story in the boy's defiant essay against school and classes and what he perceived to be excessive workloads. He had seized the opportunity made available in my friend's classroom to use language to oppose the power of school and teachers.

In *Language and Learning* James Britton writes, "For a teacher whose concern does not go beyond the ordered framework in which a class may work, there is the alternative of so managing that situation that individuals have no power and eventually no will to break rules" (270).

The framework and the management of my friend's classroom allowed students to pursue the fervor of their passions. That indignant student felt safe enough to dare to risk a direct challenge to the way his classes were run. The boy believed he could break rules. And he acted. In Britton's words, he "made important choices about himself and his work and his relationships" (272).

In *The Writing Life* Annie Dillard writes,

> One of the few things I know about writing is this: spend it all, shoot it, play it, lose it, all, right away, every time. Do not hoard what seems good for a later place in the book, or for another book; give it, give it all, give it now. (78)

Barb had given it all. So had Cal—newly enlightened about Judaism and Down's syndrome. So had my friend's resistant student Steve. And Mark—consumed with Salinger, Hemingway, and writing his own fictional dreams. So had I. We hadn't held back. All of us had demonstrated passion and faith in our own language. Although I want students to listen to others and to exercise reason, I first want them to be passionate about something. In discussing what writing teachers must know, a high school student of mine once wrote, "A writing teacher's main goal should be to open up the channels in students, to let them put their ideas and emotions and personality on paper."

In *A Place Called School* Jonathon Goodlad criticizes the emotional flatness of the classrooms he observed. In classroom after classroom, his research teams stepped into atmospheres devoid of joy or anger, elation or frustration. The researchers saw no acts of language and passion, no acts of students seizing power like my friend's student railing against homework overloads or like Barb burning with love and commitment.

I understand the lack of passion in classrooms. Passion is often misread, seen as raw, dangerous emotion with no intellect behind it, no critical stance. That is, no doubt, sometimes true. But I'm willing to risk it. In my experience, passion in students has usually led to strong positions, critical thinking, further analysis, and stirring, often eloquent language.

Passion causes ideas, images, and lines of thought to stick with you throughout the day as you shop, exercise, prepare a meal, or garden. Passion raises you from bed to jot down a phrase or a line you thought of as you were drifting into sleep.

Say the word slowly and mean it. *Passion.* It can sound dangerous, can't it? Illicit. Reckless. Consumed. Passion might lead to ecstasy, but it might also lead to entanglement, despair, and irrevocable loss.

Red lights flash.

Let's be levelheaded. Be wary of passion. If you fail when you're passionate, you'll suffer terribly. Let's have balance, moderation.

But when we strive for balance, we'd better look closely at what we're balancing. Balance the cost of recycling with continuing the practice of burying plastic, glass, and metal in the earth? Balance the right to bear arms with the millions of handguns in circulation? Balance real writing and reading with equal portions of decontextualized grammar instruction and one-right-answer reading of literature?

Strive for balance? Some things don't even belong on the scale.

Moderation didn't get *Guernica* painted, *Sergeant Pepper* composed, *Fences* performed.

Moderation didn't get Normandy invaded, the House Committee on Un-American Activities confronted, the infant born, GRE scores that soared.

Moderation didn't get the classroom converted to a reading and writing workshop.

Moderation didn't get murals painted on the gray walls of the handball courts behind school.

Moderation didn't get the scholarship extended, the job offered, the lover won.

Moderation didn't get the writing done.

THINE, WINE, AND PINE

*W*hen I was in high school in the mid-
1960s, I loved poetry, gained great pleasure
from repeating its language and figuring out
what it meant to me. This passion for anthologized poetry didn't adversely affect my status as
a member of the football and baseball teams,
either. When my senior-year English teacher
presented us with passages of poetry to
memorize, I took to the task gladly, even
though the words she had responded to were
not always the ones that carried me away. To
meet personal needs, I picked out my own
passages to learn by heart. On tests, after
writing passages my teacher needed us to
memorize, I added ones I needed to memorize.
Although the teacher never awarded me credit
for that, she never objected to my extra duty.

On one occasion, however, I thought she
might object, so I didn't write down one of the
passages I'd learned. It was meant for me
alone, anyway. I was eighteen and in serious,
dangerous love. After a year and a half, the girl
broke up with me in February, and I fell into a
prolonged, spiraling funk. When I read John
Keats, he who had died so young—too soon,
like my own father—John Keats, who had
loved Fanny Brawne more than she had loved
him, my teacher didn't have to assign me lines
to memorize. I had my own agenda. I
memorized a passage from the sonnet "Bright

Star" that John Keats, dead nearly 150 years, had surely written just for me in 1967:

> —yet still steadfast, still unchangeable,
>   Pillowed upon my fair love's ripening breast,
> To feel forever its soft fall and swell,
>   Awake forever in a sweet unrest,
> Still, still to hear her tender-taken breath,
> And so live ever—or else swoon in death.

This voice spoke hard, eloquent truth to me, as though Keats had once suffered as I was suffering and knew exactly how to articulate my feelings.

When spring came, I still dwelt in a common—though very real—brand of teenage melancholy. In May we began our senior English projects; I did mine on John Keats, naturally, throwing myself into the research and writing, the work both homage to Keats and tribute to the girl I loved. Years later, I realized that, above all, I had done the project for myself, for my deep need to work out loss—the loss of the girl, the loss of my father three years earlier, maybe even the loss of a time of my life I was leaving forever. And it was on this reading and writing that I rode out of the slough. Those spring days marked a passage both brutal and crucial, my personal adolescent experience of coming through slaughter.

I wrote the first poem of my life a week after graduation. For months I had unconsciously rehearsed the subject matter, calling on the rhythms and language in my head from four years of reading poetry in high school, most of which had been written by poets before 1900, with the exception of Robert Frost and Joyce Kilmer. No Whitman, though, no Dickinson, but plenty of Tennyson, Shakespeare, and Milton; Longfellow, Whittier, and Poe, Poe, Poe.

As I sat grimly at that tiny desk by the telephone in our apartment, gripping a pen, bent to the page of a spiral-bound notebook, I struggled with grief, loss, and regret. The emotions grew from sensual experience, indelible images, and meaningful words the girl and I had spoken to each other. The emotions I felt were timeless. The language, sentence rhythms, and notions of poetry in my head, however, were from another time. The poetic voices I knew as models were not ones that validated my late-adolescent voice:

He who has tasted wine,
Can never be satisfied with less,
So what ever be my life's success
My heart shall always be thine.
Though I am not the first to pine
For a love that had been so divine,
The longing and sorrow which around my heart is lain
Has become the foundation for unending pain.
Her touch was as soft as a new fallen snow
And her radiant smile was surpassed by an inner glow.
Since the days of her wine all others are sour
And my mortuous despair increases by the hour,
O for a basic mind and a heart of stone
That I may live peacefully alone.

A few years ago—without revealing the author—I shared this poem with high school seniors as we began three weeks of concentrated work writing poetry. I placed the poem on an overhead and read it aloud. There followed noticeable silence, a few smiles, some sniggers, and a number of serious faces.

"Unending pain," Rosanna finally said. "Man, that's a long time!"

"What's this thine, wine, and pine business?" asked Stephanie.

"Mortuous," said Eric. "Is that a real word?"

Krissy articulated the central problem. Though the despair behind the poem was genuine enough, the voice came right out of Mark Twain's Emmeline Grangerford school of poetry writing: "You know," said Krissy, "that doesn't sound like anybody I know."

It didn't sound like anybody I knew, either. And it certainly didn't sound like anybody I had known twenty years earlier.

In her book about teaching poetry writing, For the Good of the Earth and Sun, Georgia Heard often asks a child if what she has on the page matches what she has in her heart. In 1967 I would have answered yes. I'd created a match. The voice of my poem emulated the only poetic voices I knew, the voices that teachers and anthology publishers had sanctioned and promoted.

Chapter Three

FAITH AND
FEARLESSNESS

HERE IS WHAT SINGS UNRESTRICTED FAITH.

Walt Whitman

*J*ayne wrote about awkwardness with a contrite stranger in the wake of her father's death. Julie wrote about ridicule and insensitivity on the first day of high school. Barb wrote about the dark side of motherhood. Mariana captured the living image of her deceased grandfather as a boy.

I'll quote Jennifer from the first interchapter: "Writers must be brave."

Nerve must not fail. The act of writing is an act of faith—faith in our subject matter, faith that needed language resides in us, faith that our meaning making through writing is worthwhile. Indeed, writers must be brave. They don't face lions on the Serengeti. But they will face doubt, anxiety, fear—psychological carnivores that prey upon confidence.

Many people hesitate to write. It's no wonder. They see no final product, and it's frightening to start writing something they haven't envisioned. They may doubt that they have the stamina and ability to write well about what is only nebulous. So they sleep in, clean the desk, sharpen pencils, call friends, open mail, listen to *Morning Edition* while preparing a complicated breakfast—anything to avoid writing. If they read a great deal, they know that their unspoken thoughts and chaotic emotions are quite distant from evocative, precisely worded, perfectly mechanicked writing.

To write words that stick with readers you must have—or develop—faith in the validity of your feelings. You must be fearless in writing the words that emerge in your mind when you focus to compose. It is during this concentrated, unfettered act of using language that you have the best chance to discover ideas, visualize images, stumble into effective language.

In *The Long Quiet Highway: Waking Up in America* Natalie Goldberg discusses what she came to understand in the days when she was learning to write and doubting herself:

> I had to believe in my mother, my grilled cheese sandwich, opening the refrigerator, the way I felt about night and shoulders and sidewalks. My life began to become a vast field of significant value. . . . I repeated, "You must trust your own mind." I became aware that writing was based on words, that they came out of my mind, and that I had to trust what I thought, felt, and saw. I could not be afraid that I was insignificant, or stupid—or, I could be afraid, but I had to speak anyway. (40)

A STEADFAST ALLY

We don't have to remain alone in trying to sustain faith and remain fearless. An ally stands ready to help us, an ally who will never desert us if we keep faith. That ally is *process*. The process of writing is sacred. My hand moves to genuflect. The work between first flicker of idea and final tap of the print command enables us to crystallize vision. This is demonstrated to me each time I write, whatever I write, whether a letter to a cherished friend or this chapter.

During a workshop sponsored by the Utah Writing Project, Linda Rief led a group of three hundred teachers into what she called "quick-writes." Four or five times in succession she gave us a prompt and asked us to write rapidly for only two minutes, writing so fast that our language out-distanced our self-censors. The purpose of the exercise was to engage actively with language, to get thinking-starts on paper. One prompt Linda gave us was: "When I was _____." We were to select an age and begin to write. I chose the tumultuous year of thirteen (see Figure 3–1).

My handwriting can be better than that, but not much. No matter. My main concern was not the Palmer method, not even legibility to anyone but me. My main concern was writing what I most remembered about thirteen: being enamored and feeling so self-conscious that I couldn't speak anything but Italian to the girl. Of all the quick-writes Linda led us into, the words I produced for that one interested me most. The next morning I typed my

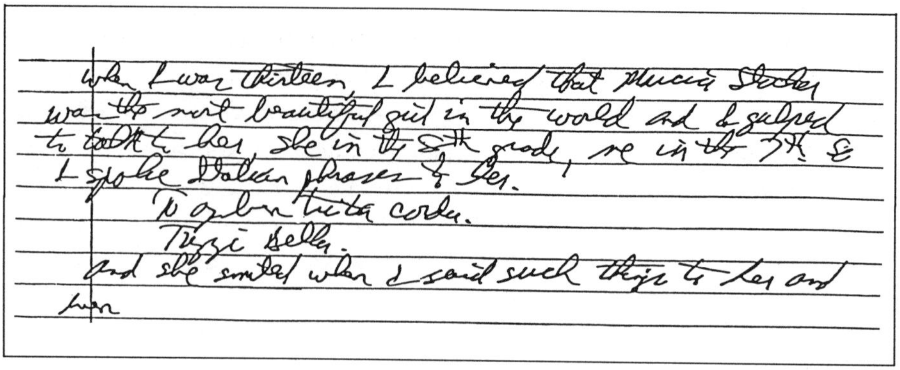
When I was thirteen, I believed that Marcia Stocker
was the most beautiful girl in the world and I gulped
to talk to her, she in the 8th grade, me in the 7th &
I spoke Italian phrases to her.
To oy ben tu ta corda.
Tuzzi bella.
And she smiled when I said such things to her and
then

FIGURE 3–1

cryptic, handwritten quick-write into the computer and fleshed out the scene with further detail:

> When I was thirteen in seventh grade, I loved Marcia Stocker, a petite eighth grader with blond hair like ripe pears and eyes so blue, a color that nobody in my family had. Only I was afraid to talk to Marcia. So I spoke to her in Italian. When I was going to my English class and she was leaving that same room, I'd catch her just outside the doorway and say, "To oy ben tu ta corda." And on another day I'd say, "Tuzzi bella." And she smiled and nodded, and although I never translated for her, somehow I knew she knew I thought she was beautiful and loved her with all my heart.

My faith in the material quickened with this writing. The simile that emerged comparing Marcia's hair to the color of ripe pears delighted me. That physical trait made me think of Marcia's other notable physical feature: her blue eyes. On the heels of that detail, the thought flashed upon me that nobody in my family—*nobody*—had blue eyes, so that information went down, too.

At this point in my writing process, I accept just about everything. As much as possible I stave off judgment, reject little, quell evaluation. I'm trying to remember and discover as much as I can, seeking to gather a body of detail to work with. Halfway through my expansive exploration of thirteen, for example, I remembered the exact spot where I saw Marcia each morning: in the hall by the door of Miss Ayer's English classroom. I stood holding my grammar book, waiting expectantly, hoping to glimpse Marcia as the eighth graders filed out of the room.

I thought this memory might become a poem, perhaps because the experience and emotion were compact and self-contained. I continued to write, visualizing, pinpointing, adding, cutting, inventing, trying to be concrete and vivid with language. In addition to tinkering with words and bulking up the text with whatever descriptions, memories, and metaphorical language I could generate, I implemented the most obvious difference between poetry and prose—I broke lines before they reached the right margin.

> When I was in seventh grade
> I loved Margaret Hansen,
> a petite eighth grader with hair the
> color of ripe pears and eyes blue
> like none of my Mediterranean relatives.
> But I was afraid to talk to Margaret,
> afraid my words would tangle and stutter,
> knew my jackhammer heart might seize the air
> from my lungs and render me mute.
> Besides, I couldn't think of anything
> to say to Margaret that wouldn't redden
> my ears like Christmas tree ornaments.
> So I spoke to her in Italian.
> In the hall I'd stop her and blurt out,
> "To oy ben tu ta corda."
> In study hall I'd walk to the pencil sharpener,
> take a circuitous route back to my seat,
> and kneel by Margaret's desk to tie my loafers.
> "Tuzzi bella," I'd whisper.
> For one month that year before she began meeting
> a ninth grader every day after school, Margaret
> smiled and nodded every time she saw me. And
> although I never translated for her, I knew
> she knew I thought she was beautiful
> and loved her with all my heart.

As I responded to the material, letting it talk back, trying to answer its needs, paying attention to lineation, my faith continued to rise. But I wasn't thinking about that. I wasn't thinking about fearlessness, either. I was thinking about thirteen and Marcia and junior high school. I was consumed with reimagining self-consciousness. I was "closing with the material" (Stafford 1986, 65), and that experience was exciting, interesting, and dramatic. Because of the details that arose in the writing—in the rendering—for the very first time in all these years I was struck by the differences between my family and Marcia's:

her Lutheran upbringing	my Catholic relatives
her Scandinavian ancestry	my Italian heritage

| her father's hourly-wage job | my father's ownership of a tavern and two bowling alleys |
| her life in a three-bedroom, two-story home on a quiet tree-lined street | my life in our apartment above the bar overlooking the town square |

I leaned on that cultural difference by giving Marcia a fictional name that sounded more Lutheran—Margaret Hansen—and by modifying my relatives with *Mediterranean*. I reached for metaphors to capture how an adolescent boy often feels when talking to an older girl he's smitten with, his breath crushed from his chest, blood rising to the surface of his skin. I invented the needless walk to the pencil sharpener to show ingenuity and desperate infatuation. I included the real detail of Margaret herself smitten with an older boy whom she later, in fact, married. Now, as I write this chapter, I analyze why I made these moves. In the heat of writing the poem, however, I engaged in no such conscious, distanced analysis. I was one with the material, right in there, dirty with images, words, and feelings, trying to make characters real, details palpable, emotions authentic.

Even after my specific enhancements, the poem didn't feel quite finished. I transacted with it further. I say *transacted* instead of *interacted*, because not only did the poem change, but I, too, changed from writing it. I saw part of my life more clearly. Synthesizing that adolescent experience enabled me to analyze it. I felt accomplishment. The difference between Margaret's family and mine offered a title. Using white space created stanzas that improved the look, ease of reading, and emphasis of the poem. With help from my daughter, who speaks Italian and lived four months in Italy, I converted the invented spelling of dialect I'd heard as a boy to orthographic regularity, a move Mariana greeted with relief. Here is the final draft:

CLASH OF CULTURES

In seventh grade I loved Margaret Hansen,
a petite eighth grader with hair
the color of ripe pears and eyes blue
like none of my Mediterranean relatives.

But I was afraid to talk to Margaret,
afraid my words would tangle and stutter,
knew my jackhammer heart might seize the air
from my lungs and render me mute.
Besides, I couldn't think of anything
to say to Margaret that wouldn't redden

my ears like Christmas tree ornaments.
So I spoke to her in Italian.

In the hall I'd stop Margaret, blurt out,
"*Ti amo con tutto il mío cuore*."
In study hall I'd walk to the pencil sharpener,
take a circuitous route back to my seat,
kneel by Margaret's desk to tie my loafers.
"*Tu sei bella*," I'd whisper.

For one month that year before she began meeting
a ninth grader every day after school, Margaret
smiled and nodded when she saw me.
Although I never translated for her, I know
she understood I thought she was beautiful
and loved her with all my heart.

Look once more at the frantic, full-steam-ahead beginning (Figure 3–1) that captures only the kernel of the emotion I felt. Read it, if you can, and know beyond doubt that process is sacred and deep faith crucial to the act of writing.

I am ever grateful to the process of writing. An image flashes to consciousness, memorable language speaks, a metaphorical connection delights, maybe an emotion surges unaccountably . . . and because you write, you get a scribble. With patience, faith, and fearlessness and with a passion for bringing language to bear on what you experience, you *may* end up with a fully realized piece of writing. The process is testimony to creativity, the generative nature of language, and the hopeful pulse beating at our wrists.

A WRITING STATE OF MIND

One spring I asked high school juniors if writing was hard for them.
"Not like it once was," said Shannon.
"That's good to hear," I said. "Can you explain why?"
"I have a writing state of mind now."
"Writing state of mind?" I said. "Tell me more."
"Like if I'm at the mall," Shannon said, "and I see an old man sitting on a bench and his coat is ragged and he needs a shave and maybe when I get closer I see that the pipe he's smoking has a cigar butt stuck in it, I think, yeah, I could write something about that, a character sketch maybe, or a story or poem or in my journal, which is what I did."

Shannon spoke truth. Develop a writing state of mind, and you need never worry about where to get ideas. Your life, as Goldberg says, becomes "a vast field of significant value." Remain brave, and everything becomes possible subject matter: abstract feelings, concrete ideas, steadfast positions, experiences both past and present. I pay particular attention to sensations, especially those that have stuck with me for years: an indelible image, maybe frozen forever or maybe containing motion, like videotape. Language linked to a face and precise moment. A scent that transports me to a memorable place, like the smell of my wife's Stone Mountain purse that made me remember playing second base with a new baseball glove. If you retain such sensory remembering, it holds significant meaning for you and is ripe for you to write about.

For example: an indelible image that has stuck with me more than thirty years involves Bobby, a boy I met in fifth grade. One summer evening when we were twelve we camped outside town. Dusk was fast giving way to night. Bobby and another boy had brought their shotguns. I retain this image of lean, sinewy Bobby: he had spotted Nazis in the trees across a small ravine and had scurried to the edge of the cliff. Crouched at the precipice, he shouted epithets into the air, the shotgun steadied at his hip. He pumped four or five resounding blasts over the ravine. As the gunblaze flashed on his defiant face, I both loved and feared him.

When I thought of this image recently, it pulled me hard. I went to the computer and wrote about Bobby. Three pages later I stopped. I was remembering why my love and fear and that pulsing flash over Bobby's face were meaningful. I began to write what turned into a prose poem triptych.

THE SILENCE THAT WIDENED

I.

Bobby ruled fifth grade when I moved into it.
"Yeah, I flunked last year,"
he said more than once. "So what?"
By midwinter he had beaten every boy
worthy of combat except one, and he had beaten them
well within the fifteen minutes of recess.
On my afternoon Bobby leapt for my head
and rode me like a rodeo steer to the ice of the playground.
He hugged me to his chest in the headlock
that made every boy give up. Bobby dug his bony wrist
into his opponent's temple, a pain focused, arrow sharp,
shooting through the brain until the inside of the nose stung.
When we slammed to the ice, I landed on top of Bobby,
squirming fast to guard my temple from his killing wrist bone.
We struggled under bloodthirsty shouts of circled boys
and, minutes later, their quiet disappointment

Faith and Fearlessness

when they learned the grim, silent, slowness of the fight.
Freezing wind whipped down our necks
as Bobby and I lay panting and straining
through the tardy bell and silence that widened between
the school buildings when the last screaming
recessor fled the playground.
"We'd better go in," I said.
"Does that mean you give?"
It didn't.

II.

Bobby and I became fast friends after that.
We shared a locker, chose each other first for teams,
vandalized wantonly at Halloween, stole outside Christmas
lights in December, drove the new music teacher
of seventh grade to such distraction she banished
us to study hall, where we sat triumphantly bored.

That same year the phys ed teacher pitted
Bobby and me against each other in wrestling.
We each scored a takedown and drew. By ninth grade,
interests, ambitions, and school-sanctioned testing
drove us apart, rockets speeding in different directions.
In the general track, Bobby never failed again.
One June we found ourselves in Washington, D.C.,
on a senior class trip. We took a midnight cab
to Georgetown, went to a disco, sat in a dark corner,
drank beer, didn't dance, and were startled
when two girls appeared at our table.
We told them about the rural midwest
and bought them three rounds of whiskey sours
before they picked up their purses and excused
themselves to the rest room ten minutes before closing.

That fall I learned about existentialism, behaviorism,
and prose stylists of the twentieth century.
Bobby forged gun barrels in a steel mill, working
so fast the union steward sat him down
for double-time breaks to make the job last.
In three months Bobby was drafted into the army.
Less than a year from the night we looked at each other
in that Georgetown bar, the lights flickering,
and knew the girls weren't returning,
Bobby was missing in action. A month later
his body was found on a steaming jungle slope.

Bobby's father and brother went to Deckman's Funeral Home.
"I wouldn't look," warned Mr. Deckman.

Bobby's father insisted. Mr. Deckman opened the casket. Bobby's brother, the one who had taught him bloodless victory through the deadly headlock, fainted.

III.

On that winter afternoon in 1959 Bobby and I
tried to find out who was better, but he couldn't
adjust the headlock and I couldn't break it.
The principal burst through the schoolhouse doors,
bellowing commands neither Bobby nor I could obey.
Mr. Daggart's tie flapped over his shoulder;
his sport coat caught the wind, billowing behind him
like a madman's cape. He snatched our collars
in large hands, yanked us to attention, choked us
into the building, down the long hallway, where he drew
his paddle and whacked us five times each.
Before the principal banged the schoolhouse doors aside,
the playground was ice-quiet, waiting as Bobby
and I strained and sweat inside our clothing.
Pressed between Bobby's back and the ice-coated asphalt
my ungloved hand burned. My butch haircut brushed
Bobby's chin, my face crushed against his corduroy coat.
Breaking loose would have been the biggest mistake.
Bobby held me so fast, so close, so safe.

Like Bobby, I worked one summer in a steel mill. We often forged rectangular chunks of metal the size of cement building blocks. In a hutlike brick oven they absorbed thousands of degrees of heat for hours. When they were white-hot, I opened the oven door, knocked them loose with a long steel hook, and dragged them out. Heat rolled from the oven in a steady wave, stinging the flesh and bringing tears to the eyes. To do the work, I wore thick gloves, a heavy, long-sleeved shirt, and a wire mask over my face. The master steel forger and his first helper held the malleable chunks of metal with tongs and shaped them under the massive hydraulic press. For as long as the metal remained soft, we worked fast and paid keen attention.

This is a good way to write, too: quickly, bravely, properly equipped, and with a little risk. Such a stance makes us alert to memories, experiences, emotions, ideas, images, associations, beliefs, and surprising language—chunks of material for writing. They are often white-hot as soon as we notice them. Or sometimes all they need to become white-hot is to lie in the oven of the subconscious. Whenever they are ready, a writing state of mind enables us to go right to work, shaping them with language, turning them into something with form and meaning.

IMAGES

Visual thinking is crucial for writers. It can spark writing as it did for me in "The Silence That Widened," even though the original, powerful image of Bobby firing his gun on the cliff appears nowhere in the final draft. Images can also sustain writing and evoke further language during revision. I sometimes ask students to map indelible images in their lives, to begin to objectify them with language. I know they'll stir up flashes of pictures, some of them recent, some of them tucked away. Figure 3–2 is an image map jotted down by Mark, a senior English education major and past nose guard on the Utah State University football team.

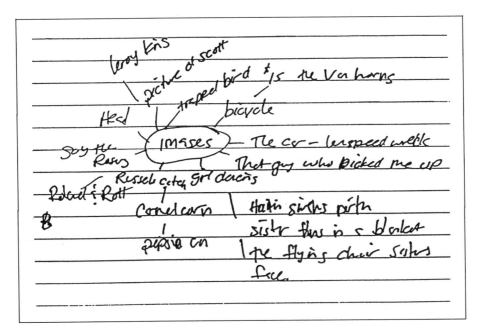

FIGURE 3–2

Among the images awhirl in Mark's mind was a "picture of Scott"—a yearbook photograph of a boy he'd known in grade school. Like inner speech, this inner image held a shower of meaning: incidents, values, social critique, language, sensory associations. Mark free-wrote immediately after mapping the images. Language carried him into his memories of Scott and a horrid story he knew but had not witnessed. After some shaping and revision, he arrived at this troubling, multiply tragic poem:

AFTER SCHOOL

Scott,
Scott something or other,

I don't remember the dude's last name.

All I know is
he killed that sea gull,
then he burnt that old Chinese woman up.

I'm sure the smell of her burnt angora sweater
was worse than the smell of her burnt skin.

Flicking
matches at her while
she pruned,

who thought she'd
go up like a Buddhist monk
freshly dowsed with gasoline.

Dixie cups
half-filled with water,
to extinguish the flames.

Her hair,
burning flash,
then black ash, like Michael Jackson's
after that Pepsi commercial.

We were only in the fifth grade,
and now Scott was off to some reform school.

What a fool,
I don't think he knew,
the matches, the flames, the screams
of pain.

He's gone now,
his youth burned
away,
like that lady's
yellow, Asian skin.

Skin
grafts
more painful
than the flames that ate
her back,

And innocence,
burnt beyond recognition.
> *Mark Johnson, Senior, Utah State University*

In Mark's class we had immersed ourselves in poetry for three weeks, reading Paul Janeczko's *Poetspeak* and writing poetry ourselves. Most of the students had never read an entire anthology of poetry before. I had also been reading them a contemporary free verse poem at the beginning of each class. The students were aswim in contemporary poetry. The rhythms, concrete imagery, and plain subject matter of it entered the bones of many of the students; some began to develop a writing state of mind.

KimberLeigh, a senior math major and English minor, was one such student. In her final portfolio she included three poems she had written and this explanation of their meaning:

> These [poems] are included because after reading *Poetspeak* a door unlocked in my mind. I knew I could write this stuff and after reading the book, I did. Before then I had locked any bit of creativity in a little corner of my gray matter because I felt my poetry was inadequate and would never compare to anything great. The poems in *Poetspeak* were great and I felt freed to attempt the writing of poetry again.

Our concentrated attention to imagery had quickened KimberLeigh's alertness. Her immersion in contemporary poetry made it natural for her to put language to indelible images she perceived. She explains how she came to write one of the poems:

> The third poem came to me in the night as I was walking from the library to the student center. Below me the ice sparkled, just like diamonds. And the words to the poem came into my mind like someone just spoke them to me.

I WALK ALONG THE SIDEWALK

I walk along the sidewalk
sides lined with lighted lamps.
Below, feet trudge through frozen slush.
I see little reflections,
small glimmers from the lamps in crystals of ice.
I walk on diamonds.

Nature is rich.
  KimberLeigh Felix Hadfield, Senior, Utah State University

A writing state of mind awakens you to varied possibilities for writing. Ideas can come from anywhere. On one occasion, I was teaching students a process strategy for answering in-class essay tests. We worked with a prompt I thought students had common experience with: "Describe the preparation and creation of the perfect hamburger." We brainstormed the task as a large group, and I filled the chalkboard with suggestions of ingredients and procedures for making a perfect hamburger. We decided which suggestions we might write about and numbered them in an order we might discuss them. Then I asked each student to write a lead for an essay—not a thesis statement, but a lead that would draw readers into their essay.

Christine started to write about how her family barbecued hamburgers over charcoal. In casting about for an interesting lead, she thought of her dad's grilling dictum: "You should flip meat only once." She heard his voice clearly in this bit of remembered language. Christine pursued her father's wont to advise and developed a poem. After finishing it, she began to think about sharing it with her father. She knew the perfect time. Her marriage was set for several weeks hence—on Father's Day—and she would read the poem at the reception. "I wanted to write this in my own voice," Christine told me, "the way you taught us. It didn't have to rhyme or be a mystery."

ADVICE

You should only flip meat once
Turn pancakes **after** the bubbles start to pop
And always cook eggs on low.

Get those shoulders back
Walk with your head high
And "if you are happy—tell your face."

Keep your eyes on the road
Don't swerve to miss animals
And "never drive over five in parking lots."

Flip your wrist when you shoot
Lean into the curve
And don't reach over the bar.

Keep your tongue in your mouth,
Your hands to yourself,
And "When I come down the stairs
Those feet better be on the floor!"

No one can **make** you angry,
Unless you let them.

Remember the past
Dream about the future
But live today.

Get off the phone.
Be home by twelve.

Get an education.
Show some respect!
Help your mother.
Smile.
Be nice.
Set high goals.
Are you listening?

Well Chuck, I can't say that I have always listened to you in the
    past, but today I did the one thing you've been telling me to do
    for years . . .

I married my best friend.

(Thanks for the advice—I love you, Dad.)
Christine Cluff Thompson, Junior, Utah State University

CONTEMPORARY MODELS

Christine had much going for her: passion for her material, closing with
it quickly, faith in its significance, fearlessness in getting language down on
paper from scribbled essay lead to advice her father had pronounced over the
years, and the pressing occasion of her upcoming marriage and separation
from the family she'd lived with for two decades.

She also had the benefit of another key ingredient to writing well: immersion. Christine had been immersed in contemporary models of poetry, just as
Mark and KimberLeigh had. The emphasis in our class was on teaching literature, but I wanted students not just to consume and criticize literature. I
wanted them to produce it. We were alert to possibilities for writing.

In addition to following passions, striving for truths, possessing faith, and
exercising fearlessness, it is important for writers to have experience with
contemporary models of writing, so they see possibilities for their voices right
here, right now, in their age.

Some students sit in English classes for years and never read contemporary voices, so glutted is the curriculum with voices from the distant past. The
old voices are important, but they are not the only voices, and they are not
likely to be voices that spur modern students of varying ability to writing of
their own.

A few years ago I taught a one-week writing seminar in Fredonia, New
York, with John Burns, an elementary language arts coordinator, and Susan
Stires, stellar teacher of primary-grade children at Nancie Atwell's Center for
Teaching and Learning in Edgecomb, Maine. On Friday John drove Susan and

me to the airport. John is well versed in children's literature and passionate about teaching writing. He knew I had been pushing poetry in my section. His own experience with poetry had been dominated by traditional examples of it he'd encountered twenty years earlier in required literature survey courses. When I talked about poetry on our drive to the airport, John shrugged his shoulders. "I never connected much with poetry," he said.

I took that as a challenge. I pulled out a book of contemporary poetry I was reading: Lowell Jaeger's *War on War*. I flipped to a page whose corner I'd turned down and read aloud "Leaving for Sweden." It's about a young man in the 1960s on the final night he spends with his family before leaving for Sweden. At eighteen, he's made the decision not to go to war. His parents know he is leaving home, sense there is something wrong in a world where sons are burning draft cards, and are puzzled by the passport he carries, but remain oblivious to his desperate plans. His mother bakes cookies. His father rocks away in front of the television, ignoring the horrific reports from Vietnam. Aboard the bus at 2:00 A.M., the boy looks out the window at his waving parents and utters the stark realization that knocks you dead:

> **I** looked hard
> at the stern, unsuspecting faces of my mother and father;
> *Fools, you fools,* I wanted to let them know
> I would never be home again.

Susan gasped.

John turned his head to me, his expression startled, troubled, serious. "I guess I've been reading the wrong poetry."

Not the wrong poetry, just not poetry that echoed and validated his contemporary voice, not poetry that invited him to become part of the enterprise of writing poems. John associated poetry with voices culturally distant, enigmatic, often inaccessible, just as I had when I was eighteen years old and wrote thine, wine, and pine.

When I teach novels, poetry, nonfiction, or drama, I am not teaching rarified, elitist appreciation of *li-tra-chure*. I have an eye on the development of writers and not just writers who write about somebody else's writing. I seek to engage student writers with contemporary examples of literature, to broaden their notion of possibilities for writing. Maybe we'll read fiction by Hawthorne, but surely we'll read fiction by Toni Cade Bambera and Sherman Alexis, too. Maybe we'll read sonnets by Shakespeare, but surely we'll read free verse by Mary Oliver and Alden Nowlan.

The world of literature is large and contains multitudes. The voices in it are too many to try to "cover," as anthology compilers and curriculum guides would have us believe we must. I don't want students to get a limited notion of possibilities for their voices as I did. And I don't want them to feel unworthy because their voices don't match some literati's of eighteenth-century England.

Christine told me that at her wedding reception when she got closer to reading "Advice," she began to have doubts. "That's not poetry," she was afraid people would say. "That's just talk."

"But I liked what I wrote," Christine said. "It was in my voice and my dad's voice. It didn't rhyme, but it was true."

THE BEST WRITING TEACHER

My best writing teachers over the years have taught me faith and fearlessness. In three years at Malvern High School Helen Romano (no relation) required me to write hundreds of pages of reports, essays, and term papers, thereby enabling me to discover my own writing processes, learn the pleasure of manipulating language, and enjoy my written voice.

Milton White at Miami University exhorted us to write about what we knew, pack our writing with detail, and "say it simply."

Don Murray of the University of New Hampshire urged me to draft fast, produce volume, write my best, develop my strengths, pursue my obsessions, and turn up the heat.

His friend and colleague Don Graves marveled at what I chose to write and, on one occasion, taught me how to finesse writer's block by writing what a chapter wasn't.

I left each of those empowering teachers wanting to write more, the very bottom line, I think, that marks a writing teacher's success.

Most recently, I've learned from my colleagues at Utah State University: Ken Brewer has encouraged me to write about the "tough stuff" and cut my language to the bone; Bill Strong has shown me how to continue the dialectic between myself and my drafts; and Christine Hult has urged me to step back sometimes, slow down, and give my all once again to important writing I've grown weary of.

My best teacher of writing, however, never spoke a word to me, only awaited my work each day, completely open to what I would write. My best teacher of writing tolerated error to such an extent that none of mine were ever mentioned. My best teacher of writing showed no emotion about my writing, either, was a perfect Zen master in that sense: no praise, no blame. I should add that I suffered no agitation or disillusionment from lack of praise, nor did I founder from the absence of explicit guidance and correction of my many errant ways. I didn't recognize when I wrote badly, but I often recognized when I wrote well and felt pleased and self-fulfilled because of it. My best teacher of writing was ever present as I followed my passions and wrote with faith and fearlessness, being as honest as I could.

My best teacher of writing was my journal. I began keeping one in 1973 after reading *Hooked on Books* (Fader and McNeil 1966). I was already hooked on books, but Fader and McNeil hooked me into paying the highest respect I could to my own memories, ideas, experiences, plans, anticipations, and relationships: I wrote about them. From 1973–1979 I was devout in my journal writing, rarely missing a day. In hard-backed composition notebooks I gave unfettered rein to my thinking. Journal writing became woven into the ritual of my day. I often wrote after school when my toddler daughter napped. Sometimes I wrote late at night when she was abed and my wife had not yet returned from the afternoon shift at the hospital. Sometimes I wrote in the morning, a cup of coffee within easy reach.

The aspect of my journal writing that was critically important to my rhetorical development was this: I practiced what I was learning through teaching writing. I didn't, for example, just *tell* about scenes from my past and present. I dramatized them, rendered their imagery, smells, sounds, textures, and tastes. I recorded the words people spoke. I packed my writing with details both remembered and invented to capture the illusion of reality. I ended entries with meaningful information that surprised the reader—me—with a jolt of understanding. What I preached in my teaching I practiced practiced practiced in my journal.

In graduate school I once used an extended passage from my journal to begin an essay. "Do you always write with such detail in your journal?" Don Graves asked. I did. Unlike now, when I write poetry, book reviews, articles, and occasionally a book, in those years I devoted my writing time to the journal. My voice evolved from self-centered whining and nit-picking into a tool for capturing the drama of people and incidents. I gained new respect for my familiar world, both past and present. I deepened my faith in the stories I knew, the perceptions I had, the ideas I found compelling.

The journal proved to be a seedbed, too. I wrote my first free verse poem in it when I was twenty-nine years old. A madly written entry about a censorship incident at school became the first piece of mine that *English Journal* published. And I wrote often about my daughter. I was twenty-one when Mariana was born on Christmas Eve, 1970. When she started talking, I began seeing the world anew. Her fresh perceptions and necessarily metaphorical language were regular topics of my writing:

Friday, 11/19/73   I sat reading in the rocker that Uncle Joe had given me. I looked up from my book to see Mariana standing before me. "Papa," she said, "get your pipe and blow doughnuts."

Late last August when we were in Canton, Mariana, Kathy, and I drove out to the Belden Village shopping mall. Mariana was fascinated with the elaborate fountains in the middle of the mall. She sat on my shoulders, looking at the water and said, "That's jumping water, Papa."

Saturday, 1/4/74   9:50 A.M.   While I was in the kitchen preparing coffee and pancake batter, Mariana stood by the table, sipping grape juice through a straw. I took the box of pancake mix from the shelf and shook it to see how much mix was left. I didn't know it then, but some of the mix flew out of the box and landed on my shirt pocket. I turned to Mariana. She looked up to me from her purple sipping. Her eyes grew wide. She pointed to my shirt pocket and said, "It's snowing, Papa!"

1-30-74   *Coughdrips*. Mariana said that she wanted *coughdrips* for her throat.

Mariana's observations, routine to her but so delightful and surprising to me, remained in my head long after I wrote them in my journal. Whenever I talked to students about relying on the perceptions and language they had within themselves, I illustrated my urging with Marianaisms, as I came to call them. But even though these linguistic gems were in my head, the journal was the place where I captured them, reemphasized them, afforded them dignity.

Fourteen years after I made those journal entries, while I was working on writing poetry with high school students, I set a time aside several days hence during which we would draft poem beginnings. I decided that I would try to write a poem about Mariana's metaphor making. For some reason the time seemed right to work with that material, maybe because of the heightened alertness to language that our immersion in poetry engendered.

At any rate, my subconscious was working on making sense of the Marianaisms. While driving home from school one day, I heard—just as Kimber-Leigh had earlier—a voice inside my head. It whispered: "My daughter wuzza poem." The orthographic irregularity was a distinct part of the voice. I repeated the sentence every so often so I wouldn't lose it. When I got home, I wrote the words on the card I kept in my shirt pocket.

When the day came to draft with the students, I wrote that sentence at the top of a yellow legal pad and proceeded down the page, cataloging the metaphors my daughter had spoken as a child, the ones I'd written in my journal years before. I didn't worry about how the figurative language fit; I just produced in a gush, hoping to start a rhythm and ride it for all it was worth. In trying to catch my daughter's playfulness, I found myself playing with language and images.

Over the next few days, I shaped the white-hot material, but I couldn't find a way to satisfactorily end the poem. At the time, Mariana was a sophomore in high school. Her American history teacher believed in the power of writing to generate thinking. She often had students write brief essays about their assigned reading. One day I found a striking essay amid Mariana's pile of books on the dining room table. The final paragraphs are shown in Figure 3–3.

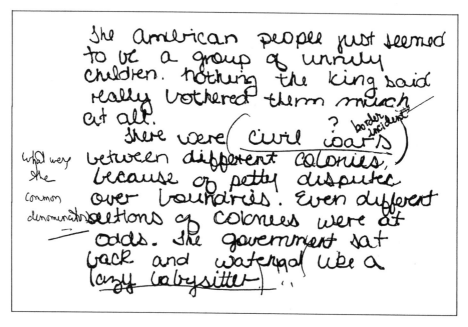

FIGURE 3–3

I used that entire excerpt to end the poem. Then I read it to Mariana. "I like it," she said, "but the ending's too dragged out." She had struck on the imbalance I'd felt. I cut and altered the words, keeping her surprising simile.

POETICS
for Mariana

My daughter was a poem.
She'd waken early, kneel near my
sleepface, wait for my eyes.
One flutter and milkbreath whispered,
"Papa, you get me cereal?"

Faith and Fearlessness

Yes, my daughter was a poem.
"Get your pipe," she'd say.
"Get your pipe and blow doughnuts."

That was eons ago, before fashion,
when she knew without doubt that
the shopping mall held
but one point of interest:
the spout and splash of the
jumping water.

Oh, she was a poem, all right.
We walked the neighborhood then,
she new enough to clasp my finger.
The daisy's petals, she told me, were eyelashes,
then asked the name of the drifty-looking tree.

Yes, my daughter was a poem and I swear that
she
(along with all poems that age)
should win perpetual Pew Lit Surprises.
When she was three feet (with no rhyme),
she saw that Saturday morning pancake flour
was really dust of snow.
On wet days we opened rainbrellas.
To soothe sore throats we sucked coughdrips.

Yes, my daughter was a poem
and may still be . . .
you see, her heart,
though carefully incognito now,
lets slip glimpses of that older identity.

She drags her weary teenage bones
home from expository school,
punches on the stereo, tables
books, folders, and a jumble of papers.
Amid the turmoil,
sticking from the pages of her history book,
a tattered fragment from a hurried essay:
"The colonists fought among themselves
like unruly children,
and King George sat back and watched—
Just like a lazy babysitter."

Is a poem.

Might I have written "Poetics" or something like it if I hadn't written
Marianaisms in my journal fourteen years earlier? Maybe. Some other process

might have slipped into gear. But I believe this: writing expressively in my journal about my young daughter paid respect to our experience, captured in print her fleeting spoken perceptions, fused love and wonder with metaphorical thinking and language development—both hers and mine.

Joy and delight were always part of my journal. I wrote about them often. But my vast field of significant value also includes experiences of pain and regret. I wrote about them too:

Sunday, 9/16/73 Early one Friday evening when I was fifteen, I said good-bye to my father. He was leaving for a bowling tournament and later on that night I was going to a high school play. May was the month. Dad wore a brown cardigan sweater. I came up behind him as he was walking down the hallway toward the back door. Dad's right elbow had caused him sharp pain since early winter. Patting him on the back, I said, "Hit about six hundred tonight, Dad."

Without turning to me, he mumbled something about trying and then was out the back door and gone.

About nine hours later, at 2 A.M., the telephone rang and I went to the kitchen to answer it.

A woman said, "Is this the residence of Philip Romano?"

"Yes," I answered.

A pause.

"Is this one of the Romano boys?" she asked.

"Yes."

Another pause, longer this time.

"Well, this is the emergency room of the Alliance City Hospital," the voice said, "and we have Philip Romano here and he's dead."

Two rooms away my mother slept, and had been sleeping for over an hour.

That was the first time—nine years after the killing experience—that I'd written about my father's death. Nine years. It felt good to write the horrid scene, to see it ordered in paragraphs, dialog, and brief description that captured the image of the last time I saw my father alive. The writing honored our time together and skewered forever the brutal way I learned of his death.

He had gone to a bowling tournament that night, had driven his new Cadillac. Four men accompanied him—three friends and his nephew. When they got to the bowling alley, they found that the tournament had been postponed. No one had notified them. My father turned onto the road for home. Less than a mile ahead, two drag racers roared side by side down the public highway toward them. Somehow the racing cars locked together as they bore down on my father. The head-on collision at 137 miles per hour exploded into the night, fusing metal, twisting lives forever. The two drag racers survived. So did the four men with my father, although they were haunted with nightmares for years. The steering wheel crushed my father's chest, killing him quickly.

Seventeen years after first writing about the incident in my journal, the reverberation of losing a father showed up in *Blindside,* a young adult novel I wrote. The main character was Nick Dasko, seventeen. Nick's father, like mine, had been senselessly killed. In the excerpt below, Nick has just seen a friend of his father, Mr. Francini, an old man Nick can't get away from fast enough. He fears that seeing Mr. Francini will make him think of his father. He's right:

Nick closed his eyes and saw his father lying in the white satin of the coffin, one hand clutching a rosary, resting on his stomach. His father didn't look at peace. He looked trapped and coerced, desperate to escape death. Too much make-up caked his face. His expression was fixed in a severe frown forever. From the lid of the coffin hung a golden crucifix, quite heavy, Nick discovered later, when he hung it on the wall of his bedroom.

Nick saw himself, fifteen then, freshman year of high school nearly over, sitting beside his mother and sister in front of the coffin. He wept and every now and then he looked up to his father. The frown. The rosary. The oppressive smell of flowers that loaded the floor and tables around the coffin. His father. Dead. His own father.

He had heard voices during those two days of calling hours, real voices that later became voices in his head. Lance came by, Lance, just two years out of high school, then, married with two children. He placed his hand on Nick's shoulder. He told Nick's mother and sister he was sorry. He said nothing to Nick, just held his shoulder. Nick didn't look up. When the pressure of Lance's hand left, Nick felt its loss.

Nick heard other voices too: old illiterate Henry Steen, bending close to his face, saying in breath that reeked of wine, "You're going to miss Papa. You're going to miss him bad." And Mrs. Kenney: "He looks like always." And Mr. Techman: "He looks good, don't he."

And Nick nodded amid all this and thought, he doesn't look good he doesn't look like always he looks dead he looks still and yes you son of a bitch I'm going to miss him and now he's gone and we argued last week and now it's too late to tell him I'm sorry it's too late to tell him I love him it's too late too late too late.

Only Uncle Mike had told the truth, Uncle Mike, the oldest of his father's six brothers, and Uncle Mike wouldn't have told the truth had he known that Nick would overhear him.

"He looks sunken because his chest was crushed," Uncle Mike

had explained to someone. "The steering wheel caved in his chest. The funeral director had a hell of a time building it up, said he'd never done anything like it before, never seen anything like it."

And then the memories moved to his mother, who had experienced the calling hours and funeral in numb terror. She had sat between Nick and Donna in front of the coffin. The three of them saw all the people pay their respects. Hundreds filed by: relatives, friends, customers. They spoke to his mother and sister and him, then they went to the coffin. Many knelt at the railing and said prayers. Nick remembered Mr. Francini genuflecting over his father. At one point Nick and his sister and mother knelt at the railing and said the Lord's Prayer, sobbing and weeping the whole time. It took all the courage he possessed to get through the Lord's Prayer, because Nick wasn't sure he believed it anymore. He wanted to believe. How he wanted to believe, but he wasn't sure anymore. Thy will be done, thought Nick. Thy fucking will be done? Was his father dead in a coffin God's will? His father clean-shaven with make-up, frowning forever. His father clutching a rosary in death when he hadn't been to Mass in years. Was this God's will?

"Forever and ever," Nick had said through overwhelming grief
forever and ever
with his hands clasped and pressing hard against his forehead
forever and ever
through tears that made his hands slick and burned the skin between his fingers
forever and ever
through the memory of his uncle Mike wrestling with the funeral director, pushing him aside, and kissing his father three times on his dead lips
forever and ever
as he broke away from his mother and sister walking from the funeral home, broke away and ran back into the room to see the funeral director removing his father's ring and the rosary and the crucifix and closing the lid of the coffin forever and ever.

CONCLUSION

To boost our faith and add resolve to our fearlessness, we have the allies of process and practice. We have another ally, too—the brute fact of development. We do not stay the same. We change. We evolve. We keep engaging in processes of writing and reading, keep talking to others—teachers and kindred spirits—about those experiences, keep risking and trying and stretching. Our minds mature as we read and write and talk for real purposes. We accumulate facts. Our vocabulary expands. We learn literary styles. Our perceptions sharpen. Our notions of the possible broaden. Our voices develop.

I've heard poets sometimes disparage the poetry they wrote as teenagers. Drivel, they call it, sentimental garbage. They seek to distance themselves from that writing, from the evolving person they were. Not me. I cherish my melancholy, searching self at eighteen. I'm glad I wrote thine, wine, and pine, no matter that no one but me saw that brave little poem for twenty-one years. Those fourteen "mortuous" lines in a voice like nobody's I'd ever known are an important part of the intricate root system that sustains my writing today and makes me sensitive to students. No thine, wine, and pine, then maybe no thousands of pages of journal writing, no "Poetics," no *Clearing the Way*, no book that you're reading now.

My father spoke only Italian to his father and mother, who died in 1945 and 1950. He also spoke Italian to the old immigrants who visited his tavern. But he never spoke Italian at home. He saw himself more new world than old. He was a citizen of the United States. He was a businessman. And I think he was happy with the life he made for himself in this country, satisfied with the way he had evolved through the early 1900s, the Roaring Twenties, the Great Depression, World War II, and the prosperous fifties and early sixties. He developed from immigrant child to prominent son to brickyard worker to poolroom operator to proprietor of the tavern and bowling alleys he borrowed money to build in 1940 and paid off three years later.

On the spring evening when he walked down the back stairs of our apartment above the bar, his elbow aching a little, his son urging on his success, he was no longer the nine-year-old immigrant child Mariana captured in "The Wooden Pony," the child who had arrived in America frightened and homesick. But if he hadn't been that child, hadn't transacted with the world, suffered defeats and won triumphs—learning and growing from both—if he hadn't developed, he never would have come to a point of equanimity that dreadful May evening, full of faith in the future and fearlessness to live life completely.

❧
WHY, INDEED

Why aren't English teaching majors required to take creative writing courses? All the writing in this world is not critical essays of authors and reviews for journals and reports of research; a lot of it is novels/poetry/ autobiographies/short stories/children's stories! I write these thoughts for this reading class (which, coincidentally, is what we future teachers are required to take the most of) because Linda Rief illustrates so well in Seeking Diversity *the hand-in-hand role reading and writing* should *play.*

The closest thing I've had to creative writing in my program is English 301, taught by Helen B. Cannon. Luckily, I enrolled in her section instead of someone else's. I hear most of the 301 classes consist of writing the traditional essay (argumentative, expositional, analytical, etc.), whereas the emphasis in her class was the personal (the freedom) essay, which made me feel as though I were a real, professional writer.

Angela Thomson Brenchley,
Junior, Utah State University

Chapter Four

FURTHER WAYS
OF KNOWING
*Dialog, Poetry,
and Song*

. . . THE VARIED CAROLS I HEAR.

Walt Whitman

*W*riting is a mural, not a snapshot. It is large and contains multitudes: meticulously developed thinking that shares vision and ideas with unknown others; scribbled, cryptic notes to trigger memory; complicated novels peopled with dozens of characters; haiku that evoke single, sensory images; dense philosophical treatises that alter nations; love letters read, reread, and placed in a shoe box for fifty years.

In academia, however, we often reduce writing to the expository— writing that analyzes a problem, explains a phenomenon, demonstrates what is known for a test. Tom Newkirk writes that once students enter secondary school they cross the "great divide" (1989, 5). Limitations are placed on what they can write about, limitations that lead them away from genres that render experience and toward genres that explain experience, particularly the thesis-driven essay. Although it is proper, Newkirk notes, for students to read about the adventures of literary characters, school doesn't often sanction students' writing their own adventures and sharing them with classmates (1990a, xiv). The further students progress through school, the fewer opportunities they are offered to write anything but exposition.

We have seen how faith and fearlessness can enable both our students and us to write stories that are pointed, imaginative, compelling, and undeniably cognitive. If we let writing that renders experience enter our classrooms and take a rightful place alongside writing that explains experience, then possibility opens like a flower. Students can express what they think (and what they come to think) through various genres. In modes of writing that come naturally to them and in modes they never dreamed of trying, students can develop facility with written language.

DIALOG

Conversation is a neglected rhetorical device in classrooms. Students might write for years and never know that essays may contain dialog. Modern essayists use the sound of voices in their essays whenever they need to. Even Michel de Montaigne, the sixteenth-century Frenchman credited as the father of the essay, included other voices in his writing by quoting earlier writers and philosophers.

In the first weeks of my beginning fiction writing course, we consciously practice using pointed dialog that provides information, characterizes, adds tension, creates rhythm, and injects varied voices into the fiction. Many students must not only learn to use dialog effectively for sense, they must also learn to punctuate it. Dialog, students tell me, is something they've never used in their previous writing.

Just as dialog amidst prose is a neglected rhetorical device in school, drama may be academia's most neglected genre. Our daily living, of course, is wall to wall with talk. Although school may not feature much genuine dialog, may, in fact, be dominated by monologs from teachers, still, students' experience is alive with dialog at home, in the corridors and lunchrooms of school, and during time spent with friends outside school. I say this even though I've heard some teachers claim that *their* students are so culturally deprived, so linguistically bereft, that they don't have language with which to write and speak. I don't believe this. The problem of the mute student is more likely the problem of a threatening audience. In 1834 Emerson wrote:

> Do not think the youth has no force, because he cannot speak to you and me. Hark! in the next room his voice is sufficiently clear and emphatic.

Dialog is a natural mode of expression. The major thing students need to learn about it for purposes of writing is the difference between written and spoken dialog. I'm talking here about more than spelling and punctuation. Dialog on the page dispenses with small talk. From writers we don't see much,

"Hey, how are you doing?"

"Pretty good. How are you?"

"Oh, just about par."

"Well, I'd better be going."

"OK, see you soon."

Don't think of dialog as mundane chitchat. Think of it rather as a dramatic encounter (Romano 1987), an encounter that reveals emotions, examines ideas, explores issues, expresses desires.

Dialog is kin to expository argumentation. Two thousand years ago Plato fashioned his arguments into dialogs. Doing so was a natural. With its give-and-take structure, its to-and-fro motion, dialog pushes thinking forward.

One voice asserts.

A second voice questions.

The first voice answers.

Both voices articulate further about matters they may have felt were settled when conversation began.

Through dialog, writers may narrate, describe, reason, argue, persuade. And as Shakespeare shows us, dialog may render experience in such a way that the language becomes poetry.

Whether that happens or not, the important thing to remember is that dialog is universal. We all engage in conversation. Writing dialog lets students write in a form close to their speaking voices. It offers them a nonthreatening genre to explore personally important topics, just as Marcia, a high school junior, does in the following piece, creating two sure voices that encounter each other and make readers think about a topic in the forefront of teenagers' minds:

This Is Serious

Gary: Can we talk?

Cathy: Sure. What is it?

Gary: It's about tonight.

Cathy: You're breaking our date?

Gary: No. I just thought maybe we could do something different.

Cathy: Oh? Like what?

Gary: We've been going together for a long time now, right? I've never said anything to you about it before. I didn't want you to rush into something you weren't sure about. But now, I mean, if you really care . . .

Cathy: Boy, when you said *different*, you weren't kidding!

Gary: This is serious, Cath.

Cathy: This is really important to you, isn't it?

	Silence
Cathy:	Why? Why is sex so vital?
Gary:	It's not like we're *strangers*. We've been together for months.
Cathy:	Is that why you've stayed with me so long?
Gary:	That's not fair!
Cathy:	Is it true, though?
Gary:	Would you stop! You're acting like a kid.
Cathy:	Okay. I'm sorry. (Pause) Gary, do you love me?
Gary:	You're very important to me. I need you.
Cathy:	But do you *love* me?
Gary:	Why is that so important: Love doesn't have that much to do with it. Look, it's a part of nature. Everybody does it.
Cathy:	That sounds so cheap!
Gary:	Please don't be this way. What's the problem? Are you afraid?
Cathy:	There is no problem. I just want more out of it than a cheap thrill.
Gary:	Why don't you come off your cloud? The world is not as sweet and pure as you think.

	Silence
Gary:	This isn't how I planned it to be.
Cathy:	I'm sorry.
Gary:	I hate to say this, but if you won't, somebody else will.

	Silence
Gary:	You would if you loved me, Cathy.
Cathy:	Love doesn't have that much to do with it, remember?

Marcia Stapleton Snively, Junior, Edgewood High School

Marcia's dramatic encounter was written in my English class, but it could have been written in health class or sociology. Dialog is a useful tool for writing in any content area. Through dialog students can synthesize facts and concepts. Teachers and students can take advantage of the natural dialectic that conversation offers to explore topics under study and/or show what they know about them.

Here is what one American Literature student wrote when she was asked to imagine a dramatic encounter between two poets—one who turned free verse loose on the world, the other a Quaker, abolitionist, and staunchly traditional versifier who wrote "Snow-Bound," one of nineteenth-century America's most popular narrative poems. In this imagined dramatic encounter Missy shows what she knows about the poets' work, personalities, poetic styles, and philosophies. And she filters all this through her satiric sensibility.

Why, hello, Whittier. Pardon me for excluding your first two names. They seem pointless to me.

Walter Whitman—

It's Walt.

Uh, Walt, I have something I'd like to discuss with you.

Come in. We'll sit the warming hearth about.

It's about *Leaves of Grass*.

Are we referring to the first, second, third, or fourth edition? There are nine, you know.

Yes, and every one just as filthy as the first.

How can you say that? All poetry is beautiful. Everything is beautiful.

You must revise that book at once. This time leave out the filth. Even Emerson says you should.

I told him and I'll tell you, the filthiest book is one which has been changed to suit the whim of others.

Walter—

Walt.

Walt, be reasonable. You can't just write down and publish everything that comes into your head.

Don't worry. I saved some of the ideas for later use. I didn't think anyone was ready for them yet.

If nothing else, change the blasphemy against God.

I won't change a word.

You sacrilegious fool!

Oh, it's snowing out. If you don't leave soon, you'll be snowbound here. I know. I'll sing myself for you.

I'm leaving, but don't think for a minute that your book will be forgotten.

And it wasn't.
Missy Lee, Senior, Edgewood High School

POETRY

This poetry stuff scares me to death. I have never written any, and I did not "get it" in high school.
Melissa Farnsworth-Warnick, Senior, Utah State University

Perhaps no other genre is as misunderstood as poetry. On one hand, it is demeaned and maligned. In many English classes, writing a poem may get extra credit, but the act is not usually part of the substantive work of the course. Many see poetry as airy-fairy stuff written by delicate, cloistered women and men with ruffled sleeves. A recent television commercial for an after-shave featured shots of a young man seen pulling a T-shirt off his muscled torso, fixing a car, soaking in a hot bath. A seductive female voice-over informed us that real men are back—and you'd better believe they'll "pass on poetry."

Poetry suffers the other extreme, too. It is routinely inflated. During one graduate class I taught, one of the students (a community college teacher) and I disagreed fundamentally about the role of poetry in the English curriculum. So upset did he become with my position that he refused to participate when we tried our hands at writing poems.

Poetry, I believe, is for all of us. I lead students of all ages into writing poems, not just reading them. Getting students both to consume and to produce poetry is my strategy for moving contemporary poetry into people's bones.

The teacher's position on poetry was quite different from mine. A writer of poetry himself, he believed the genre sacred. Students might befoul essays with their shoddy thinking, imprecise grasp of written English, and ineloquent diction, but they would not get the chance to soil poetry. Not in his classes.

I wasn't always so committed to bringing students to poetry as writers as well as readers. For years I was an inflater of poetry. By the time college literature teachers finished with me, I knew beyond doubt that writing poems was beyond my ken. From the poems teachers had me read and the way they intellectualized them, I believed that poetry represented a kind of abstract, arcane, symbolic thinking that wasn't my way of knowing. Despite my freshman composition teacher's touting of MacLeish's "A poem should not mean but be," all the tests and lectures sent me the unmistakable message that poems did indeed *mean*, and they invariably meant something I didn't "get."

I remember a peer who talked about the poetry-writing class he was taking. I was impressed and fearful. Not me, I thought. I wanted no part of writing poetry. Later, as a novice teacher, I never even entertained the idea of having students write poetry. In fact, I was afraid of any poem I didn't have a teacher's manual for. Students could write poetry on their own, I reasoned, but if they waited for *me* to lead them into writing poetry, they wouldn't write poetic word one.

Because I eventually started to write free verse myself, I came to understand that students could benefit greatly from seeing their world through poetry's indelible images, rhythmic wording, precise language, and purposeful use of the page. Working with poems can sharpen perception—the writer's *and* the reader's.

More than prose—more even than prose that renders experience—poetry uses concentrated, metaphorical language. Creating and extending metaphors can lead to surprising insights and connections, thus furthering and deepening the writer's understanding. This goes for students as well as for poets appearing in the latest issue of *Poetry*.

I sometimes charge students to develop metaphors, to look at one thing and see another—as young children so readily do, as Mariana did in those remarks of hers I used in "Poetics." I ask students to be profligate in making associations, some of which may lead to extended poetic metaphors that will help us see.

As Edward Lueders writes in "Your Poem, Man ..." (1969, 37):

Tell it like it never really was,
man,
and maybe we can see it
like it is.

Gerald, for example, a high school senior, conveys the serious nature of our profession when he melds simile with Biblical allusion to express his take on teachers and education:

Some teachers are like the money-changers in the temple.
They defile the holy grounds of teaching
with their sinful loans of personal opinion.
They should be thrown out on the street
for their educational hypocrisy.
    Gerald Van Winkle, Senior, Edgewood High School

Rhonda, a junior, uses metaphor to see a time of day. Although I love to work in the early morning, she makes me feel a rueful bitterness toward it that I haven't felt since I was a teenager. Rhonda's poem, too, demonstrates how a perfect word can make a poem satisfying and memorable. In this case, the metaphor drove her to generate it.

Dawn is the threatening
shadow of a thief,
slyly breaking into
your mind,
filching your dreams.
    Rhonda Dines Howard, Junior, Edgewood High School

Poetry certainly has no monopoly in getting students to speak from personal experience. Every genre can do that. But because of poetry's bent toward imagination, figurative language, and innovative form, it is an exciting and natural place to link the powerful generative forces of language with personal experience and passion, as Gerald did in having his say about classes in which his opinions mattered little.

In the poem below, high school sophomore Ted brings a strong, urgent voice and a knack for creating metaphor to a topic he knows from the inside. Ted's poem makes me believe deeply, even thrill a little.

ADRENALIN

With the
first taste
you're either
addicted or
repulsed
it's a drive
from deep
within to
flirt with
death and
pain
it's a steely
taste
and a heady
smell
Adrenalin
coursing through
every vein
at the sound
of whining
concrete
or the touch
of an angry
fist
it's the rush
of hearing
death snapping
at your heels
the thrill of
keeping
one step
ahead
dear god
don't let me
SLIP

Ted Hymer, Sophomore, Edgewood High School

Ted uses form to enhance meaning. The narrow, plummeting lines of the poem make me think of the arrowlike, instant hormonal surge that calls us to action. We can take this notion of fitting form to meaning to greater lengths. Some poets occasionally mold words and lines into a shape that suggests concretely the very topic of their poem. Though I am not good at this myself, some students can adroitly use "shape" or "concrete" poems to express themselves.

A poem by Philip G. Tannenbaum in our literature anthology (1984, 419) was all the nudging Joe, a sophomore, needed to write a concrete poem of his own. I was delighted with "Priming the Poem," but must admit that the fourth line confounded me. I couldn't shake myself from reading its first word as *can't,* even though such a reading renders the next word unintelligible:

PRIMING THE POEM

```
          writingis
          likeapu
          mpyou
           cantugatth
         e armal    ld
       a     ywith
     o       utadr
     o       pbuti
   f         youad
 d           alitt
           lewat
           eritw
            illfl
          owandfl
          owandflow
```

Joe Prushing, Sophomore, Edgewood High School

Sometimes poems build slowly and work their way leisurely into your understanding. Other times poems strike; writers deliver the goods sans discursiveness. Through poems students can synthesize bits and fragments of their knowing without the elaboration required in exposition. Heather, for example, creates a persona who blusters and commands, stating a position opposed to her own. She doesn't talk her topic to death, though, explaining cultural blindness, sexist crippling, and antiquated stereotypes. She doesn't need to. The absurdity and crassness of her persona's mind-set speaks for itself.

HEARD BY WOMEN ONLY

C'mon, woman,
    Do you need any help?
        CRAZY broad drivers!
Women are to be (ob)seen and not heard;
    Blond-haired diz
        Only good for two things!
          BAREFOOT and BEARING!
Feed me, wash my dishes, and while you are at it
    Get my beer:
        Who needs women's rights . . .
         You credit card disaster!
           NO BALLS, NO BRAINS . . .
Heather Smith, Senior, Edgewood High School

The poems I have shown you so far have been tightly controlled and well developed. But there is also room in poetry for the nonlinear, for wheeling flights of imagination, for thinking that does not march so much as soar. Writing poetry invites students to play with language and free-associate. In *Word Weaving* David Johnson writes:

> Creating by letting go . . . is especially suited for any writing that is exploratory, that seeks new associations and connections. It means beginning the process of writing without preconceived ideas about the direction and end of the process. It means being as open as possible to the flow of one's consciousness from image to image, pattern to pattern. It takes a kind of faith not to control or force the material but to *let go*, to discover in the process of writing itself what it is you are writing about. (52)

In the following poem Jeff uses free verse to romp on the page, playing with a common name, using it as a way of connecting some of the wide-ranging knowledge in his head. Through his fooling, he satirizes mythology, popular culture, cliches, religion, and childhood sex games:

IN THE NAME OF BOB

Bob
    bob
shiskebob
 Beelzebob
        Ratman and Bobin
Bob-bob-bobbin' along
Robert
    Rob

Bob
    Bobby
        Cindy
           Jan
              Marsha
Corn on the bob
           thingamabob
Bob spelled back
   ward is boB
Sha-na-na-na
      Get a bob
          Bob?
In the big inning
Bob created the Heavens
and the Dirt
        Let there be bob
eat Bob
     sleep Bob
        Baptize in
          the blood
            of Bob
Frankly, my dear, I don't give a Bob
bob
   Bob
      I'll show you my bob
if you show me yours
        Bob
   Bob
Who the
    hell
  is Bob
Jeff West, Senior, Edgewood High School

My method for inducing students—middle school through graduate school—to write poetry is to surround them with accessible modern free verse, contemporary voices that reflect their own. I place transparencies of effective poems on the overhead, hand out minicollections of poetry I've gathered, bring in books I've bought. As Ralph Fletcher says, I seek to " 'marinate the kids in lots of great poems before they start to write' " (1991, 175). Along with the marination, I make sure students know they are free to write about anything they want, to pursue passions in whatever direction they like. And then I provide the most important element. Wynnde, a college undergraduate, realized the importance of that element when she reflected on the work we had done reading and writing poetry:

This experience taught me a lot about teaching poetry. The most important concept, to me, is time. We had two weeks to compose our poems. It wasn't like we had time to spare. . . . No, these poems that we worked through took time and the majority of the time was spent on the process: peer response, self-evaluation, free writes, etc.

Wynnde Spalding Whittier, Junior, Utah State University

Although I believe firmly in immersing students in the genre and then letting poetry of many forms and topics emerge, occasionally I use an exercise or a specific type of poem to jump-start students into putting language on the page. Stephen Dunning and William Stafford's *Getting the Knack* (1992) offers provocative suggestions that students might try. One kind of poem that has led some of my students to productive poetry writing is what Dunning and Stafford call the confession poem (171).

This kind of prompt led Melinda, a thirty-five-year-old mother of five children and a college junior, to a serious, emotion-charged subject. In her quest to nail down her thinking, she came to an organic stanza shape for her poem.

CONFESSION

I must have done something to deserve this;
You were right—I asked for it,
I earned it.

I confess: I was a bad wife.
I studied while you watched TV.
I worked nights while you slept—
But not alone we now agree.

I threw a dish once and
It shattered against the counter.
(PMS)   you smugly said
It was dishonest to send the shards
Back to Corelle for replacement.
But it wasn't supposed to break! I said.

I smoked pot in high school.
I didn't keep the house clean enough.
I wasn't patient enough,
I wasn't loving enough,
        enough, enough, enough.

No one knew you were unhappy.
If you had said so I would have changed—
But your flight for perfection

Will warrant you nothing
But loss of your eternity.

Pain hurts. But it's better than lies.
Better than being bedwarmer
Instead of lover and wife.
(By the way—thank you for the children.)

Your orgasms were expensive.
Masturbation would have been cheaper
For us all.

I must have done something to deserve this.
Melinda Nutt, Junior, Utah State University

Not all students respond with such success to specific assignments. The safety valve is to make sure that a student's accomplishment in writing poetry does not ride entirely on whether or not she clicks with some particular assignment. The prompt for the confession poem was merely one part of the poetry writing we did for two weeks.

Given the time to write, an immersion in poetry, and the freedom to choose important subjects amid an accepting environment in which taking risks isn't all that risky, students can write startling, effective poems. The genre lets students assert their emerging power in compact, direct voices that use image and figurative language as allies of expression. The poem below was created in just such a concentrated high school poetry writing workshop that featured time, immersion, and freedom. With its controlling extended metaphor, direct language, and definitive ending, "Thermal Years" is the equal of any essay a student might write that explains the emotional and psychological shackles adults place on teenagers in the name of protecting them. Tari captures the boldness, vulnerability, and determination of adolescence.

THERMAL YEARS

I slammed the
        door shut on my
        winter squall
        and drank the
        warmth of
        future's fire.
        Then I undressed.

First off,
        my blood-red toboggan,
        too tight around my head,
        a gift from my preacher.

It's muddled righteousness
confused my soul, and
anyone, with a tug, could
pull it over my brow
and blind me.

Next,
　　the sunset scarf,
　　knitted by my grandmother
　　of ancient fears and
　　pigeon-holed paranoia.
　　It strangled my voice
　　and gave easy reins
　　to anyone wanting a
　　pack mule.

Then,
　　the straightcoat Dad bought,
　　"To keep you warm and safe."
　　It's bulky hug
　　tangled my arms and
　　made traveling from home
　　too hard.

Now,
　　the concrete boots
　　Mom, on my sixteenth birthday,
　　gave me to keep me
　　firmly
　　on the ground
　　and out of love's heaven

Then, finally,
　　I peel off
　　layer upon layer
　　of thermal underyears
　　and toss them away.
　　I'm naked.
　　And once more,
　　I turn and
　　walk into the fire.
　　Tari Shepherd, Senior, Edgewood High School

SONG

Students are attuned to song. They wear headsets, dance through con-
certs, crank up car stereos, buy extensive sound systems, set five CDs for

random play. Song lyrics and rhythms fill students' heads. I've seen students write down line after line from a song, not stopping until they have unreeled all the lyrics. On oldies radio stations I hear a song I'd forgotten existed, from thirty years earlier, and find myself singing the words. Some students go beyond simply consuming music and perform it, becoming quite sophisticated vocalists and instrumentalists.

I have sometimes invited, sometimes required students to try their hands at song writing, a particular kind of song writing: blues—that indigenous American music with roots in the slave quarters of southern plantations and in the African and European rhythms "that evolved . . . from the common musical practice that undergirt the work song, the prison song, the street cry, as well as the spiritual" (Collier 1978, 35), that sad, often sexy, sometimes tongue-in-cheek music that "was a cornerstone on which jazz was built" (43). Blues lyrics lend themselves well to teenage angst and the turmoil that literary characters encounter.

As we begin investigating processes for composing blues songs, I immerse students in the genre through the music of Eddie "Cleanhead" Vinson ("I Had A Dream" and "Juice-Head Baby") and Loudon Wainwright III ("I'm All Right"). After the blues singers have wailed on the boom box, we take a close look at the lyrics so we can talk about the structure of blues songs, their use of rhyme, rhythm, persona, humor, and surprise.

Graduate student Jim Mims felt Henrik Ibsen's *A Doll's House* had been ahead of its time, a premier drama to introduce modern readers to issues of gender. Below is a blues song Jim wrote based on Torvald's character:

DOLL HOUSE BLUES
(sung by Torvald)

(Standard Blues Riff)
My little squirrel left me.
My lark flew the coop.
I'm here all alone,
and you know I feel like poop.

But I am a proud man, baby,
I will survive.
The last thing I need
is some embezzler's jive.

You macaroon junky,
you screwed up real bad.
Walked out on sweet Torvald,
the best you ever had.

But I'm a big man, baby.

I'll let you live in my house.
You can see your children,
seem an obedient spouse.

Come on home, sweet Nora,
get in here outta' the cold.
I'll treat you like a doll, babe,
just like I did of old.

'Cause I'm a good man, baby,
though you've made me so sad.
Return to the Doll House, Nora,
and you'll make me so glad.

(Slower)
Return to the Doll House, Nora,
and you'll make me so glad.
            Jim Mims, Graduate Student, Utah State University

In a high school writing class, I asked students to collaborate in writing blues songs. On the Thursday and Friday students began drafting their lyrics, I was out of town. The writing workshop ran as usual, the bemused substitute teacher wandering about the room, students told me. With the new week, I returned to "End-of-School Blues," "Stranded-in-the-60s Blues," "Lil'-Sis Blues," "Acid-Washed Blues," "Fix-Your-Hair Blues," "I-Hate-My-Life Blues," and others.

For all our lesson plans, assignments, and classroom management procedures, the brightest moments in education are often serendipitous. Sweet spontaneity turns the mundane miraculous. The day we shared blues songs, Brian showed up with his acoustic guitar and strummed standard blues riffs. Before long, peer pressure and my cajoling worked their good effect: twosomes scattered about the rug mumbled their songs in practice, rehearsing to sing to Brian's accompaniment. I turned on my portable tape recorder, and we were in business.

At lunch I played the blues songs for my colleagues. They were as delighted as I.

"You ought to get Amy to sing 'End-of-School Blues' at the awards assembly," someone said.

Of course! "End-of-School Blues" would be perfect for lightening the tedious, overlong awards assembly held each spring in the "cafetorium," a room in which heat steadily rose throughout the evening until people-steam hissed from beneath the doors.

And wouldn't this be a wondrous leap for Amy? Bright, talented, somewhat reluctant Amy, whose voice so often quavered when speaking in class.

I cleared the idea with the principal, ran the lyrics past the vice principal, whom the students referred to as *Buck*—the administrator charged with enforcing the blue-line, anti-hall-roaming rule; cement-block parking rule; and tardy rule. With a bit more coaxing and the assurance that Brian would accompany her, Amy agreed to reprise "End-of-School Blues," only this time on stage with a microphone, three hundred parents and fellow students expecting the main things from her.

The next night, after two hours of academic awarding, just before the much-needed intermission, our principal introduced a special treat. Onto the stage walked Brian carrying his guitar and Amy wearing sunglasses, her one concession to the shyness of her soul.

The audience buzzed with wonder. The academic awards assembly, although gratifying in fleeting moments to parents and their children, had never featured something for everyone, had never admitted the students' culture into the program. Tonight it would.

Amy warmed to the audience, and the audience took immediately to her appealing intellect and natural humor. She began singing in the wrong key, at which point she stopped abruptly and said, "Let's start over."

The audience laughed along with her. Amy began again, in the right key and with a soulful, lamenting quality to her voice that the audience didn't know she possessed. The words and emotions Amy and her friend Wendy had written into the song became vivid. Amy squeezed every ounce of humor and I-been-oh-so-wronged sentiment from the lyrics. In moments, the audience of tight collars, ties, and dresses began swaying and clapping to the beat.

END-OF-SCHOOL BLUES

Get up Monday mornin'
Alarm clock blarin' in my ears
Gotta face another school day
after twelve long gruelin' years.

Try to wake up in the shower
Soap is burnin' in my eyes
gotta chemistry test in an hour
but all I wantta do now is die.

I got the end-of-school blues
Thank God you're not in my shoes
These days are draggin' like molasses
up to the last days of school.

Drivin' along in my dump truck,
Pull in the parkin' lot

End up gettin' yelled at by Buck
'cause there wasn't no cement block.

The two-minute bell is aringin'
I'm dashin' on down the hall
I almost make my locker
but I trip on the steps and fall.

I got the end-of-school blues
Thank God you're not in my shoes
These days are draggin' like molasses
up to the last day of school.

Gotta detention at lunch time
for steppin' on over the blue.
I'm so darn sick of those blue lines
Hallelujah! I'm almost through!

I got the end-of-school blues
Thank God you're not in my shoes.
Nothin's goin' right, I'm all full of spite
up 'til the last day of school!

Wendy Hartman Tuttle and Amy Whitacre White,
Seniors, Edgewood High School

❧
First Day of School

The wide-eyed students, the stifling heat, the newly waxed floors, the blaring P.A., the bells, the surprising silences, the blaring P.A., the cramped hallways, the slamming lockers, the new clothes, the stacked textbooks, the blaring P.A., the shy questions, the cool facades, the practiced saunters, the three-month reunions, the blaring P.A., the rules, the rules the rules, the rules the rules the rules the rules . . . .

Lind Williams, Teacher, Provo High School, Provo, Utah

Chapter Five

Breaking the Rules in Style

From this hour I ordain myself loos'd of
limits and imaginary lines.

Walt Whitman

*D*uring the time I was writing *Clearing the Way,* I discovered a book
that profoundly influenced my conception of what writing was, what it could
be, and what I would teach. The book was *An Alternate Style: Options in
Composition,* by Winston Weathers, now out of print.

Certainly, the book is for composition scholars who seek greater knowledge of rhetorical theory. But the book is also for all who love linguistic
innovation, stylistic experimentation, boundary-breaking written expression,
and, above all, glorious human diversity.

Weathers describes two ways of writing in this book, two "grammars of
style," as he calls them: Grammar A and Grammar B.

Grammar A you're familiar with: standard written English, traditional
rules of style. It holds up the SAT English-usage hoop that students must jump
through. Grammar A is eminently acceptable and generally quite conservative.
Fidelity to Grammar A has prompted many of us to say to students things like,
Never begin a sentence with *and* or *but*, when we know that professional
writers break that pseudorule whenever they must.

That's Grammar A, the grammar that we—among a phalanx of English/
language arts teachers—see to it that students learn from kindergarten through

graduate school. But according to Weathers, Grammar A is not alone. Also at large in the kingdom of writing is an another grammar, an appealing rebel, illicit in most eyes, yet ubiquitous and purposeful. We English teachers should be forthright and honest and acknowledge this other way of writing, this other grammar of style: Grammar B, Weathers calls it, "an alternate style."

Grammar B breaches the social amenities of Grammar A, taking liberties with Grammar A sentence structure, syntax, spelling, voice, and form. Grammar B breaks the rules of standard written English as a means of communicating powerfully. And it does this breaking, altering, and smashing with panache.

Don't be alarmed. Grammar B does not presage the decline of the West. Neither is it linguistic anarchy or grammatical promiscuity. Grammar B is nothing new. We've seen it in the writing of

Emily Dickinson	e. e. cummings
Tom Wolfe	Gertrude Stein
D. H. Lawrence	Jon Dos Passos
Virginia Woolfe	Richard Brautigan
Walt Whitman	Joan Didion

et al.

Grammar B is no youngster, either. Weathers's earliest citation of alternate style usage in fiction is Laurence Sterne's 1760 publication of *The Life and Opinions of Tristram Shandy*, in nonfiction, William Blake's prefatory remarks to each book of *Jerusalem*, published in 1804. Writers have been using Grammar B for years, but especially since the mid-1960s when "new journalism" announced its presence through the work of Tom Wolfe and Truman Capote.

> [Grammar B] is a mature and alternate (*not* experimental) style used by competent writers and offering students of writing a well-tested set of options that, added to the traditional grammar of style, will give them a much more flexible voice, a much greater communication capacity, a much greater opportunity to put into effective language all the things they have to say. (Weathers 1980, 8)

Assuming the persona of a student who is learning to write, Weathers asks that

> [I] ... be exposed to, and informed about, the full range of compositional possibilities. That I be introduced to all the tools, right now, and not be asked to wait for years and years until I have mastered right-handed affairs before I learn anything about left-handed affairs. That, rather, I be introduced to all the grammars/vehicles/tools/compositional possibilities *now*

so that even as I "learn to write" I will have before me as many resources as possible. I'm asking: that all the "ways" of writing be spread out before me and that my education be devoted to learning how to use them. (2)

I was excited by Weathers's inquiry into what many might consider this profane area of rhetoric. I developed a sense of urgency about my writing and teaching as I saw him treat with respect the unconventional stylistic maneuvers I'd admired over the years but never tried myself. Weathers approached his research in a scholarly, academic fashion. He cataloged the stylistic techniques of Grammar B, described them, and demonstrated how they might be used.

I found that Grammar B seeped into my own writing. Although no chapter in *Clearing the Way* is about Grammar B, I was immersed in learning about it when I wrote Chapter 11, "Literary Warnings." You can see the influence of my study in the alternate style in which the chapter is written. My urgency about Weathers's research made me determined to bring Grammar B to my high school students. But before I made such a bold move, I needed to talk about it.

I sought out Mark, my widely read friend and former student of eleven years earlier, Mark of the uncollected J. D. Salinger stories. I told him I'd never seen anything like Weathers's explanation of the alternate style, hearkened to the work of Tom Wolfe, e.e. cummings, and Ken Kesey we'd admired and discussed over the years. "I'm hoping Grammar B will spur students to take chances," I told him. "I want them to astonish themselves. I want them to smash conventional rules of writing and cut loose."

Mark raised his eyebrows. "Looks like you're going to do what you've always done."

I blinked. He was right. For years I'd sought to free students from restrictions, to create an atmosphere that removed impediments to exploration and communication. But I'd never actively and single-mindedly pushed students to break conventional rules of writing as a way of writing effectively.

Even though I hadn't, however, over the years there had been those memorable students with irrepressible voices who had surprised me with risk taking and originality. They were bellwethers. They knew intuitively that any rule of writing could be broken if the end result was writing that worked.

STYLE-MAKING BELLWETHERS

On a final essay exam in a high school American literature class, I asked students to write informative, well-supported essays in which they discussed five pieces of literature they had read over the semester:

Breaking the Rules in Style

1. The piece that revealed something startling or surprising about America's past
2. The piece they found most enjoyable
3. The piece most artfully put together
4. The piece that caused them to gain sympathy for a character they normally might not care about
5. The piece that most challenged their ideas or beliefs.

Students could range freely over any of the poems, stories, essays, and books they had read during the semester. In fact, I listed the titles of everything we'd read to help jog their memories.

Here is a paragraph from David's essay:

Another book that shows just how much change has happened is *The Electric Kool-Aid Acid Test* (you're probably tired of hearing me talk about it). It was well written. I liked the way it looked on paper. How many books can you say *that* about? It looked good on paper. It had run on sentences in parts where the action seemed like it could go on forever and he just kept dragging the sentence out to keep you reading on, and on, and on. Then. All of a sudden. He would toss in a fragment sentence. He also had poems, songs, and the thoughts of the characters thrown into fully italicized paragraphs.
David Van Cleave, Junior, Edgewood High School

I hadn't taught the alternate style in that American literature class, but David had read Tom Wolfe on his own. That was enough. David had learned about writing through reading. He was delightfully infected by Wolfe's exuberant voice that demonstrated possibilities for supercharged prose.

In the same batch of papers was an essay from another junior, Becki. Ten months earlier, she had missed the first week of my writing class, each day sitting in the guidance office trying to talk a counselor into letting her drop the course. When the counselor wouldn't comply, Becki and I spent the next few weeks at loggerheads: she sullen and recalcitrant; I righteous and unyielding.

As the semester progressed and Becki grudgingly wrote, her strong voice piqued my interest. We softened our positions and gave each other a chance. Becki enjoyed writing; I enjoyed her feisty intellect and fearless yawp. Second semester she elected to take my American literature class. Here is Becki's final essay exam, written in about thirty minutes—a double-twisting one-and-a-half off the high board, no second chance, no revision:

The reality. The pain. The loneliness. All the endurance and loyalty involved with war is what I got from the novel *Johnny Got His Gun*. I never realized the true horror of war until this story. I cried when he did, laughed when he laughed, and felt the pain of being abandoned. Which is why "Richard Cory" ended his life. He wasn't happy with all his material things, no, not by far. He needed and so desperately yearned for love. And all he got was a lot of "oohs and ahs" by the peasants. He was at the end of his rope in the cold *[In Cold Blood]* damp basement. His son witnessed his murder. Then, shortly, his own. His wife lay sobbing in her bed awaiting death, as did her daughter. Her daughter turns her face to the wall so as not to look death in the face when BANG. The cold hard iron doors shut. *[Sonny's Blues]* Shutting out the rest of the world. His brother never wrote him. His parents were dead and he was in jail. Sitting and thinking, thinking and sitting. I felt sorry for the poor guy. Growing up in *[Blood Brothers]* the city can change a man for the worst. Unless you're Stony Decoco. Then you deal with life the best way you can. Day by day. Not getting too attached to anyone or anything for fear of change. Raising hell and earning money are two of the most important things to Stony. Who cares about love? Stony did. He loved Cheri so much that every breath he took reminded him of her. Then she left him alone to face the world and being a survivor, he did.

Becki Strunk Thompson, Junior, Edgewood High School

It took me awhile to catch on to Becki's sophisticated discussion, which deftly blended one piece of literature into the next, one character into another. At one point—jumping the gun—I was saying to myself, Wait a minute, "at the end of his rope in the cold damp basement"? Richard Cory didn't hang himself. But I read on and was rewarded by Becki's subtle creation of language, literary interpretation, and compassion.

She expected me to have brains. Becki knew I had read all the literature she referred to. She had her audience pegged, but this was, after all, the final exam. So when it wasn't clear in her text which piece of literature she was writing about, Becki wrote the applicable title in the margin next to her discussion: Truman Capote's *In Cold Blood*, James Baldwin's "Sonny's Blues," and Richard Price's *Blood Brothers*—rhetorical elbows in the ribs in case I didn't get it.

So thoroughly delighted was I with Becki's linguistic performance that I telephoned her mother to extol Becki's stellar synthesis of literary knowledge, personal connection, and language use. When I called, Becki answered the telephone, rock music cranked up in the background.

"Mom's at work, Mr. Romano, I'm kicked back, listening to music and drinking a pop. School's out, man!"

"You deserve some laid-back time," I said. "I called to tell your mom about your excellent essay."

"Yeah?" she said.

"Yeah, indeed," I said, "it made me sit right up and take notice."

Becki laughed. "I thought you'd like that."

For years my best writing students had been showing me that you *can* break rules of standard written English and write exceedingly well. With their example, my own delight in playful, innovative writing, and Winston Weathers's solid academic discussion of alternate style techniques, I was ready to bring Grammar B to my students. I've been doing it ever since, nine years now, with students junior high through graduate school.

GRAMMAR B STYLISTIC TECHNIQUES

The remainder of this chapter demonstrates some of the stylistic techniques Winston Weathers discusses in *An Alternate Style*, principally

Repetition
the sentence fragment
the labyrinthine sentence
orthographic variation
double voice
the list

REPETITION

Grammar B certainly has no monopoly on the use of effective repetition. Repetition is a staple of effective writing regardless of genre or style. Our lives thrive on repetition: our lungs expand and contract, expand and contract. The pulse at our wrists beats steadily on. In writing we love cadence and rhythm and rhyme. In Grammar B, however, repetition takes on even more importance. Grammar B, Weathers tells us, uses repetition "to achieve a kind of momentum in composition" (1980, 28). Here is a high school junior playing around with repetition in a homework assignment:

There were pans, there were pots, there were plates, there were glasses that had to be washed.
    So I rubbed, scrubbed, polished, and rinsed the dishes clean.
    I put them in the dish drainer to drip dry and they dripped in the sink.
    Then I had to wipe the table, wipe the stove, wipe the sink.
    I had to put the mound of dishes away in the cabinet under the counter.
    Paula Perdue Cox, Junior, Edgewood High School

I love saying this piece aloud.

"Cabinet under the counter."

"Wipe the table, wipe the stove, wipe the sink."

Paula repeats sounds, words, and parallel patterns of phrases and sentences. And she knows intuitively that repetition is effective and then more effective when the repeated pattern is varied:

There were pans,
there were pots,
there were plates,
there were glasses that had to be washed.

The arrangement of the words makes me want to beat out their rhythm.

Writers in the alternate style also repeat ideas, even forms. They use everything from simple repetitions to repetends. (The repetend is the unexpected repetition of a word, phrase, sentence, or passage. Remember "So it goes" in Kurt Vonnegut's *Slaughterhouse Five*?)

THE SENTENCE FRAGMENT

Elevating words or phrases to the level of a sentence—albeit a fragmentary sentence in the eyes of Grammar A—"suggests a far greater awareness of separation and fragmentation" (Weathers 1980, 19). A sentence fragment is a word or phrase torn from a continuous flow of discourse. It is no longer merely one word working with five, ten, twenty, or thirty others to create meaning within the confines of a traditionally defined sentence. The sentence fragment is isolated, emphasized, granted the integrity of beginning with a capital letter and ending with a period. *usually* Look at the lead to Chapter 7 of Richard Wright's *Black Boy*:

Summer. Bright hot days. Hunger still a vital part of my consciousness. Passing relatives in the hallways of the crowded home and not speaking. Eating in silence at a table where prayers are said. My mother recovering slowly, but now definitely crippled for life. Will I be able to enter school in September? Loneliness. Reading. Job hunting. Vague hopes of going north. But what would become of my mother if I left her in this queer house? And how would I fare in a strange city? Doubt. Fear. My friends are buying long-pants suits that cost seventeen to twenty dollars, a sum as huge to me as the Alps! This was my reality in 1924. (178)

I've shared this passage with teachers and asked them to speculate why Wright used sentence fragments. Some have said that the fragments emphasize the fragmented nature of his life at that point, the overwhelming nature of loneliness, fear, and doubt. Others have said that sentence fragments mirror thinking—the Vygotskian notion that inner verbal thought is composed of bursts of significant words that contain a shower of meaning for the thinker.

I asked students to experiment with sentence fragments in their writing. Chris, a senior, wrote this:

> I. Once. No. Many times.
> Tried to ignore it.
> But woke still. With my cat.
> Walking. On my chest.
> Licking. My face.
> *Chris Hardin, Senior, Edgewood High School*

Chris's compact, radical use of sentence fragments startled me. Other students had used sentence fragments judiciously, mixing them in with complete Grammar A sentences as Wright had done. Chris, I think, had been influenced by samples of writing by Gertrude Stein.

Why, I asked him, had he taken sentence fragments to such extremes?

"I wanted you to read every word," Chris said.

He achieved his purpose. I didn't skim the catwalk.

THE LABYRINTHINE SENTENCE

At the opposite end of the sentence-length continuum from the fragment is the labyrinthine sentence—not a lawless, poorly punctuated run-on sentence, but a finely crafted aggregation of words that weaves in and out, accruing information, riding rhythms of parallel sentence structure, tacking on phrases, clauses, and grammatical absolutes to form a sinuous sentence perfectly suited for some things we might describe or discuss.

Here is Tom Wolfe in *The Right Stuff*, describing what it was like for test pilots in the 1950s to take jet planes beyond Mach 1:

> To take off in an F-100 at dawn and cut in the afterburner and hurtle twenty-five thousand feet up into the sky so suddenly that you felt not like a bird but like a trajectory, yet with full control, full control of *five tons* of thrust, all of which flowed from your will and through your fingertips, with the huge engine right beneath you, so close that it was as if you were riding it bareback, until you leveled out and went supersonic, an event registered on earth by a tremendous cracking boom that shook windows, but up here only by the fact that you now felt utterly free of the earth—to describe it, even to wife, child, near ones and dear ones, seemed impossible. So the pilot kept it to himself, along with an even more indescribable

... an even more sinfully inconfessable ... feeling of superiority, appropriate to him and to his kind, lone bearers of the right stuff. (30)

Weathers describes the labyrinthine maneuver as an "almost picaresque sentence" (1980, 18). Indeed, the sentence is a generative adventure, requiring the writer to provide more and more information to sustain it. The writer winds up her voice and lets spin. Here is a high school senior describing what it's like in midwinter to catch a Toronto metropolitan bus to school:

> Waiting. For the bus. It takes a long time. In fact, it seems to take so long that your feet turn blue and your fingers become so numb that the book you were reading and were halfway through is now finished but the pages are stuck to your fingers so you have to pretend that you're still reading as you sway in and out of the bus shelter doorway hoping to catch a glimpse of the red rocket but instead your nose gets frostbitten and ice particles form in your hair, and as you return to safety your scarf blows away and you start coughing while out of the corner of your eye, you see the feeble lights on the bus approaching so you step up to the bus stop but the light turns yellow so the bus must stop and you feel the breath freezing in your throat and constricting your lungs, when all of a sudden the bus lurches forward and ... CHARTERED.
> *Jennifer Alderson, Senior, Woburn Collegiate High School, Toronto, Ontario*

ORTHOGRAPHIC VARIATION

Weathers notes that one frequent characteristic of Grammar B is "a pressing against the walls of ordinary/orthodox vocabulary, a playing with words/word forms to achieve a special kind of lexical texture—a reading surface that is exciting and rebellious all at once" (1980, 30). That pressing against the walls is probably never more evident than it is in alternate stylists' use of orthographic variation.

And we teachers shudder.

Is there any surface feature of writing more glaring to the eye than spelling errors? If parents, administrators, and school board members have complained about any error in students' papers more than misspelled words, I don't know what it is.

A parent's concern you will *not* hear:

"Ms. Dickson, I have a complaint about the writing my son is doing in your class."

"What's that?"

"His writing has no voice. It reads like the minutes from a meeting. I notice, too, that he doesn't use active verbs consistently. And there's an overall lack of concrete detail."

But you will hear plenty of carping about poor spelling, even though professional writers have been altering the way words look on the page for years. Here is John Dos Passos writing in *The Big Money*, describing the heinous rigors of assembly-line production in Henry Ford's automobile plants:

> At Ford's production was improving all the time; less waste, more spotters, strawbosses, stoolpigeons (fifteen minutes for lunch, three minutes to go to the toilet, the Taylorized speedup everywhere, reachunder, adjustwasher, screwdown bolt, shove in cotterpin, reachunder, screwdown bolt, reachunderadjustscrewdownrea-chunderadjust until every ounce of life was sucked off into production and at night the workmen went home gray shaking husks). (56–57)

We want students to attain orthographic regularity in their writing, keeping in mind, of course, that standard English already permits some variation. On one high school student's paper I had routinely circled the word *alright* and told him the words he meant to spell were *all right*. He didn't see the point. I directed him to the dictionary. Later in the period, I came by his desk and asked what he had found.

He raised his eyes wearily. "They got yours; they got mine."

He showed me the citation. Sure enough, in that dictionary it was alright to spell *all right alright.*

Horrors, right? Slipshod standards. Riffraff corrupting our beloved English language. The same thing happened once when I circled *judgement* on a student's paper (an intelligent, capable student, I should add).

Good lessons for me from the populace. A poor speller myself, I'm all for simplifying English spelling whenever possible. During the copyediting of *Clearing the Way*, I argued for *dialog* instead of *dialogue*. And won. Then the copy editor upped the ante and pointed out that I should also use *monolog* instead of *monologue* and *catalog* instead of *catalogue*. I felt the sudden guilt and fear of conspiring in something unlawful. But I was giddy from the opportunity to help evolve the language.

Orthographic variations in Grammar B do not occur only when dictionaries grudgingly permit alternative spellings. Alternate stylists employ orthographic variation to meaningfully jolt readers (e.g., "The rule in one English Department was that three errors on a paper automatically equalled an F. Therefore, if a student's paper contained three spelling errors, the teacher assigned it an F—*automaniacally*.").

The proper word for orthographic variation, Weathers tells us, is not *misspelling*, but "calculated and controlled respelling" (1980, 30), which doesn't relieve teachers of their responsibility to continue to move students toward orthographic regularity. I nervously imagine a scene in which a parent storms into a classroom, righteously waving her child's paper rife with spelling errors.

"How can you accept this writing?" demands the parent. "It's a spelling disaster!"

The teacher leans back in the chair, disdainfully waves a hand, and says, "Not to worry—those seeming errors are merely respellings."

It is, in fact, orthographic regularity that enables orthographic variation to be effective.

Consider Erin, a young woman I met during the final semester of her senior year of high school. Erin was bright and polite. Her precisely clipped blonde bangs corresponded to her meticulous daily attire. Her writing was cautiously restrained with no significant problems in grammar or usage. The only thing missing, for my taste, was a distinctive voice, a bond between meaning and style that would make her writing memorable.

At the time I met Erin, the high school featured a dynamic girls basketball team. A number of the players were my students, so I went to a game. Erin, I found, was the point guard. In a basketball uniform she was daring, confident, and canny. She'd dribble the length of the court, pass the ball off to the corner, take it back at the top of the key, and launch an eighteen-foot jump shot. Erin played basketball with a distinctive, undeniable voice.

Where, I wondered, was this young woman in my writing class? The labyrinthine sentence gave Erin a chance to blend her personas of outgoing, risk-taking athlete and reserved, obedient student. In the passage below, she used a labyrinthine sentence to cut loose a roller coaster that rose with fond description, plunged to righteous indignation, and leveled off to a hard-won tranquility. In addition to achieving full-voiced prose, Erin used orthographic variations and sentence fragments to highlight double meanings and communicate quiet commitment. Erin wrote about spring vacation in Florida, quite a contrast for students in the dreary, grimy-snowed winter of southwestern Ohio, where the biggest nearby body of water is the Ohio River.

> The waves are crashing down on white, sandy beaches as we take our morning walk, for the third day in a row, to celebrate the spring break and a get away from city, schools, and familiar neighbors who seem to know all that happens whether at school, on a date, or inside our house, where no body should interfere, especially not

those that are jealous because we get a Florida vacation while they sit at home, dreaming about the palm trees, the shining sand, glistening water and savage tans. The sights are many and varied and fill me with memories of things I might never see again. Return soon though. Eye will never forget these seven daze of onederful sites, clear beautiful sees, and a gorgeous state. Can't wait to come back. Will come back. Planning.

Erin Kash Allen, Senior, Edgewood High School

Erin's wrongfully right use of *eye, daze, onederful, sites,* and *sees* makes me stop and take note. Her multiple meanings emphasize the visual chasm between coastal Florida (with its beaches, palm trees, and expanse of blue sea) and southwestern Ohio in early spring (with its muddy hog farms, low rolling hills, and long stretches of brown-black earth waiting to be tilled and planted with corn and soybeans). Erin's orthographic variation puts me on my semantic toes, jolts me to attention.

So closely do I consider her surface text and meaning that by the time I get to *state*, I do not think *Florida* alone. Psychological state, I'm wondering? Emotional state? State of being? I don't know if Erin intended these meanings, but her playfulness alerts me to language. Seeming is not being. An intellect lurks behind the language play, an intellect that expects me to think.

DOUBLE VOICE

Although we teachers press students to focus their writing, to straddle no fences, to argue either one side or the other in essays, Weathers notes that sometimes contrasting ideas are valid and opposing points of view equally interesting. Such complexity does not obfuscate or confuse meaning, but rather adds richness to it. Psychologist Jerome Bruner reminds us that often "depth is better achieved by looking from two points at once" (1986, 10).

Issues can be complex, and walking this earth are complicated people driven by motives both simple and multilayered. When we're being fair, we know that each story has two, three, and four sides. Instead of discussing or rendering one point of view or idea, then its opposite, or minimizing one in favor of the other, a writer may employ double voice, a stylistic maneuver that presents two sides simultaneously. Scott, for example, engages double voice to indicate a hormonal dilemma and the probability of double-dealing:

Girl friend . . . . . Girl friend
I love you.
Only one for me
Always and forever.

> Who's she?
> Always be together.
>   Is she new here?
> Spend eternity together.
>   Do you know what her name is?
> *Scott Robinson, Senior, Edgewood High School*

Writers may achieve double voice in many ways. One voice may appear in regular type, the other voice in italics or within parentheses. Voices may alternate sentence by sentence or paragraph by paragraph. Often double voices are set side by side in columns or paragraphs to emphasize the duality of two ideas or points of view. Such arrangement further suggests *synchronicity*—"all things present in the present moment" (Weathers 1980, 35)—another characteristic of the alternate style, one which accounts for its plentiful use of present tense.

When my students experimented with the alternate style, I did the homework assignments right along with them. I needed to feel firsthand what purposeful, stylistic rule breaking was like. When we explored double voice, I created my homework assignment the period before class met—just as many of the students did. As I watched my American literature students take a test, I wrote what was on my mind:

The room is silent. Twenty-five American Literature students ponder, dig into their minds, work hard to formulate coherent thoughts that will impress me with their extensive knowledge of Henry David Thoreau.	Oh, Jesus, Thoreau—what a conceited ass. He's badgered me for two weeks. I shoulda read them essays!
Thoreau believed in the power of the mind to plumb the depths of thought and imagination, to deal with intellectual subjects.	God, did Julie look good last night! Her hair, her eyes, her wonderfully luscious mouth, her

Radical political ideas, the individual's relationship to government. That's what Thoreau dealt with in his seminal essay, "Civil Disobedience." And my astute essay question will lead students to confront crucial issues.

My stomach is rumbling like a distant thunderstorm. Pepsi for breakfast? Why did I do that!

Nothing can stop an individual who is determined, who advances confidently in the direction of his will, who leaves material possessions behind and seeks to know truth.

Time's awastin'. Better crank up the ol' B.S. machine.

The voice on the left is Teacher Tom. The voice on the right, I like to think, is George, the smart, likable, hulking wag, sitting in the last seat in the row by the windows. But soon after I wrote this, I realized that both voices were mine, the one on the right the sixteen-year-old Tom who still lives in me.

THE LIST

A list allows a writer quickly to confront readers with abundant detail, enabling them to see an untainted, holistic picture. In list making, syntax and logical connections of language are not important. Simple, unexplained, occasionally poetic, the list usually appears in a column, one item per line, much like a grocery list. For practice the students and I did a quick-write and listed things we love. Here is the list I made:

Students who speak the rude truth
RX 7s
gliding through water 900 meters into a swim
flesh
Mary Oliver
a book that makes me forget I'm reading

Wasatch Raspberry Wheat Beer
finding the precise word
Papa Bear's Pizza Oven in Canton, Ohio
GAP shirts
raw cherrystone clams
calamari
old photographs
Luciano Pavarotti
the 1930s
my daughter, upbeat
paper clips
my address stamp
newsy, full-voiced letters
Harry Crews
clear, honest intellects
connections that teach

Weathers explains that when making a list the writer simply provides "the data, the evidence, the facts, the objects." The reader is left to bring meaning to them. The writer presents "a 'still life' of objects without indication of foreground or background, without any indication of relative importance, without any suggestion at all of cause-effect, this-before-that, rank, or the like" (1980, 20).

Chad, one of my high school seniors, who held Tom Wolfe in high regard and loved to write, play soccer, and deliver announcements over the PA system, dismissed the columnar list as "too much like a poem." In an alternate style piece about his visit to a college campus, Chad lists items that capture the feel of a young man's dormitory room:

> So after the coach leaves, I get a feel for what a college dorm room is like: Snipped-snaps of Jordan, Kareem, Bird, Tony Perez, a goldfish tank, paper, an Algebra III text, Diadora's crusted with dry mud, phone hung upside down on the wall, stereo singing softly with four speakers, a picture of a girl, Athens license plates tacked to the wall, Mousse and soap and toothpaste and speedstick wedged tightly into a basket, draped with a towel like warm bread, a Nerf basketball hoop jutting from the wall, a dead sock hanging on a makeshift clothesline, Tide.
> *Chad R. Pergram, Senior, Edgewood High School*

Weathers writes about the objectivity of the list, about its nonjudgmental nature. It certainly can be that way. But the list can be calculated, too. The writer includes some items and excludes others. He orders the chosen items,

Breaking the Rules in Style

too, maybe randomly, maybe not. In Chad's list I can't help but see both clutter and direction with "Tide" mentioned last to clean up the entire room.

Indeed, the list offers the writer opportunity to amass pointed detail in a particular context for devastating effect. Below is a poetic list rendered by a high school teacher as part of her research paper on Margaret Sanger, pioneering leader of the birth control movement in the United States:

1913 METHODS FOR BIRTH CONTROL

rue seed, castor beans
foam from a camel's mouth
pine bark and seaweed
stepping three times
over a grave

pomegranate peel
parsley and thyme
cedar oil
crocodile dung
churchyard luck

cabbage blossoms
root of spotted cowbane
holding the breath
great care and restraint

  Dana Rickets, Teacher, Cottonwood High School, Salt Lake City, UT

In the example below, graduate student Jennifer's list takes the form of a help-wanted advertisement for a cosmetic specialist in a fictional department store. Jennifer's absurd advertisement singling out the tacit qualities demanded of female cosmetic workers zings with social critique:

HELP WANTED
NYMENS COSMETIC SPECIALIST

Attractive women ages 21–39
with prior cosmetic experience.
Must have excellent communication
skills. Single, non-mothers
preferred. Must be able to work
anytime Monday–Sunday including
holidays. No wrinkles, age spots,
facial scars, or bad teeth. Heavy
foundation, panty hose, high heels
and hairspray required. No sick
pay or personal leave time. Over-

weight applicants and applicants
with physical handicaps need not
apply. No job security unless you
maintain sales goals. Aggressive,
self-motivated, persistent women
only. Big-busted blondes encouraged
to apply. Actresses and anorexics
preferred. Please contact Sherrie
Airs at 231-2343 for an appearance
interview.

Jennifer Pickering, Graduate Student, Utah State University

Taking Weathers's definitions and the examples of alternate style maneu-vers I'd found in literature, I created a packet that introduced high school students to Grammar B. We discussed Weathers's definitions, read aloud the examples, and sometimes puzzled over what was happening with the language (Gertrude Stein had us thinking hard). For homework assignments we wrote lists and double voice pieces; we experimented with repetition, orthographic variation, and sentence form, both fragmentary and labyrinthine. Each day we shared writing, sometimes reading in a circle, sometimes putting our efforts on the chalkboard, opaque, or overhead. Our purpose was not to see who had done it right and who had done it wrong. Rather, by sharing the writing we saw the linguistic and personal variation that could exist in each Grammar B stylistic maneuver. That sharing became an instructive delight; the students' enthusiasm for rule breaking often turned those brief assignments into satis-fying pieces of writing.

In the next chapter I will discuss "the crot" and "collage/montage," larger pieces of the alternate style that enable writers to create fully-realized pieces of writing.

❧
BEYOND BOUNDARIES

Third grader Justin is one of the best writers in class. He loves reading, revels in language, crafts stories that leave me in awe of his eight-year-old imagination and skill. In his latest piece of writing, one sentence reads, "I ate blugurt in the morning."

"What's blugurt?" I ask him.

"You know how you can put two words together to make one?" Justin says. "Like can *and* not *make* can't?

"A contraction."

"Right. Well, blugurt is my combined word for blueberry yogurt."

Ninth grader Dianna's paper about the Cleveland Browns' miserable losing streak has received 82%. Nine errors are marked; no teacher comments appear on the paper.

In one spot Dianna has written, "When asked about the Browns' record, quarterback Brian Sipe said, 'I don't know. There's just something wrong with the Browns.' Something wrong indeed!"

Something wrong indeed!—that nicely timed rhetorical phrase revealing Dianna's voice and ironic sensibility had been dutifully labeled "Sentence Fragment."

Patty, a high school junior, is reading The Color Purple, *written primarily in protagonist Celie's African American dialect. One day I ask students to explain what they have learned about writing from the novels they are reading. Patty writes, "Alice Walker taught me that you can break the rules of writing I learned in tenth grade and write one of the best books ever."*

Chapter Six

Evolving Voice Through the Alternate Style

Gently, but with undeniable will,
Divesting myself of the holds that
would hold me.

Walt Whitman

*T*wo more elaborate Grammar B stylistic maneuvers that Winston Weathers (1980) describes—"the crot" and "collage/montage"—enable writers to create fully realized pieces of writing in the alternate style.

The Crot

The *crot* gave my high school students the most trouble. The concept is so big, so basic, and subsumes so much that many students couldn't conceptualize it. Fooling around with spelling they understood. Stretching sentences to endless lengths or chopping them off before nouns and verbs got acquainted they saw. But *crot*? What was crot? Robin, in fact, refused to say the word. She thought it sounded obscene.

"Crot," Weathers explains, "is an obsolete word meaning 'bit' or 'fragment.' . . . A basic element in the alternate grammar of style, and comparable somewhat to the stanza in poetry, the crot may range in length from one sentence to twenty or thirty sentences" (14).

Written crots are not connected to other text by transitional words or phrases. In fact, they are nearly always "separated one from the other by white space." Although a series of crots is meant to create a cumulative effect, each crot in the series "should have a certain integrity" that enables it often to stand alone, end abruptly, make a point in itself, possess "some sharp, arresting, or provocative quality." Because it is self-contained and does not require transitional words or phrases, crots accommodate "rapid transition from one point of view to another." A piece written entirely in crots "is similar to a slide show," each slide unique in composition, clear in image, precise in idea (14–15).

The second year I taught the alternate style, I solved the conceptual dilemma my students had with crots. I arranged an in-house field trip in which students traveled in pairs. I armed the teams with hall passes and off they went to various places in school to observe and write brief pieces about what they experienced: the raucous shouting of physical education students playing dodge ball, two sullen freshmen waiting stiffly in the office to be disciplined, band students readying their instruments for rehearsal, cigarette smoke wafting above a rest-room stall, and more. The students returned to class and read their pieces. Taken together, they became an alternate style narrative essay of our school. Each team had created a crot—in this case, detailed, focused linguistic slides of life in our high school.

"Very brief crots," Weathers explains, "have the quality of an aphorism or proverb, while longer crots may have the quality of descriptive or narrative passages found in the traditional grammar of style" (15). Thus, Chapter 2 in this book ("Truth, Risk, and Passion") is composed of a series of larger narrative crots capped by an expository one. In Chapter 5 Chad's list of the contents of the slovenly dormitory room, ending ironically with "Tide," is a crot that captures one part of Chad's weekend at a college campus. And the preceding interchapter comprises three crots—the self-contained, language stories of stylistic rule breakers Justin, Dianna, and Patty.

COLLAGE/MONTAGE

Collage/montage is the form and effect often achieved when we assemble a series of crots. In collage/montage "diverse elements are patched together to make the whole composition" (Weathers 1980, 37). Think of the wonderfully vivid and provocative visual collages students create by cutting photographs from magazines and newspapers and mounting them on large pieces of cardboard. Some of the most sophisticated, comprehensive, and satisfying responses to novels I've seen have been done when students created such visual collages.

The collage/montage effect also makes me think of "now films" of the late 1960s and early 1970s. In these films directors often edited together footage of photographs and live action in a visual, nonlinear, usually rapid-paced montage. I think of Saul Bass's masterful—if gender-biased—exploration of creativity, *Why Man Creates* (1968) and Charles Braverman's *American Time Capsule* (1969) and *Braverman's Condensed Cream of Beatles* (1973).

Weathers maintains that collage/montage "is a stylistic effort at synthesis, distinguishable from Grammar A's effort, nearly always, at analysis" (37).

I would argue, as I do in Chapter 1, that analysis, too, takes place when writers synthesize experience, ideas, and learning. Analysis occurs both before and during synthesis. In creating the montage of Chapter 2, for example, I wrote from strong feeling about disparate examples of passion I've encountered in academic settings. As I worked with those scenes, fleshing them out and objectifying them, I began feeling the need to comment about *moderation* and *balance*, concepts that had been on my mind since the previous summer but that I hadn't felt the need to explicate until I was immersed in the act of synthesizing so much passion.

The act of synthesis
  is the act of analysis
    is the act of synthesis.

Weathers differentiates between *collage* and *montage*. "As the compositional units to be 'synthesized' become larger, more substantial, and more complete within themselves, we come to a sense of montage," Weathers writes, "a presentation in sequence, side by side, of compositional units less fragmental, yet fairly disparate so far as form or content is concerned" (37).

Considering this distinction, the previous interchapter might be considered a collage, while Chapter 2 is a montage. But differentiating between the terms is not critical. What is important, I think, is for writers to grasp the idea of putting together fully realized pieces of writing through collage/montage, of assembling verbal slides—fragments of meaning in which the writer's synthesis speeds readers to experience and analysis, as a good novel does.

Below is an excerpt from Karen Ballinger's collage/montage titled "The Art of Learning Nothing," an alternate style exposé of high school education. When she wrote this, Karen was near the end of her senior year. She was never more linguistically and critically mature as a high school student than she was in those final months. Karen was living the flip side of senioritis. She was neither jaded nor mired in lassitude. Karen was soaring. Confident in her intellect and critical powers, she took on contemporary secondary education. The collage/montage form emerged organically as Karen developed crots of various subject areas, crots that contained lists, labyrinthine sentences, orthographic variation, sentence fragments, double voices. The series of crots fragments the essay, just as a high school student's day is fragmented:

THE ART OF LEARNING NOTHING

Biology—How to etherize tiny bugs so we can stare at their tails and wings and guess. Male or female? Which is more dominant?

25% chance of wrinkled winged female 25% wrinkled winged male 25% red-tipped female 25% red-tipped male ... except red-tipped is a female trait so your whole experiment is now screwed up.

REASONS WHY MY EXPERIMENT SCREWED UP

1   bugs etherized to death
2   bugs reproduced so much they changed color
3   bugs fried to death in incubator
4   bugs (male) were fags
5   stupid lab partners' fault—give them the F—not me
6   I don't have any idea
7   all of the above

What Was Avogadro's number again?
Kelvin's number?
Melvin's number?
H'm'ny MOLES ... Molality. Molarity. Molecule. Molecular. Mole Method. What's the difference? I forget.

Charles' Law $\dfrac{V}{V_1} = \dfrac{T}{T_1}$

Boyles' Law $\dfrac{V}{V_1} = \dfrac{P_1}{P}$ put them in a pot and mix laws together

and you get a V that equals $V \cdot \dfrac{T_1}{T} \cdot \dfrac{P}{P_1}$ and Dalton's Law says the

total pressure of a mixture of gases is the sum of partial pressure and I'm totally drowning in the sum of equations.

Try something new.
200 + some pages of Indian history.
Wounded My Heart at Buried Knee.
Wounded My Knee at Buried Heart.
Buried My Knee at Wounded Heart.
Then 284 pages of torturous philosophies for future scholars of the universe.
"However this restriction may be opposed to natural right and to the usages of civilized nations, yet, if it be indispensable to that system under which the country ..."

What was that?

Again.

Sigh.

"It is difficult to comprehend the proposition that the inhabitants of either quarter of the globe could have rightful original claims of dominion over the inhabitants of the other, or over the lands they occupied or that the discovery of either, by the other should give the discoverer rights in the country discovered . . ."

You said it. Great book you picked for us. Slam.

English can be fun. GRRammar!

We, us, them, they, their, there, they're, are, our, idea, idear, ideal.

Students scrunch over their desks scribbling and scratching their papers.

With pencil in hand and mouth, I nibble on the eraser and I sit . . .

        and sit . . .

               and sit . . .

Finally—

"Birds chirp at my bedroom window . . ."

No.

"Love, like a cancer—never a full recovery . . ."

Yuck. No.

"To be or not to be . . ."

That's not my question. No, that won't work either.

Nibble . . . Nibble . . .

      Chomp!

I spit the eraser from my tongue and stare at the dammed paper.

  Let's try clots

crots!

crots, crots

sorry

"autonomous unit characterized by the absence of any transitional device . . ."

huh?

D. H. Lawrence

my work	my crot
my crot	my life
my life	my crot
my crot	might rot

Karen Ballinger, Senior, Edgewood High School

Because of the range of Grammar B techniques, the diversity of human beings, and the variety of writing topics, alternate style pieces can look very different on the page, can take various forms. Here is an alternate style meditation, written by university teacher Teri Faulkner during a ten-minute, nonstop write in a workshop on Grammar B.

Midnight. The laundry.

 whites
  colors
   darks
    towels
     special wash

Sort into piles and carry downstairs.

Load, wash, rinse, spin
Out of the washer, into the dryer
        softener, soap
Load, wash, rinse, spin

Three degrees, three children, I
struggle to rebalance parts of my life,
meditate through the cycles at 3 A.M.
in the basement with a stack of papers
yet to read but one daughter needs
her uniform and another needs
jeans sometimes Life's choices
are pretty basic—fold and stack.

Load, wash, rinse, spin
Meditate, mediate, mediatate?
        Immediately.
        NOW

Dr. Faulkner,   Mom,
when can we   is my
expect our   flannel shirt
papers?   clean
                                   yet?

                (Damn!)
                Soon . . .

A stray red sock bleeds into the whites
as Teacher, Mother, Scholar, Wife
spill over, color one another.

Sometimes pink is a nice color.
Sometimes not.
  Teri Faulkner, Teacher, University of Wisconsin-La Crosse

Here is high school junior Teri Baumgartner's description of a place rendered in Grammar B:

'Tucky House

It got its name when my brother was learning to talk. I spent half of my childhood there.

> Little red house on the hill
> overlooking a field of
> Bluegrass.
> Fresh scent of honeysuckle
> spread by the breeze.
> No T.V.
> No telephone.
> Only a wooden swing on the front porch.
> Large garden in the backyard:

potatoespotatoespotatoespotatoespotatoes.

tomatoestomatoestomatoestomatoestomatoes.

lettucelettucelettucelettucelettuce.

onionsonionsonionsonionsonionsonionsonions.

strawberries!

"Uncle Dale." A man of seventy-five years. He had white hair and whiskers to match. His crystal blue eyes sparkled beneath droopy eyelids. A grin continuously covered his face. The only outfit I can remember him wearing consisted of faded overalls, rugged work boots, and his old engineer's cap. Every time he saw me, he would tease and threaten to spank me. I knew he was only joking.

"Aunt Libby." Dale's wife. A tall, slender woman. Her silver-gray hair was swept into a bun, and a warm smile accompanied her piercing brown eyes. She always stopped by with a strawberry or peach cobbler for the "young-uns" (Yum, yum!).

When Kentucky is mentioned, many people think of hillbillies running around barefooted with a pig under one arm, trying to lead a stubborn old mule up a hill to the barn.
It's not like that.

Mornings. I roll over beneath the cozy blankets, yawn, and lie motionless. Sausage crackles in the skillet and the aroma fills the house. I open my eyes to be greeted by the sun's rays that gleam through my window.

Evenings. I sit on the back porch while Granny retells favorite stories of her childhood.

"When I was a youngster—about ten or twelve, there was this hillbilly singer—Red Foley, and his daughter was married to Pat Boone, well, when someone died, he stayed at our house in Corbin and wanted a chicken for the funeral, so my mother sent me out to get a chicken from the chicken coop, and the rooster got all roiled up, so later when this hillbilly guy was on the radio giving the names of people he wanted to thank, he didn't mention me, and I thought he should've 'cause of the trouble I went through gettin' his ol' chicken, well that just didn't do much for me . . ."

Horse and buggy . . .
milkman . . .
iceman . . .
walking to school . . .
Sunday drives . . .
sleigh ride down Cordon Hill . . .
camping in tents . . .
no cooler . . .
army cots . . .
courtin' at Cumberland Falls . . .
trip to Jelico . . .
bridge out . . .
Grandpa's coal mine . . .
not allowed in . . .
Carrol town . . .

               Blink
            Blink
        Blink
"Look, Granny.
the fireflies are out!"
Blink
        Stomp!
Blink
        Stomp!
         Stomp! Blink
          Clap!

           "Gotcha!"

Relatives stop in unexpectedly. They are welcomed warmly and urged to stay for dinner and a good night's sleep. No matter how many people are crammed into the little house, the motto is: "The more the merrier!"

When I see a "Home Sweet Home" sign, I think of my Old Kentucky Home—'Tucky House.
Teri Baumgartner, Junior, Edgewood High School

For additional examples of the alternate style, see the personal essay in Appendix A and the short story in Appendix B. You can read them now if you'd like.

CAN STUDENTS GET IN TROUBLE FOR THIS?

After a workshop I conducted on Grammar B, a sixth-grade teacher told me he had shared the poetry of e.e. cummings with his students. They read the poems aloud and discussed the unconventional punctuation, spelling, and forms that cummings invented to communicate powerfully. The students delighted in the poet's rule breaking. Near the end of the discussion, however, one concerned soul in the back of the room raised a hand and asked, "Can e.e. get in trouble for this?"

It's a legitimate question. Will students get in trouble when they leave classrooms where Grammar B is permitted, even encouraged? One teacher accused me of teaching students to write "maverick essays." That sounded exciting, actually. But I knew what she was referring to. In judging students' advanced placement exams, when anyone at an assessment table encounters an essay that breaks the standard or deviates from normal form, that essay is branded "maverick" and passed to the leader of the assessment table. My accuser believed this means curtains for the paper. Friends who have served as table leaders have told me, however, that if a Grammar B essay has a chance of scoring well with anyone at the table, it is likely to be with the leader, whose conception of effective writing often encompasses more than the traditional, thesis-driven, argumentative essay.

Never have angry or disenchanted former students contacted me to complain that I'd led them down a stylistically irresponsible path. Never that I know of has a student failed a future class because of our three-week foray into the alternate style. The worst that has happened involved one young woman who came back to visit the high school after her first semester of college. Cheryl told me that in her freshman composition class she had cast her first assignment in the alternate style. Her teacher found the essay interesting but didn't know what to do with it. He asked her to write conventional essays for the remainder of the semester. She agreed to. I applaud the teacher's openmindedness and straightforwardness. I applaud Cheryl's exuberant boldness and pragmatism. Four years later she became an English teacher.

Part of what we must teach students, of course, is sensitivity to audience, whether that audience is a teacher, an ailing grandparent, a newspaper's readership, a government bureaucrat, a grant-funding committee, or what have you.

I must admit, however, that socialization to the amenities of standard written English, both in surface features and in form, is not my major concern as a teacher of writing. In fact, I'd like to see more students using Grammar B writing techniques and purposefully breaking rules and pseudorules of standard style a lot more often in their writing. I'd prefer they do whatever necessary to generate original thinking and language than to slavishly heed the amenities of Grammar A.

As writing teachers, I don't think we have to fret much about socializing most students to the conventions of standard style. That socialization will occur *if students participate often in real literacy engagements*—writing frequently for their own purposes, reading frequently from the vast world of print. The bulk of what students read—particularly from textbook publishers— is written quite conventionally. Combine that reading experience with the patient teaching of editing skills within the context of their own writing and most students will steadily move toward mastery of many standard conventions of composition.

In fact, purposeful rule breakers may be even more attentive to standard rules. The students keenly aware of various school rules are not the student council representatives. It is the rule *breakers* who know the ins and outs of school rules—like those two sullen freshmen waiting stiffly in the office to be disciplined, like Mark who smoked dope with his buddies under the pretense of practicing his trumpet in the band room.

What we teachers should worry about, however—what I am most concerned with—is our students' linguistic confidence. I want students to develop a willingness to be bold with language, to press forward with words. I want them to be versatile, daring, and practiced enough to interact readily with their writing and to do so with imagination, logic, and originality.

For many students the alternate style was a liberation akin to the women's suffrage amendment. It was long overdue; it emboldened them; they were never the same. Cheryl, the student who confounded her freshman composition teacher with her Grammar B essay and later became an English teacher, echoed the sentiments of her classmates when as a high school senior she wrote,

The alternate style adds freedom to do what we've always wanted to do but we always felt we'd get an F. This style enabled me to get what I really thought down on paper without worrying about structure. All of our class pieces came out more truthful and, I think, interesting in the process.
Cheryl Eby, Senior, Edgewood High School

The students broke rules of writing and began ruling writing. In their alteration of standard style, they wrote with more purpose than ever before, paying closer attention to punctuation, word choice, and the forms they organically created. In paper after paper I saw evidence of intellect and intent, of students who were vitally aware of their role as writer, as maker and shaper of meaning through language.

"For the first time," wrote Teri, "I began thinking about the way my writing would look on the page."

Jon, a talented writer who had no trouble weaving flawlessly punctuated complex sentences, believed that purposefully using sentence fragments made him begin to think about the power of individual words. His voice expanded to include, as he put it, "terser sentences."

One student kept mis-saying the alternate style term. Grinning and excited, he'd stride up to me before class. "Mr. Romano," he'd say, "are we working on our ultimate style papers today?"

That made me nervous. For many students this paper *was* the ultimate style. Grammar B was freedom, license, escape from constraint. They saw Grammar B as a genre in itself, the ultimate genre. And what else could I have expected students to think? I'd driven them toward such thinking by doing an alternate style unit that required each of them to write an alternate style paper. I'd created a dichotomous monster. The students thought

there was straight writing over here, conservative, staid, safe, and sometimes boring.	But over here . . . over here was this "other" kind of writing— dangerous, rebellious, free of inhibitions.

I looked upon the alternate style differently. I saw Grammar B as a resource that offered writers further stylistic options—nontraditional ones, to be sure but, as Weathers makes clear, no less legitimate and with ample precedent in our diverse literary heritage. In articles, in talks, in book reviews, in theses and dissertations, as well as in fiction and poetry, we can often push the envelope, be a little more daring and adventurous in how we put words on paper. I wanted Grammar B techniques to become part of a versatile rhetorical repertoire that each of my students possessed, equally as useful, depending on content and audience, as conventional spelling, topic-sentence-controlled paragraphs, thesis-driven essays, and argumentative idea development.

It seems to me that the most important aspect of Winston Weathers's Grammar B has little to do with crots, orthographic variation, or labyrinthine sentences. Of critical importance is the *spirit* of the alternate style, the implications it holds for nurturing all student writers, kindergarten through graduate school.

High school or university students whose writing reflects their reading of Virginia Woolf and Allen Ginsberg often employ alternate styles of writing as they evolve original voices. Elementary school students whose writing repertoire includes invented spelling, drawings, speechmarks, and supplemental talk are also employing alternate styles—eminently appropriate ones—and they, too, are evolving original voices.

Iowa first-grade teacher Chris Rinner knows how his students readily create nontraditional techniques and forms: "They see writing as a way to make their point." And they make their points by using everything their new learning makes available. Weathers, in fact, maintains that Grammar B "is probably the fundamental and essential style, out of which a secondary Grammar A has been developed for specialized logic/clarity goals" (51).

One of my high school students pointed out that the alternate style "really helps writers understand their voices." I think he's right. My students—both in high school and in college—pushed beyond boundaries of written expression, boundaries imposed both from without and within. They astonished themselves and learned about limits. Such self-understanding of the power and range of our voices is crucial to our maturation as writers. Voice is the vitality of a writer, both the root and the point of growth. We write about personally important matters in many different genres and through a lifetime develop our voices.

We extend them, we adapt them, we learn with them. The alternate style options explained by Winston Weather lets students participate in this development in new and exciting ways. Their visions become expansive, their language adventurous, their use of line and page inventive. Instead of wearing ruts in safe, beaten paths, my students break new trails when their purposes demand it. They trust both instinct and intellect, practicing possibilities, evolving their voices.

CLEARING THE WAY

After my first-period class, I hoofed it up to the office to see my principal, Gene Smith— former math teacher and basketball coach, a man whose leadership and past decisions had earned my steadfast loyalty. When I stepped up to Gene's door, he sat at his paper-covered desk, holding aloft a folder in each hand, wondering where, it looked to me, he could safely put them down.

"Got a minute, Gene?"

He glanced up, relieved. "Come in, Tom. Sit down."

I did.

"How are your classes going?"

"We're off to a good start," I said. "But I've got my mind on next semester."

Gene's expression said say more.

"I've got a project I want to try in Advanced Writing. It's based on a book I read titled The Collected Works of Billy the Kid.

Gene smiled. "Billy the Kid's collected works?"

"Not really. Michael Ondaatje is the author. He writes in a style I've never seen before. I don't know what genre the book is, but there's one thing sure—he knows the last couple years of Billy the Kid's life inside out."

"He's done his research."

"Exactly. I thought the students and I could read the book, see how the author wrote

about his research, then the students could research people of their choice and write papers in the style of Ondaatje."

"So they'd write research papers," Gene said.

"Not traditional ones. They'd write . . . well . . . I've been calling Ondaatje's style multigenre. They'd write multigenre research papers."

"I've never heard of that before," Gene said, leaning forward.

"I'm not sure what these multigenre papers will look like," I said. "I just know this book excited me."

"What's the title again?"

"The Collected Works of Billy the Kid."

He laughed and leaned back. "Never read anything like that when I was in school."

"Me either," I said.

"The project sounds challenging."

I nodded.

"And the Advanced Writing class," he said. "That's a perfect place to give it a whirl."

"That's what I thought. There's usually a mix of a few scholars, a few rebels, and some others who just want to write."

"Sounds good to me."

"One problem, Gene, and it could be a big one."

Gene raised his eyebrows.

"I didn't decide till this summer to do the project."

"That doesn't sound like a problem," he said with a wave of his hand. Your curriculum is flexible."

"It's not the curriculum." I cleared my throat. "Like I said, I want students to read The Collected Works of Billy the Kid before they do their research."

"That makes sense," Gene said. "This kind of research paper will be a real departure for them."

"My problem is that I need a classroom set of books, but I didn't order them last spring when requisitions were due."

"How many copies we talking about?"

"I checked the enrollment. If everybody stays in the class"—I swallowed—"twenty-seven."

Gene raised his eyebrows and puffed out his cheeks. "That's a lot of students. How did so many get in there? Aren't we supposed to keep writing classes small?"

"Brenda checked the price of the book," I said. She was our media specialist.

Clearing the Way

Gene lifted his pen from his shirt pocket. "How much?"

"Seven ninety-five each."

That sounded expensive, especially for books ordered months after budgets had been set, especially in a community that frequently exercised its right to veto the only tax increase it had any say over.

Gene, the old math teacher, was delightfully multiplying numbers on his desk blotter. "Twenty-seven students," he mumbled. "I don't see how that happened. I'll have to talk to the counselors, see if we can lower that before next semester." He scribbled a final figure. "We better order thirty books, just in case. Let's see. That's two hundred thirty-eight dollars and fifty cents."

The sum emerged from his mouth in magnified slow motion, tumbling through the air toward me. I wanted to duck.

TWO HUNDRED

THIRTY-EIGHT DOLLARS

AND FIFTY CENTS.

My ears tingled. The figure sounded like a huge amount for one class in one semester in one rural school district in southwestern Ohio.

" 'Course they can't charge us tax on that," said Gene, "and we get a discount too." He circled the figure on the blotter and laid down his pen. "Tom," he said, "buying the books is not a problem."

The space between my eyebrows unfurrowed. I straightened in my chair.

"We can't use the regular textbook fund," Gene went on. "That's only for orders at the end of the school year, but," and at this point a rare but unmistakable shade of smugness entered his voice, "I have an emergency principal's fund I can dip into for worthy projects." Gene smiled.

In less than a minute my spirits had gone from resignation to disbelief to the exuberant realization that the project was a go.

"What was that title again—The Collected Dead of Billy the Kid?"

"The Collected Works of Billy the Kid," I said. "Through Penguin."

"That's some title," he laughed. Gene stood up. "Get Penguin's address. Brenda can help you there. Make a purchase order for thirty copies, and hand it directly to the secretary. Be sure to tell her it's not to go through as a textbook order. It needs to go through the special principal's fund."

I nodded, a little bewildered.

"Here, wait a minute," he said, "I'll warn her it's coming."

Gene headed for the door, then stopped and looked over his shoulder. "Think you'll have the purchase order this afternoon?"

"This morning," I said.

He stepped next door to talk with the secretary.

I sat alone in Gene's office, relieved, exhilarated, and also this: I felt I was the most valued teacher in the state of Ohio.

Chapter Seven

THE MULTIGENRE RESEARCH PAPER
Melding Fact, Interpretation, and Imagination

I AM LARGE, I CONTAIN MULTITUDES.

Walt Whitman

*P*erception is all.

Ways of seeing.

Ways of knowing.

Ways of learning.

Sometimes I see the world through poetry: a bit of cadenced language suddenly saying itself in my head, an indelible image ever sharp, a surprising metaphor with extensions following close behind.

Sometimes I see the world through prose: a description that holds in place an unforgettable scene, a pointed story that clarifies experience, a monolog that marshals points I wish I'd made during a disagreement.

Sometimes I see the world through dramatic encounters: before a student arrives for conference, I play out the dialog that might occur between us; I talk with my father, he dead now three decades.

Each genre offers me ways of seeing and understanding that others do not. I perceive the world through multiple genres. They shape my seeing. They define who I am.

* * *

In Stratford, Ontario, at the Shakespeare festival, between "Good night, sweet Prince" and the hurly-burly of the "dead butcher and his fiendlike queen," I visited a wonderful house of a bookstore called Fanfare Books. In the jam-packed poetry room, my head tilted to scan the book spines, I saw a title I just had to pull from the shelf: *The Collected Works of Billy the Kid*.

Author Michael Ondaatje created a treasure in his rendering of the last few years of outlaw Billy the Kid's life. The book won Canada's prestigious Governor-General's Award for Literature. Although Ondaatje takes his material from a real person and true events, his book is far from conventional biography. In fact, the subtitle Ondaatje provided in the original Coach House Press publication was *Left Handed Poems*. The Library of Congress catalog entry lists the book as poetry *and* fiction. Despite this, *The Collected Works of Billy the Kid* is loaded with fact.

Ondaatje thoroughly researched the vengeful, bloody life of William H. Bonney—alias Billy the Kid. The author's inquiry easily matches that of a dissertation. Out of his learning, however, Ondaatje did not write exposition. Instead, he created a complex, multilayered, multivoiced blend of genres.

In his "learning journal" one of my high school seniors wrote a good description of the work:

> This is a fantastic book. . . .
> Ondaatje manages to balance the terrifying and gruesome with the bizarre and hilarious. Sometimes, he did it all in one scene. . . .
> As a whole, the book worked very well for me. Though I'm still confused about some of the picky details of Billy's life, I feel I know him, now.
> Ondaatje is uncompromising. He shows us characters from every angle. He switches smoothly between personas—from Billy to Pat Garrett to Sally Chisum . . . and sometimes he steps back and writes simply as "the author."
> Blending stream of consciousness, narrative, verse, monolog, even newspaper style dialog, he leaves nary a stone unturned. — And it all is effective.
> While sometimes author techniques run dry by book's end, Ondaatje builds on you. The more I read the more I understood.
> *Jon Graham, Senior, Edgewood High School*

In addition to the genres Jon mentioned, Ondaatje includes songs, thumbnail character sketches, an authentic comic book legend from The Five Cent Wide Awake Library, imaginative creations of moments that could have occurred, even photographs and drawings from the era.

Each genre reveals a facet of Billy the Kid or of the characters who moved in and out of his life. Each piece is self-contained, making a point of its own, and is not connected to any of the other pieces by conventional transitional devices. The book is written in crots of many genres. The reader enters this different kind of book and drifts and puzzles and makes sense. Reading it is like listening to jazz: the reader feels something satisfying and meaningful, but may not be able to articulate what it is immediately. The multiple genres, the nonchronological order, the language rhythms, the condensed imagery—all these the reader adjusts to and begins to work with. Intellectual and emotional understanding mounts. As Jon said: the more you read, the more you understand.

After reading and rereading the book, I began to *what if* ... what if students wrote in Ondaatje's multigenre style? The notion was so big I carried it around with me for nearly a year, talking with friends and colleagues in the Ohio Writing Project and the University of New Hampshire Summer Writing Program. Look at this book, I'd urge them. Look at the poetry and fiction, the character sketches and songs, the pictures and scenes. Listen to all the voices. Have you ever seen anything like this?

They hadn't. And they probably grew tired of my obsession with *The Collected Works of Billy the Kid*. I was grateful for their indulgence. I later realized I had used them as an audience to talk myself into understanding the book and grasping the possibilities it might hold for writing.

I wondered: could Michael Ondaatje become my students' "distant teacher"? Vera John-Steiner uses that term in *Notebooks of the Mind* to describe those—living or dead—who teach from afar (37). When I was nineteen years old, for example, Ernest Hemingway became my distant teacher when a professor sent me to the library to read "The Short Happy Life of Francis MaComber." The ending of the story knocked me on the seat of my pants. I read "The Killers," too, and "Indian Camp," "My Old Man," "Wine of Wyoming," and "Fathers and Sons." I started to write about the world I knew, the people I grew up with in small-town Ohio. My prose became leaner, less adverbial. Marge Piercy became my distant teacher, too. After reading *Hard Loving*, a collection of her poetry one of my former students had given to me, I went to my journal and wrote my first free verse poem. I was twenty-nine. Distant teachers have enabled me to risk and grow and learn. Maybe Michael Ondaatje could become the distant teacher of my students.

Enrolled in a junior/senior elective called Advanced Writing, these students represented a wide range of writing development, experience in English classes, and reasons for taking the course. Jon intended to become a playwright; Lila had taken a class from me her sophomore year and wanted another; Bobby had little interest in writing but thought he'd enroll in the course since his sister had taken it two years earlier. Although ability and motivation varied among the students, none were the academically alienated. The majority were bound for some kind of post–high school study the following year, however short-lived that study might be.

Could these students pick interesting people, research them, and then report on that research *not* in traditional, expository research papers but rather by employing Ondaatje's multigenre mode of writing? I believed they could. I also wondered if the students and their audience would perceive and feel more deeply through the multiple ways of seeing and knowing that various genres offered.

In *More Than Stories* Thomas Newkirk quotes Donald Murray's warning about genre:

> Genre is a powerful but dangerous lens. It both clarifies and limits. The writer and student must be careful not to see life merely in the stereotyped form with which he or she is most familiar but to look at life with all the possibilities of the genre in mind and to attempt to look at life through different genre. (1989, 5)

Newkirk explores an implication of Murray's assertion:

> It would follow that a child who has mastered a repertoire of genres has a number of lenses with which to view experience: genres, while constraining, are also cognitive instruments for making sense of the world. (5)

We began our project by exploring *The Collected Works of Billy the Kid*. Ondaatje readied us for the work ahead. One senior wrote,

> This book is different from any other I have ever read. I like the poetry mixed in with the bits and pieces of story. It flows better. This book is almost like a movie which just shows the highlights of the story line. It is vivid and doesn't "beat around the bush." You'd think Ondaatje was by Billy's side the whole time. I like how he improvises on what they (Billy, friends, etc.) would have said or done. He takes a factual situation and makes a believable story of it. You get to know the characters better this way, as opposed to a boring documentary. I can see why you suggested this book. Now we know we can be more imaginative in our reports.
> *Krissy Farler Daniels, Senior, Edgewood High School*

After our joint work with Ondaatje, the classroom turned into a workshop for six weeks: these twenty-seven southwestern Ohio teenagers read, wrote, researched, and conferred about personages they were drawn to for one reason or another. Student choice of whom they would research was imperative to the success of the project. I didn't realize that initially. In the months before the project I entertained a thought that would have usurped a large part of that choice.

Multigenre research papers were so different from traditional research papers, so far beyond the ken of anything I had ever asked students to write, that I began to have pedagogical qualms. Perhaps, I thought, I should restrict students' research to American or British authors. That would at least give the project canonical legitimacy. It took me a few weeks to resolve that skirmish in my head. If students were going to fly as high and as far as they could with this project, they needed complete freedom of choice, unfettered opportunities to pursue their own driving interests.

Here are the people my students chose to research: Elvis Presley, Marilyn Monroe, Ken Kesey, Maya Angelou, Charles Manson, John Lennon, Bob Dylan, Jimi Hendrix, Robert Plant, G. Gordon Liddy, Jim Thorpe, Tom Seaver, Willie Mays, Bette Davis, Betty Grable, Carol Burnett, Mary Wilson of the old Supremes, Alan Alda, Helen Keller, FBI-undercover-mafioso-investigator Danny Brosco, Amelia Earhart, Tennessee Williams, and, in the spirit of nascent feminism and with a mother's cautious approval, Linda Lovelace.

One requirement of the research was that students read a biography or autobiography. From there they were free to explore any other information sources they could find. I didn't ask students to fill out note cards on their research, but I did require them to keep learning journals. Each week I asked them to write at least a thousand words about their research. I wanted students to use their personal language as a tool to "audit" their learning (Berthoff 1987, 11). Such auditing I knew would organize information and uncover new thinking.

Here's Amy rummaging around in her research:

Went to the library today and found a couple of magazine articles on Carol Burnett. Nothing spectacular, just an article on her chin surgery in '83 and another article about the movie "Between Friends" that she'd played in a few years ago. I found some interesting pictures that compare what Carol's chin looked like before, and after her surgery. You can certainly see a difference. The surgeon added four millimeters to it. I don't figure I should write much about it though, it's not really all that significant to the part of her life that I'm focusing on. But it's evident that to her it is in fact a "big deal." So I don't know whether I should or not (what do you think). I did note one important point. In the article, at the end, Carol comments that the best thing she likes about "getting a chin" was that when it rained now, she could feel it on her chin. And I thought that was neat because I was watching videotapes that Brian loaned me on Oprah & Donahue and she made the same comment. The article was written about five yrs ago and the videos were taped a year (or less) ago. I guess it was the way she said she could finally feel rain on it, that got me, all through her book she mentions rain here and there. She's got some sort of fascination with it. She says rain puts her in a good mood. And brings her good luck. So I'm going to use rain here and there in my piece. I'm thinking about titling the whole thing

"Carol Burnett: The inspiration reigns on." Something like that, I don't know.

Amy Whitacre White, Senior, Edgewood High School

The bulk of writing in the learning journals was what James Britton calls "expressive writing" (1993, 8)—informal, personal, unpressured words on paper by writers seeking to recover information, make connections, and generate thinking with their close-to-speaking-voice language—the best learning tool available to them.

Learning journal entries that scrapped about for meaning, reported, connected, and speculated the way Amy's had were excellent work. But I had an additional agenda. Because of the magnitude and atypical nature of the multigenre project, I also wanted students to experiment with various genres in their learning journals, not simply wait until their research was completed to write their papers. I wanted students to play with possibilities, to try the untried, to develop their papers *as* their research was in progress. Initially, I suggested they do this, then I nudged, then I pushed.

Wendy dived deeply and quickly into David Henderson's *The Life of Jimi Hendrix: 'Scuse Me While I Kiss the Sky*. In her learning journal she made brief prewriting notes aslant the top of her paper then wrote this poem about Hendrix's early career and a key person in his life:

FAYNE, JIM HENDRIX, AND HIS GIRL

The first time you heard
    Jimi Hendrix play
you could have been sitting in the cramped New York
                  night club
         dangling a cigarette between red,
            chipped fingernails
      leaning back in your chair
      soaking in the music.
You may have been wearing a blue cotton dress
         sleek black shoes
         and cheap pearl costume

jewelry
Maybe you wanted to get up
        out of that stiff chair
and dance
       wildly to the beat
           surging into your feet
           pounding into your mind
But the world wasn't ready for you yet.
And I know you realized Jimi's talent
         eating up conservative ways
         paving roads for
           free music.
You felt all of Jimi's pain
        in each whining note
         of his girl.
No doubt you were wrapped up
        in the sounds
          of the frantic guitar
No doubt you felt free.
And I know at the end of Jimi's gig,
        you nodded your head yes
     to the
        crazy music
          you'd never heard
    before.
But the world wasn't ready for Jimi yet.
So you, the girl from Harlem
       with the foxy smile,
stood up for Jimi and his girl
      to the audiences
        and Big names.
    You understood him
    always laughing to forget those who
          didn't understand
Laughing about silly things like
how short poor Jimi looked in the white trousers he
         bought for his gig.
   Wendy Riley Brown, Junior, Edgewood High School

In the earlier example of Amy's expressive writing, she discussed the importance of rain in Carol Burnett's life. Imagery and language were building in her. In the excerpt from her learning journal shown in Figure 7–1, Amy drafted a poem complete with misspellings, vivid verbs, figurative language, and a new word tried on for size.

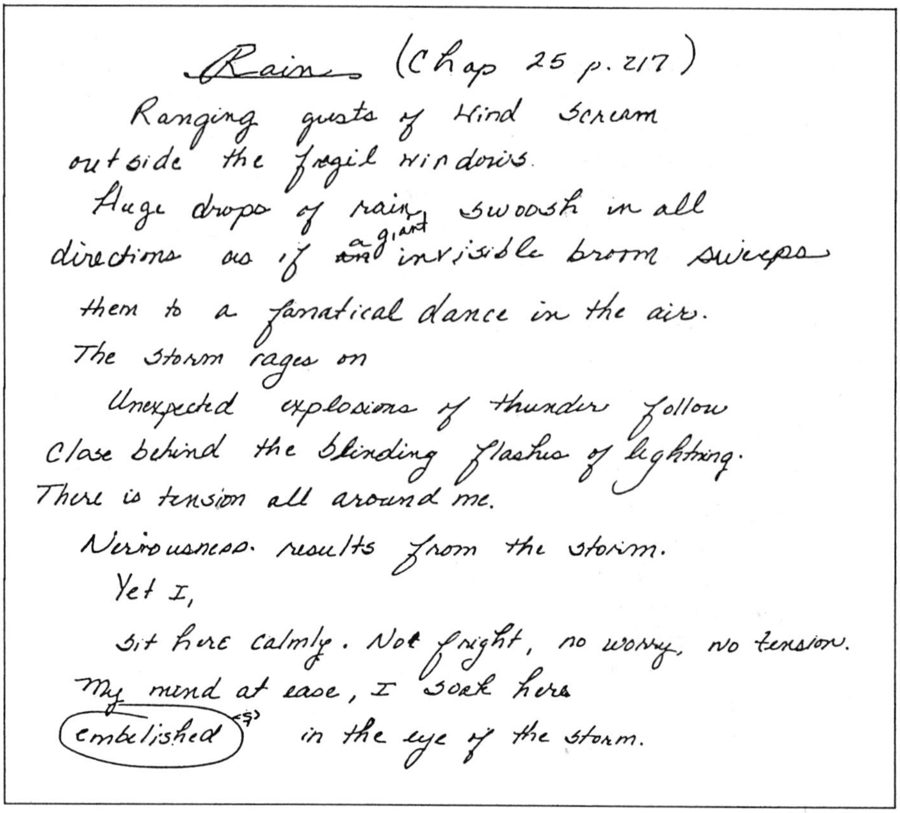

Rain (Chap 25 p. 217)

Ranging gusts of wind scream
outside the fragile windows.
Huge drops of rain swoosh in all
directions as if a giant invisible broom sweeps
them to a fanatical dance in the air.
The storm rages on

Unexpected explosions of thunder follow
close behind the blinding flashes of lightning.
There is tension all around me.

Nervousness results from the storm.

Yet I,

sit here calmly. No fright, no worry, no tension.
My mind at ease, I soak here
embelished in the eye of the storm.

FIGURE 7-1

While researching Elvis Presley, Donna began to understand the mania teenagers developed about Elvis. In her journal she wrote:

I had this idea come to me as I was looking back over some notes.

A DEVOTED FAN

I love Elvis Presley!
If I could only meet him!
Oh, I'd do absolutely anything!
OH! Elvis! I love you!
I've spent all of my allowance
on everything about you.
In the morning I put on
Elvis Presley bobby socks
Elvis Presley shoes
Elvis Presley shirt
Elvis Presley blouse or

Elvis Presley sweater.
An Elvis Presley charm bracelet
dangles from one wrist,
An Elvis Presley handkerchief
goes in my Elvis Presley purse.
I go to school,
Chew some Elvis Presley bubble gum
And use an Elvis Presley pencil.
After school,
I change into my
Elvis Presley jeans or
Elvis Presley shorts
(both have Elvis's face on the pocket or tag).
I can play an Elvis Presley game
While I drink an Elvis Presley soft drink.
Before bed,
I put on my Elvis Presley pajamas
To write in my Elvis Presley diary
With my Elvis Presley pen.
I play "Hound Dog"
(About ten times)
Before turning off the light
To see my Elvis Presley
"Glow in the dark" picture
before I go to sleep and dream,
About Elvis.
    Donna Hatten Buzan, Senior, Edgewood High School

I urged students to play with extended metaphor when writing about their topics. Metaphorical thinking, I thought, might lead them to surprising connections and offbeat understanding. We took fifteen minutes one morning to generate metaphors and follow promising ones with a line of language. Sally wrote about cult leader and mass murderer Charles Manson, a man she grew quite sick of after five weeks of intense research.

Weeds growing up the vine going all over uncontrollably—poison ivy spreads first infecting a little, the blister busts and the pus pours out all over there's no stopping it. There's no cure like a disease. The healthy object green—turns brown and molds. Manson molded their minds. The smell of mold is everywhere. Infection spreads.

    He needed attention when he was younger like a plant needs water but he didn't receive it— turned brown, hard edges, stiff.
    Sally Friday, Senior, Edgewood High School

Journal entries turned into instructive mini-lessons (Calkins 1986, 168). I made transparencies of these genre experiments and, at the beginning of a class period, placed them on the overhead so that everyone could tap into the classroom's "creative current" (Romano 1987, 171). After we discussed these genre experiments, the student writers revealed the genesis of the idea and talked about their writing processes. By sharing these ongoing multigenre creations, we sparked ideas in our community of writers, taught each other what Donald Murray calls "the geography of possibility" (1985, 88).

I urged, cajoled, and pushed students to use their journals to try genres. And I was successful, for the most part, except for Mary Beth. She had her own way of writing. Her final paper was a sensitive, spare, poetic examination of Marilyn Monroe. In her written evaluation of the project Mary Beth acknowledged the usefulness of her learning journal, but admitted that she hadn't used the journal for experimenting with genres:

> **I** really didn't try different genres in my journal, but maybe once because when I write, I just write with no "pre" to it. I know this eats you up, but that's just me. In my journal, I wrote about considering a poem, but I never wrote anything until I wrote my poem. (Rough draft, only draft)

Mary Beth's writing process was not my process. It wasn't what I was trying to teach her. And it did eat me up—a little. But Mary Beth achieved quality results with her no-pre-to-it process of composition. Here is an excerpt from her paper, "The Simple Life":

SOMEDAYSOMEMONTHSOMEYEAR

walked on the beach for hours watching the
water come and go just as i do with Marilyn
and Norma Jean but who am i really i
know i'm not Marilyn because i wasn't
born Marilyn but i'm not Norma Jean
because i wasn't born well i was born her
but i wasn't her once i got my "big break"
my big break that broke me in two or three
or however many i am who in the hell
am i i'm a flower a moth a spider a
bird a well i guess i'm everything everywhere
everyone i'm a sex symbol sex is strange
but it's all mine it's all i have to give
i haven't slept my way to the top i've
slept my way to your heart you love
me for my sex and why you like it i don't
know i hate it it's not for me it's not

me it's your pleasure not mine but that's
all i'm for is your pleasure
a trademark a fool
     a lonely lonely
         fool who wants
             to die

Mary Beth Shepherd, Senior, Edgewood High School

I showed Mary Beth's prose poem to a high school's group of "lay readers"—community volunteers who collected class sets of papers from teachers, marked every error they could ferret out, and returned the papers for students to recopy correctly. After I read "SomedaySomemonthSomeyear" and projected it on the overhead, one volunteer reader raised a hand and said with a skeptical squint of one eye, "Did she really mean to leave out all that punctuation?"

Not only did Mary Beth intend the passage to be unpunctuated, but she had also learned from Ondaatje a sophisticated use of stream of consciousness, its ability to move readers inside a character's mind and, in this case, communicate disillusion, confusion, and desperation.

No pre to it? I've got to believe there was plenty of pre to Mary Beth's writing. It just took place in her head where no one—perhaps not even she—knew it was happening.

When the students neared the end of their inquiries, we spent a day working with mapping as a strategy for gaining an overview of their research and revealing topics to write about. I wanted to bolster their confidence. That would happen, I believed, if they showed themselves the great extent of their knowledge. I also used the mapping strategy so they could supplement the linearity of their learning journals with a decidedly nonlinear way of accessing their knowledge.

We tried a whole-class, collaborative mapping activity. The first time I demonstrated this strategy, Ronald Reagan had just completed his presidency. I placed a clear transparency on the overhead and wrote his name in the center of it. Then the students brainstormed details from Reagan's life. In minutes I filled the transparency with Reagan facts, some, no doubt, that Reagan boosters would rather the public forgot.

Next, we speculated: suppose we were writing a multigenre research paper that would illuminate the character of Ronald Reagan. What genres would be appropriate for writing about some of the crucial facts and events we had mapped on the overhead?

Todd suggested a simple list poem of the names of important figures in Reagan's life.

Jon thought an interview would be revealing, one between Nancy Reagan and Jane Wyman, Reagan's first wife.

A thumbnail sketch of Reagan's would-be assassin, John Hinckley.

A stream-of-consciousness passage from Reagan's point of view in the moments when he was shot, pushed into a car, and hustled away.

And—if you spend time with teenagers, you know that many of them are just a step away from broad, indelicate satire—a tabloid piece à la the *National Enquirer*, accompanied by a close-up of Reagan's cancer-blighted nose.

The students then took ten minutes and let fly without self-censorship, rapidly mapping crucial facts, people, and events from their characters' lives. Senior Margaret Colaw's mapping of Mata Hari is shown in Figure 7–2.

As the deadline for their drafts grew near, the students began asking familiar questions: What should these multigenre papers look like? How should they begin? What should be in them? And, of course, how long should they be?

I had no answers. This was new territory. None of my previous students had ever written multigenre research papers. Neither had I. And I wasn't so sure I wanted to tell them precisely what to do anyway. A memo, it seemed, was in order. About time, I thought, that these older teenagers received a memo.

To: Advanced Writing Students
From: Romano
Date: 3/10/88
Re: Your research and final pieces of writing

First of all, what is it you should create based on all the research, reading, sharing, and writing you have done? Fact is, I don't know what it should look like or how many words it should contain.

I do know that I want it to be deeply textured (Ondaatje showed us that), interesting, vivid, specific, insightful, diverse with many genres (we have worked very hard on that), intelligent, bold, experimental (I want to see your imagination and intellect turned loose), and comprehensible. When I finish reading, I want to really know your person through your perceptions. I want to be gasping for air from the excitement of reading you.

I want a lot. But I think you can do it if you're willing to risk and work (writing always involves both).

And I want to help you as you craft your writing, your vision.

If this memo seems flip, remember that it reflects one teacher's personality and relationship with a particular group of students. Even though it didn't

FIGURE 7–2

tell them anything about length, lead, format, or content, the memo assuaged their trepidation, which it was meant to do.

It took the students about a week to assemble, create, and write drafts of their papers. I read them and conferred with the writers; the writers conferred with each other in small groups and pairs. Then they revised. A week later, I collected the final versions.

Below is one of the papers. When it was published in *Menagerie*—our high school creative arts anthology—we saved room by double-spacing between each crot, and I present it that way here, too. In his original version, however, senior Brian McKnight followed Michael Ondaatje's example, granting integrity to each genre, however brief, by placing it on a page of its own.

THE LONG AND WONDERFUL ODYSSEY OF THE WALRUS
A HEART PLAY

Unfinished Music #1—John

He hit the pavement
ass-first
Yoko raised
his
head.
He wanted to embrace her
but a hundred people
were
standing on
his arms.
    Oh God, Yoko, I've been shot.

The Death of John Beatle

Outside the Indica Gallery, the world still oppressed ideas, fought wars, and censored news.

Inside, however, it was like nothing he had ever seen. It had only been eight years since he had graduated from Liverpool Art College. He hadn't been in an art gallery since. And he had never been in one like this. White nails half driven in a white block of wood, white vases with white flowers sitting on a white table in a white corner. He saw a white, half-eaten apple on a white pedestal. (When he was a kid and had had a bad day, his aunt Mimi always gave him an apple. "There now, don't you feel better, then, John? Of course you do, now give your aunt Mimi a kiss.") The apple felt as smooth as glass in his hand—so white and smooth and pure.

"Don't touch anything, please." She stood menacingly in the doorway. "The show doesn't open until tomorrow, so you better not mess anything up."

"Yoko, this is John Lennon. The Beatle."

Lost in the gallery, John had forgotten Tony was there. He took John by the arm and led him to the dark figure in the doorway.

"John, this is Yoko Ono."

John stood there like a prize being awarded to someone who wishes he hadn't won in the first place.

Yoko didn't move. Her all-black outfit and long black hair contradicted the all-white gallery. The artist herself. She looked deep into John. Past his round-rimmed granny glasses, past John Beatle

and into John Lennon. "Well, whoever you are don't touch anything."

Whoever you are?

But surely, he thought, everyone's heard of John Lennon, the
Beatle. This Jap was daft! Didn't she know who she had in her
gallery?

"I just wanted to look around, all right?"

She nodded and pulled her long hair away from her perfect,
pristine Oriental face. John made his way past Yoko and into the
other room. He stopped at a white ladder leaning against the white
wall. Suddenly she was at his side, holding a magnifying glass.

"Here," she said, "climb up and look."

He pushed his spectacles back on the bridge of his nose. Now
she thinks I am bleedin' Sherlock Holmes.

When he arrived at the top, he raised the spyglass gently to the
ceiling.

And he looked down at her.

And again the magnified word: YES, it said.

He smiled.

Two Virgins

A New Age
awoke
with the
Two Virgins.
Confusion and ignorance
were wiped away
with
the sleep in their
eyes.

Dressed all in
white
they paraded their
love
for the world to
see.

The Two Virgins
were wed
March 20, 1969
on the
Rock of Gibraltar.
The world was invited
to their bed-in
for the consummation.

From a maharishi
to
primal screaming
to
heroin
to
NEW YORK
The Two Virgins
arrived in
New York
to be welcomed
home
by a
family
they'd never
seen.

The Rotting Apple

"This is it. I want a divorce."

Paul was stunned. He looked across the table to see himself, mouth open wide, in John's spectacles.

"What do you mean?"

"Just that. I want a divorce. I don't want to be a Beatle anymore. I just want to be with Yoko. I'm tired of the pressures and the people and all the bullshit. Your bullshit, Paul."

"John, come on, Man. Don't do this. Listen, fine, if *you* want to be with Yoko, that's okay, but don't say anything to the press. It'll look bad ..."

"I don't give a bleeding damn about how it looks!" Apple Corporation had become a pain in the ass. He ran his ragged fingers through his long, unkempt hair and beard. He straightened his white jacket and fixed his white turtleneck. "Fine. I'm gone, but I won't say nuthin' to the press. You deal with 'em. You're better at that shit anyway."

It took him a while, but four months later the news hit the stands: PAUL McCARTNEY QUITS THE BEATLES.

Solo LP due out soon.

BEATLES BREAK UP; McCARTNEY, ONO TO BLAME

LONDON—A High Court ruled today that singer-songwriter-musician-Beatle Paul McCartney and screamer-songwriter-artist-Beatle-lover Yoko Ono were jointly responsible for the destruction of the greatest band in the history of music.

"Well, she's a bitch," replied Judge Len N. Fann, when asked about his decision. "She took John away from good music and turned him into something sick and perverted."

Paul McCartney, meanwhile, has been hiding out at his Scottish retreat, changing diapers, breast feeding, etc.

"It wasn't my fault," he said in a statement to the press. "We [the Beatles] just didn't get along anymore. They got real rebellious. They wouldn't play their instruments the way I told them to. But don't worry, I'll have another number one single out in no time."

Ms. Ono was unavailable for comment.

NO. 9 NO. 9 NO. 9 NO. 9 NO. 9 NO. 9 NO. 9 NO. 9

Born on the 9th He
NO. 9 Dreamed of the 9th Revolution beginning
on the 9th
Recorded on the 9th: Love Me Do: Parlophone R4949
All We Are Saying Is Give Peace A Chance
His son was born on the 9th to John Lennon
Who was born on the 9th who met
Sean's mother on the 9th
One after 909.

NO. 9 NO. 9 NO. 9 NO. 9 NO. 9 NO. 9 NO. 9 NO. 9

Unfinished Music #2—Yoko

She kissed him hard on the mouth.
She could already
taste
the blood
the blood
The blood
was thick and
made her sweater
heavy as
she held him
close
   Hold on, John, please hold on.

New York

Like a rose
New York City
opened its bud to
JohnandYoko.
Each crimson petal offered a
new opportunity to
live and love and grow.

Their home at the
Dakota Building
was the magical epicentre
of an ever extending
sea of possibilities.
Each ripple grew
larger and larger
picking up
ideas.

New York
pulsated and breathed just for
JohnandYoko.
It was the heart that
kept their spirits alive.
It was the safe place
that protected them
from
the rest of the world.

America

"Hey, John, how's the new album?"
"Yo, Johnny, —where's Yoko?"
He was
free
in New York.
No hassles, man.
Sign the occasional
autograph
and move on.

Unfinished Music #3—The Reaction

The ambulance
barreled around
W. 72nd St.
Oh John
she screamed
Move out of the way, ma'am.
Where are you taking him?
Roosevelt Hospital,
   9th Ave.
They loaded his
heaving, dripping
body
into the ambulance.
   Holy Shit, man. This is John Lennon.

The Coda

Flashbulbs
popped off a
morbid papparazzi
as
Dr. Lynn
spoke.
"John Lennon ...

John Lennon
was
brought to
the emergency room of
Roosevelt Hospital
shortly before
11 p.m.
He was
dead
on arrival."

"And in the end—the love you take is equal to the love you make."
—*John Lennon/Paul McCartney*

   Brian McKnight, Senior, Edgewood High School

I had never read anything like these multigenre research papers before. Most of them were genuinely interesting in style and content. The visions were complex, the writing versatile. Brian's paper was one of six or seven I found astonishing. All was not glory, though. Three of the papers were disappointing, showing little depth, breadth, or commitment. And rest assured, like Reverend Dimmesdale, I did a requisite amount of self-flogging: What did I do wrong? What could I have done?

In retrospect, I do see things I could have done. The disappointing papers didn't emerge from nowhere. The three students' learning journals had revealed puzzlement or a lack of commitment early on. I could have given those students greater support, feedback, and direction. I could have been a better companion for their words.

I think of William Stafford and cringe a little:

If I go to a class, I feel I'm meeting a succession of people to whom I owe individually total allegiance and commitment. I'm not looking for the ones who are going to enhance the school or my reputation or their own. That's nice, but as a teacher I believe that if there is such a thing as the lowest one in the class, they deserve the same level reception and cordiality as anybody else. (1986, 85)

ROOM TO ROLL YOUR SHOULDERS

This multigenre project did not appear in a district curriculum guide. There was no state mandate involved, no national multigenre standard to meet. It didn't appear in a teacher's manual. It didn't even appear in the curriculum guide I wrote for the course. Make no mistake. I am glad to have been entrusted with the responsibility of deciding the curriculum for Advanced Writing, but that document, which enabled me to analyze my students' needs and synthesize my thinking, became dated a few months after I wrote it.

I am not static. I am evolving. The multigenre research paper was born out of my own literacy pursuits, the dynamic connection between my students' needs and development and my own wonder and delight with literature and writing. If I'd had to adhere to an inflexible, overloaded curriculum, a research project of this magnitude would never have occurred to me. I want a curriculum I can roll my shoulders in.

To do this multigenre project required seven weeks of steady work. I felt guilty about that for awhile. More than one third of the semester had been devoted to this multigenre project. Some things in the curriculum had to go— a book review, an alternate style paper, an essay of complaint. The guilt didn't linger, though, when I considered all the reading, research, note taking, drafting, revising, peer interaction, and teacher-student conferences that took place.

STUDENT INFORMANTS

My own brand of action research yielded some unexpected understanding. One of my original research questions was, How will students decide which genres are appropriate for their multigenre papers? We had emphasized genre; the students knew they were expected to write in a variety of them, but I hadn't mandated that students use a certain number of genres or any one genre in particular.

A few of the students described systematic processes for choosing genres—what I thought I'd find across the board, since we had been so systematic in identifying the genres in *The Collected Works of Billy the Kid*.

Some students mentioned the appropriateness of their subject matter for certain genres. "I picked genres that I thought would fit the piece," wrote Susan. "For example: When Maya was considering suicide, I thought a stream of consciousness would be best because all kinds of crazy thoughts were going through her mind."

Brian worked in a similar way: "First I would pick an event in John Lennon's life, like the Big Beatle Breakup. Then I would decide—poem or prose or what? In this case, I thought that since the world read about it in the news that I'd write a short news story."

Brian and Susan came closest to how I assumed students would work and write in selecting genres. But most of them didn't work and write that way. Most of them worked in a manner reflected by the comments of Tari: "To be honest, there wasn't any specific way that I decided on which genres I used. The [Ken Kesey] material I read was so powerful that certain things just grabbed me and I had to write about it, my genres were almost picked for me."

I asked students to tell me about the benefits and drawbacks of creating multigenre research papers. Nearly all the students believed that composing them was far more difficult than any writing they had done before. This was true for students who remained close to the ground during their research as well as for those who stretched and discovered wingspans that carried them to places they'd never been. "The only drawback that I can think of," wrote Bobby, "would be that it makes you think a lot harder. It is a lot easier to write a standard research paper."

Most of the students linked "standard research papers" with boredom, perfunctory reading, and a kind of writing that offered little opportunity for surprise, inventiveness, and individuality. "I've done plenty of research papers with the old encyclopedia," noted Tari. "They're boring to write, read, and hear."

"A term paper or your basic social studies report would have been easy," wrote Holly, "because it requires no creativity."

And I want to weep. In the minds of so many of our students, reporting on research is divorced from creativity. I'm not talking about an airy-headed, flowers-by-the-babbling-brook, ooo-wee-ain't-we-clever creativity. I'm talking about the real thing—when intellect, emotion, and imagination merge; when analysis and synthesis are one; when writers, painters, sculptors, dancers, composers, physicists, ecologists, historians, take that which is outside them and bring it inside, intimately, then give it back with form, imagination, and meaning, stamped indelibly with their own personal voice and vision.

The act of researching and reporting is no less than the creative act of living. We perceive through our spirits. Our past experiences guide us, our self-awareness, our knowledge, our dreams—however grand or humble—and we live our lives, putting our own personal stamp on them every step of the way. So it is when we bring our entire selves to investigate something. I research and write and sound a particular way because of all that I am.

Many students believe that when turning themselves to research and writing about it, they must leave the realm of self. They have learned that lesson well in school. They believe they are expected to feign some pure though unattainable objectivity. Facts become ashes in their mouths, choking their voices. Routine, perfunctory behavior in thinking and writing lock into autopilot.

The multigenre paper is not the cure-all for research paper woes. Traditional research papers, masters theses, and dissertations can be exhilarating to read. They can be lively, colorful, and provocative. They should be.

The multigenre research paper I've described in this chapter requires that creativity and imagination be part of research. Personal stamps are what I want to see. I value the diversity of the students. When they understand that their individuality is valued, the modus operandi in classrooms becomes risk taking, that priceless straying from the beaten path—the way Albert Einstein did and Martha Graham, Thomas Edison, Dian Fossey, and Henry David Thoreau (that consummate researcher of the countryside of the soul).

The multigenre research paper recognizes that there are many ways to see the world, many ways to show others what we see. Shakespeare saw the world through plays and poetry and poetry amid plays. I'm grateful that his spirit was indomitable, that no one compelled him to forget those ways of seeing, and, instead, to write only prose chronicles in *reporting* what he had learned and imagined about the Scot and the Dane.

THE SILENCE OF LOSS

*G*reg *stepped to the lectern.*
He was seventeen, four months shy of
   senior year.
A first-year teacher in sport coat and
   properly knotted tie,
I sat at a desk in the back of the room,
   jotted Greg's
name, prepared to make notes on his book
   talk of
The Catcher in the Rye.
Greg gripped the sides of the lectern,
   rambled about plot:
Holden losing the fencing team's foils,
   Allie's baseball mitt,
the duck pond in Central Park . . .
Greg stammered to a stop, stared at the
   lectern.
I put down my pen, had hoped he would
   do better.
Greg picked up the book, held it before
   him, an offering.
"Holden wanted to save the children." He
   stopped again.
"Phoebe. His sister Phoebe. It shocked
   him
what a little kid had to face in the world."

Greg looked out at the class, his eyes
   frightened birds.
He swallowed, then turned his back to us,
   walked

to the blackboard, picked up yellow chalk, pressed
hard against the newly washed surface,
wrote letters three feet high:
F . . . Oh, no, I thought . . .
U . . . Good Christ . . .
C . . . And I'd recommended the book to him . . .
K . . . Now it was my turn to swallow.
Greg stepped to the lectern, gripped those sides again
to steady himself against thirty amazed faces.
"Shocking, isn't it? That's what Holden found written on the
wall of Phoebe's school. Little kids weren't safe anywhere."

Two boys sniggered. No one spoke. No one dared
look back at me where I sat in my properly knotted tie.
Greg raised the book above his head. "I never
read a story like this before. I didn't want to read
it when Mr. Romano gave it to me. I'm glad I did. Holden
tells the truth. You should all read it."
Greg stepped from the lectern. "Just a minute," I said.

War waged in my head: a young man moved by a book,
shocking us out of our late afternoon drowse,
just as Holden had been, just as Greg himself had been.
Adolescence and literature had converged and soared.
That fact fought my properly knotted tie.

I began my own ramble about Holden's self-consciousness,
compulsive lying, disdain for phoniness. Greg
waited, one hand resting on the lectern,
his eyes staring at the floor. Students lowered
their heads as though in prayer.
My properly knotted tie crushed my throat,
but I kept talking.

When my words wound down, the silence of loss filled
the classroom. I granted Greg permission to take his seat.
"Why don't you erase the board?" Becky said.
"Yeah," said Angie, "people won't understand." Greg did.

Chapter Eight

PROBLEMS, ISSUES, DILEMMAS OF THE MULTIGENRE RESEARCH PAPER

IT IS NOT UPON YOU ALONE THE DARK
      PATCHES FALL,
THE DARK THREW ITS PATCHES DOWN UPON
      ME ALSO.

Walt Whitman

*T*eaching the multigenre research paper was not without problems. Some were particular to the kind of new work we were doing. Other problems, like the problem of slang speech, what many people, in fact, consider profanity, could have arisen in any class with any assignment.

APPROPRIATE LANGUAGE

In the previous chapter I showed the no-pre-to-it stream of consciousness that Mary Beth wrote from Marilyn Monroe's dazed yet incisive first-person perspective. The version you read, however, wasn't the way Mary Beth originally wrote it. One word had been changed. Here's the pertinent section of the original:

> i'm a sex symbol sex is strange
> but it's all mine it's all i have to give
> i haven't fucked my way to the top i've
> fucked my way to your heart you love
> me for my sex and why you like it i don't
> know

In writing about Marilyn Monroe, Mary Beth was empathic, melancholy, and frank. She pulled no punches. *Fucked* seemed appropriate. *Fuck* is the word that television doesn't use, even though the promise and allure of sex is the core of so much of its programming and advertising.

Mary Beth's use of the word caused a problem: the editors of the yearly creative arts anthology and I wanted to publish three pieces from Mary Beth's multigenre paper. Marilyn's stream of consciousness we especially wanted to use. But *fucked* would provoke consequences, possibly catastrophic ones. It wasn't that we'd never published expletives before. Although we occasionally heard grumblings about *damn, bitchin'*, or *hell*, in fourteen years the anthology had never officially been censored by the administration or school board. We had never, however, published the lightning-rod word that elicits telephone calls and packs school board meetings.

So I, Tom Romano, Mr. Clearing the Way, who urged students to draw upon their passions and speak the rude truth, to look at all aspects of life— wherever their strong feelings pulled them—and write honestly about what they saw, felt compelled to ask a student if we could somehow eliminate Marilyn's casual and thoroughly appropriate use of *fucked*.

Mary Beth lay on the rug in my classroom, writing in her journal. I knelt beside her. She sat up and crossed her legs.

"We want to use three of the pieces from your Marilyn paper in the creative arts anthology."

Mary Beth smiled and her eyes brightened.

"They'll fit perfectly on one page," I said. "Thought we'd title it 'Three About Marilyn.' Could we do that?"

"Sure."

"There's one problem," I said.

Mary Beth raised an eyebrow.

"We want to use 'SomedaySomemonthSomeyear.' But if we print *fucked* in the creative arts anthology, I'm afraid the administration will either stop subsidizing it or insist on approving everything we plan to publish in the future."

An I-knew-it expression formed around Mary Beth's lips as she shook her head. "You know," she said, "if I'd written that in any other class, I'd have gotten in trouble. But in your class I knew I could use it."

I smiled. But inside my head controversy raged. One voice screamed, "She doesn't respect you! Your class is loose and undisciplined!" Another voice soothed, "Calm down, Tom. She's complimenting you."

"I was wondering if we could come up with a synonym," I said.

Mary Beth wrinkled her forehead.

I had thought about synonyms the night before. They all sounded insipid or inappropriate in the context of the desperate, doomed, and tragic stream of consciousness: *have sex*, *fornicate*, *make love*. Heaven help me, I even considered *screw*!

"How about *slept*?" said Mary Beth. "i haven't slept my way to the top i've slept my way to your heart."

From the time my daughter was a little girl, I'd taken the position that there were no "bad" words. Imagine the absurdity of a word being bad, disobedient, wicked, a behavior problem: Send Bastard to it's room. Wash Prick's mouth out with soap. Sit Asshole in a chair for an hour. And Fuck? Suspend Fuck. Better yet, expel Fuck.

I told my daughter, however, and I tell my students that there are social situations to consider when choosing language. We flout those considerations at our own risk. Depending on the words we use and the context we use them in, an audience might become alienated during a speech. A letter to the editor might go unpublished. A client might be offended. A superintendent might reprimand. A school board might not renew a contract. A poem might not appear in the creative arts anthology.

Although I recognize the reality of language in social situations, another side of me resists anyone dictating the language I may use. That side knows that Hemingway's *A Farewell To Arms* was banned in Boston, Vonnegut's *Slaughter House Five* was burned in Drake, North Dakota, and half my beginning fiction writing students at Utah State University were offended by the soldiers' talk in Tim O'Brien's *The Things They Carried*.

Emerson urged us to speak the "rude truth." I take that urging seriously. I take Emerson's rude truth to refer to the language we use as well as to the subject matter we choose to write about.

But we must be aware that we speak and write our rude truths in particular social settings. We have to be willing to face consequences our words might trigger. I wasn't willing to live with the possible consequence of the creative arts anthology's demise. Mary Beth wasn't willing to live with the consequence of her poems going unpublished.

Mary Beth knew she could write the words she needed to in my class. She also knew the quality and honesty of the pieces in the creative arts anthology. She chose *slept*. I don't think "SomedaySomemonthSomeyear" is as effective with that substitution. But it isn't hurt much. And *slept*—rather than *fucked*—allowed more people in our school community to vibrate sympathetically to the emotion of the passage.

When I have presented my action research on the multigenre research paper at conferences and workshops, a few teachers usually want to know how to obtain a copy of *The Collected Works of Billy the Kid*. I tell them. But I also tell them that students can write multigenre research papers without reading it, that the book is, as Jon wrote, "uncompromising."

One Saturday afternoon after the books had arrived, a friend of mine, John Gaughan, lounged on the couch in our family room. He picked up a copy of *The Collected Works of Billy the Kid* from the coffee table.

"So this is the book you've been talking about."

He began leafing through it, stopped, and read a passage aloud—a blunt sexual passage. My jaw dropped. John turned randomly to another passage. "Oh, Mr. Romano," he said, "what does this mean?" Then he read a passage even more explicit than the first.

I read a book holistically. I hum to the voice, visualize scenes, tense to the drama. Sometimes I mark passages of powerful content, compelling style, or effective language. Sometimes I bend down page corners, but I don't often remember words or content that might offend someone whose thoughts about language and appropriate subject matter for literature don't match mine.

Now that my friend had pointed out specific passages that might be problematic, however, I began to worry. I wanted desperately to use *The Collected Works of Billy the Kid* with my students; I believed its multigenre model would cut loose their writing and alter forever their visions of what a research paper could be. But my friend had me thinking about censorship upheavals and shouting matches at school board meetings where the first amendment counted for naught and Emerson could keep his rude truth to himself.

I wouldn't be using the books for several months, so I began talking to others about my dilemma. One experienced teacher and fellow member of the Ohio Writing Project advised me not to make a big deal about the book. Just teach it as I would any other book. He told me, though, to articulate thoroughly my rationale for using *The Collected Works of Billy the Kid* and to detail its literary merit. If objections to the book arose, deal with them then. But don't stir up problems that might never happen.

That sounded sensible. I couldn't doubt the success he'd had with this tack. For years he'd taught without incident *The Catcher in the Rye* and *One Flew Over the Cuckoo's Nest*. Even so, his advice rested uneasily with me. I hated being caught doing something I was worried about.

I talked to another friend—Jane Hansen, professor of reading and writing at the University of New Hampshire. I told Jane about the singularity of Ondaatje's book, the aspects of it that worried me, what I hoped students would do with their own research after we'd read it.

Jane waved her hand in a much-ado-about-nothing gesture. "Oh, Tom," she said, "just tell the students what you're worried about."

I reread *The Collected Works of Billy the Kid* and wrote about it in my journal, the place I could dump my vexations, learn what I thought about them, and figure out what to do. My journal writing about my rereading evolved into a direct letter to the future students.

I still think Ondaatje's *The Collected Works of Billy the Kid* is fine writing, art of great craft, language skill, and imagination. Some poems in it, even some prose poem passages, I didn't understand well. I wanted more meaning from them. Many other places left me with a sense of completion and satisfaction that I strive for in my own writing.

But I am worried about how the book might be perceived by students and parents. I know there isn't a school board in the land that would adopt *The Collected Works of Billy the Kid* as a text.

Although the book deals with the sexual aspect of Billy, I remembered it as poetic, even ambiguous. But upon rereading, I found two or three parts that were explicit. I still don't believe they are pornographic or gratuitous— Ondaatje took the boy-man Billy the Kid all in all, dealt with him straight, put many of the strands of his violent life on the page—sex, blood, drunken binges, characters, killings—all of it, straight, no cautions. Ondaatje wrote *his* book, as he should.

And, of course, I forgot he had used that most controversial, explosive four-letter word of them all—more than a couple times— all in the context of the story and none I see as unwarranted.

And then a surprise: I realized another aspect of the book that might cause problems (it disturbed me more than the sex)—the incredible scenes of violence, the horrid violence of men killing men, not a glamorized picture of gunfighters and the West as we have watched too often at the movies and on television. We find what shootings were really like, what bullets did to brains, what amorality means when acted out— the existentialist nightmare running amuck among people.

So how will I deal with this book when I ask students to join me in reading it?

1. I'll be blunt about my concerns and how I read, how I look at language. Often the impact of a book is what stays with me—I

don't read with censorship in mind. I look at language and at the things that human beings do in public and behind closed doors as simply "that which exists in the world."

2. I'll tell students about the idea that gradually grew in me after I read the book, that Ondaatje demonstrates a writer performing at a height of creative and artistic freedom, blurring genres, using language to shape and create a multitude of impressions and scenes out of his learning and reading.

Can't I have my students do that—urge them, push them to grasp a similar freedom of creative expression? Yes, I purposed.

So I asked Mr. Smith if I could purchase the book. He asked no questions, trusted me, and knew that in the past when he let me go with my enthusiasms, good usually came of them—a film course, an advanced writing course, a fourteen-year-old creative arts anthology called *Menagerie*, a student film festival, a new way to teach sophomore English.

Order the books, he said

I did.

And then I reread the book January 30. And I was surprised to find that although all the art and genres were present, the violence I knew was in the book was rendered more vividly, more brutally than I remembered. The sexual references were there, but even more than references, I found two or three scenes, brief, but rendered in blunt, graphic detail. Billy apparently loved a prostitute, and it's pretty hard to write about that with honesty and not be blunt.

I knew there must have been some cursing, some slang, but I didn't remember that the big, controversial mama of all curse words was used, say, a dozen times (even though I believe they are all in context, nothing like Eddie Murphy's constant use of the word in concert).

So now I am left with a dilemma. I don't want to offend anyone— you or your parents. I'd like for all of us to read *The Collected Works of Billy the Kid* as literature, judge the characters, see what Ondaatje is doing with writing to achieve his effects, evaluate what works and what doesn't, talk about how various passages hit us, what they mean to us, and thus enrich our understanding.

Can we do it? You do not have to read the book if you find it offensive.

I read parts of the journal entry to the students, appealed to their maturity as juniors and seniors in high school who were deeply interested in the written word (rash generalizations, maybe, but I was desperate). I read aloud the opening pages of *The Collected Works of Billy the Kid*; we talked about what happened in our heads as the words did or didn't become part of us. I asked the students to read the first twenty-five pages of the book and to write a specific response to what they read. I added the caveat that anyone who was offended by *The Collected Works of Billy the Kid* should tell me; I wouldn't require them to read it.

And it worked. Not a peep of protest from parents, administrators, or students.

I know ... I should have felt guilty. I had stacked the deck, skewed the outcome, been underhanded and manipulative. I'd created a situation in which students pretty much *had* to acquiesce to my designs. I appealed to their maturity and indicated what mature behavior would be (students don't for one instant believe they are immature). I enticed them with the possibility of the profane (and students know beyond doubt that they are progressive and open-minded, hipper by far than parents and school personnel). All this I did to achieve my purposes. I'd do it again. I don't know whether a little Machiavelli resides in us all, but there's certainly a generous dollop in me.

After we had read and discussed *The Collected Works of Billy the Kid*, I asked students to write about their ability to handle its content. Here's what some of them wrote:

> This book was tough. I know you warned us but I figured that was just teacher talk.
>
> I found it hard to concentrate on Billy's life with all of those offensive sex scenes. I didn't want to know that! I feel like when two people have sex it's between *them*. Not the whole world.
>
> Violence was okay, because violence is nothing new to me or anyone else, because we see it every day.
> *Missi Howell, Junior*

> Unless students live in a cave, this stuff about sex & violence won't affect them. Except it might come as a little surprise since we usually don't read nothing like that in schools.
> *Kelly Hollister, Senior*

> The book expressed the rawness of those times, and without such explicit sex and violence, it would be just another book that deprives the reader of the truth.
> *Lisa Simpson, Senior*

> I really had no problem with the explicit sex and violence in the book. Sex is a part of life and we wouldn't be here if there wasn't sex. Violence was a part of the old West so I realize that's some of the things that happened back then and it happens now days too.
> *Bonnie Stoffregen, Senior*

We've been very sheltered for most of our lives by living in urban boondocks. After we graduate it'll be a big shock. And the violence—except for some very graphic description—you can see on TV or in the movies. But violence is reality. Like I said, we shouldn't be sheltered all of our lives.

Tammy Honesty, Junior

We were all pretty much afraid of the sexual parts of the book and didn't bring them up. Society is still very conservative.... I didn't think the book was so bad, this is how life was back then ... the R-rated truth. I don't think people should be so affected by these passages because without entire truth there are only lies.

Bryan Hilch, Senior

What lesson in this about appropriateness of literature, pedagogy, and a teacher's agenda?

The world of literature is large and contains multitudes. Many of the stories, poetry, and books we bring into our classrooms might be—and sometimes are—objected to on someone's moral, political, or religious grounds. I strive to be sensitive to my students' cultural upbringing and evolving values, but I also see my duty as a teacher to stretch myself and my students beyond the worlds we know well—in this case, to stretch accepted notions of how research might be reported, of how intellect, emotion, and imagination might be boldly fused in an academic work.

As a language arts teacher my responsibility is not to censor, but rather to discuss the language people use and the diverse topics they write about. I seek to put language and subject matter into an intellectual context so we can talk about them. What Bryan said was true, however: "We were all pretty much afraid of the sexual parts of the book and didn't bring them up."

That was as much my fear as the students'. I was so glad we were reading the book that I shied away from dealing forthrightly with all aspects of it. The old social biases of our culture were at work: as Missi said, it is all right to talk about and show violence in public, but not sex. And this too: what goes on in students' imaginations is all right, as long as it is not expressed in the classroom.

I'll try to do better in the future. Teenagers need to talk about controversial matters in open educational atmospheres where accurate information is available, diversity of thinking is tolerated, and exploratory talk is the norm. One mark of educated people is their ability to talk about anything and remain open-minded while entertaining new and sometimes conflicting ideas. We might talk about racial stereotypes. We might talk about the genocide of Jews during World War II or American Indians during the conquest of America. We might talk about AIDS and condoms. We might talk about the physical and psychological problems that can accompany involvement in sexual intercourse at an early age.

If ranting parents had descended on school waving a copy of *The Collected Works of Billy the Kid* over their heads, I know I would not have required their son or daughter to read it. And such an incident may very well have caused an administrator to cave in (or to see his own moral and pedagogical obligation— however you choose to look at it) and decree that none of my students continue reading the book.

But that didn't happen. My friend who alerted me to the potentially explosive passages in the book says I am blessed. Maybe. What I do know is that I am left with my own lights. I try to be sensitive and responsible and at the same time true to my own passions about reading and writing, teaching and learning, bringing to my students what is appropriate, challenging, provocative. And my ideas of those things might not be the same as the teacher down the hall.

At one NCTE convention I was carried up an escalator, while an acquaintance of mine was carried down the escalator to my left. I waved to her. She had been in one of the first groups of teachers I shared the multigenre project with. Her expression this day communicated her worry about my rashness. "*The Collected Works of Billy the Kid?*" she said, shaking her head as we passed. "Never in my school district."

DOCUMENTATION

While reading that first batch of multigenre research papers, I began to get nervous. Scholarly documentation was abysmal. Students had gathered information from biographies, autobiographies, articles, and videos, but only half of them listed their sources on a reference page. None of them wrote footnotes or endnotes to reveal specific information about individual pieces. My anxiety increased several notches when I saw that some students—usually those who had read autobiographies—had written first-person pieces that made me wonder about intentional and unintentional plagiarism.

Despite my delight with the papers, part of me felt academically irresponsible. Was I teaching students to be blithe researchers? Was I promoting a cavalier attitude toward source material once it had been mined? I shuddered and blamed myself. The students had sniffed out my passion. They knew I was primarily interested in multiple genres. We had spent considerable time picking out various genres, examining how they worked, experimenting with them in learning journals. We had spent little time on documentation. I remembered exhorting students two or three times to make sure they cited their sources. Not good teaching, I thought, and shuddered again.

With the next class that wrote multigenre papers I did what teachers do when they want students to pay attention to something: I made a big deal about it. I devoted class time to documentation. I made overhead transparencies. I talked about the need for academic responsibility. We discussed how students might document their sources. They didn't want to clutter their papers with footnotes amid the text, even with the relatively simple *Chicago Manual of Style* method of noting author, year of publication, and page number in parentheses. After all, Ondaatje hadn't.

This discussion prompted us to attend closely to what Michael Ondaatje had done with references and documentation in *The Collected Works of Billy the Kid*. His work was essentially a research paper taken to a maximum level of literary sophistication. He had researched; he had written out of his learning; he had made art.

On the copyright page of *The Collected Works of Billy the Kid*, Ondaatje had written a paragraph of "credits." He cited four research sources, mentioning specifically that from them he had used a particular scene, two characters' reminiscences, a piece of dialog, and photographs. Then this last sentence: "With these basic sources I have edited, rephrased, and slightly reworked the originals. But the emotions belong to their authors."

The students were satisfied with this kind of documentation. The integrity of their texts would not be compromised. I agreed, but wanted students to get tighter and more specific in their actual crediting of sources for specific portions of their papers. In addition to a bibliography, I asked students to write a note page that explained some of the nitty-gritty, the ins and outs of particular pieces. To show them what I had in mind, I created a hypothetical note page, along with some general advice:

HYPOTHETICAL NOTE PAGE

1. The scene in which Maya describes her rape (10) I composed with some of the key words and phrases found on pages 62–66 of *I Know Why the Caged Bird Sings* by Maya Angelou.
2. The phrase "Somebody up there likes me" that I employ as a repetend throughout the piece was actually spoken by Rocky Graziano to Art Rosenthal, reporter for the *New York Times*.
3. The interview between Ernest Hemingway and the reporter I composed almost entirely of Hemingway's actual words from

the following sources: Holly Jackson's "Profile" in *The New Yorker*; Chapter 6 of A. E. Hotchner's *Papa Hemingway*; and Hemingway's own *Death in the Afternoon*.

> The key is to be responsible. If you quote someone or use someone else's ideas or material in shaping your own work, acknowledge that. Give him or her credit. They deserve it, just as you deserve credit for your ideas and hard work.
>
> Furthermore, a complete list of your sources and notes demonstrates (to some degree) the amount and quality of your work.
>
> The thing about research is to be open and candid, not secretive or sloppy.
>
> If your documentation is irresponsible, readers might think your research is of no value. Worse, they might think you have plagiarized. That can lead to big problems: F's for students, lawsuits for professional writers.

A year after my multigenre work with high school students, I mentored a University of New Hampshire student—Meg—who was creating a multigenre paper on Mary Wollestonecraft Shelly for her senior honors English project (Romano 1992). The coordinator of honors English sent word to students that they could have a second reader for their project if they liked. Meg thought that a capital idea and chose for her second reader Elizabeth Hageman, the English department's nineteenth-century British literature scholar. A shot of fear ran through my bowels. Oh, well, I thought, traditional academia versus the multigenre research paper. I knew who would lose.

But I was wrong. Hageman loved the project, had never seen anything like it before. She had only one suggestion regarding Meg's documentation:

> Typing the endnotes as footnotes at the bottom of each page would have helped the reader keep up with you (after I realized that there were endnotes to read, I found myself constantly wanting to know what they would say, and so my second reading of your project was interrupted by my leafing back and forth between text and notes); one of the really special things about this project is how you have used your research to create an imaginative (and true) portrayal of your protagonist—as an admiring reader, I wanted to watch that process at work as I read. (1990)

The response made perfect sense. Hageman knew the territory of Meg's research; as she read she wanted immediately to see the origins of the writing, the notations about sources, the particularities of Mary Shelly's life. For me, endnotes and a bibliography sufficed.

GRADING

Evaluating the work represented in these multigenre projects was sticky, stickier even than evaluation usually is. The seven weeks of reading, research, and multigenre writing would represent one third of a semester grade. I was concerned about that. I wanted to be fair. I wanted to recognize process and reward good-faith participation. I also wanted to hold students accountable for quality multigenre products.

Initially, I weighted various aspects of the project this way:

1. (20 percent) Written responses to Billy the Kid material (handout and Ondaatje's book).
2. (30 percent) Four weeks of learning journal entries regarding research.
3. (10 percent) Draft of multigenre paper.
4. (40 percent) Quality of final multigenre paper.

Let me explain my thinking in actually arriving at letter grades, the part of teaching I was cocksure about during my first years in education, the part I've become less and less comfortable with as I learn more about process, learning, and development.

The students' learning journal responses to the Billy the Kid material and to their research I graded this way:

Four satisfactory responses: B
Four responses, one exceptional: B+
Four responses, two exceptional: A
Four responses, three exceptional: A+
No response: 0
Perfunctory response: F

I didn't grade individual responses. I read them, though, and checked them if they were satisfactory. In my estimation, satisfactory work is good. Good is B. A satisfactory response, I determined, deals specifically with the material and searches for understanding. It makes assertions. I know the writer has read and connected.

If a response was exceptional, I scribbled a star at the top of the paper. When I recorded that response in my grade book, I wanted something to jog my memory about its exceptional nature. An exceptional response is specific, probing, inventive, risk-taking, surprising, scrappy, or incisive in its thinking. An exceptional response might include all of those adjectives or only a couple. Even though it is single-draft expressive writing, the language of an exceptional response might even be skillful and arresting.

In the previous chapter, Amy's response to the Carol Burnett material was exceptional; so, too, were Wendy's poem about Jimi Hendrix and Donna's poem about Elvis.

As I read the responses coming in, I knew I had to teach a vocabulary word: *perfunctory*. An assignment that looks as though it has been done in the cafeteria a minute before the bell is perfunctory. A response that skims the surface and offers little more than generalizations is perfunctory. A short response that only grazes significant issues is perfunctory.

A perfunctory response is decidedly not good-faith participation. It demonstrates little engagement, a shying away from thinking. I need students to engage as I am engaged in order to have substantive interaction with them. They need total engagement if their peer group and pair discussions are to be productive, too.

I weighted the draft of their multigenre paper at 10 percent and evaluated it this way:

Suitable draft on time: A +
Late draft: B
Poorly developed draft: D–C

Although I don't place grades on drafts, I did note the appropriate credit in my grade book and informed students when their drafts were not suitable. My judgment of drafts bears explaining: I value time in class to work; I also value deadlines. I've been meeting deadlines for years, have in mind, in fact, the deadline for delivering this manuscript to Heinemann. I know also that there can be extenuating circumstances, perfectly valid reasons for missing deadlines. In some instances, students and I negotiate missed deadlines individually. A key is that, if possible, students talk to me beforehand about a problem that will necessitate a late draft. The most conscientious example of this occurred when a pregnant young woman from a class I taught at Utah State phoned me in the morning to tell me she had just begun labor and would miss class that afternoon.

I grant full credit for a suitable draft. *Suitable* means appropriate in length, experimentation, and quality—students had, after all, been working for six weeks. Some parts of the multigenre draft might be well developed, others might not. In some parts the language might resonate and be memorable; in others it merely holds an idea in place or slogs along wordily. Some scenes may be dramatized fully, others may be sparsely rendered. A suitable draft provides language and ideas I can interact with. Enough decisions have been made on the page to spur my thinking. Then I can confer productively with the writer.

I judged the quality of their final paper to be worth 40 percent of the project grade. This is my recognition of the importance of final products. Again and again in school and in the workplace students will be evaluated by their final products alone. An outsider will judge their work without any consideration of learning, growth, and process.

Because I am a teacher and value the trip as well as the destination, I want to apologize for this subjective judgment of quality but can't. My own poems and articles are judged regularly. In the last year I've sent out my writing eleven times to journals and publishers. Two I haven't heard from yet. Two have accepted my writing. Seven have rejected it.

Sometimes a rejection comes because the work I've sent is not suitable for a particular style or audience. Sometimes the writing is rejected because what I've sent is similar to something else published recently. Most often, I suspect, the editor decides that what I've sent is not good enough. When I was a student, such judging of final products was often the bulk of a class grade, maybe 90 or 100 percent of it. I've shifted the emphasis in my classes to make the bulk of students' grades their good-faith participation, their work within process. But I also look for the quality of students' final products. And this I grade subjectively, just as my editors do.

As an educator, though, despite how much I thrill to fine products, I am most interested in students' learning and development. That's why I've added a fifth part to students' multigenre project grades.

The quality of final papers now counts as only 20 percent of the grade. The remaining 20 percent is allotted to my assessment of the student's portfolio—not a literacy portfolio or a working portfolio or a showcase portfolio, but a portfolio that admits me into a student's learning. This kind of portfolio—I call it a learning portfolio—gives students the opportunity to inform me about their work and growth, about things I couldn't possibly know from merely grading final multigenre papers. This take on evaluation asks students to use portfolios to dazzle me with their learning, to give me, as Mary Oliver writes in her poem "The Ponds," a look "into the white fire of a great mystery."

OTHER POSSIBILITIES

The very things that empower me limit me. I love writing that pushes boundaries of acceptability. My conception of the multigenre paper came out of that love and a respect for all the various genres we might write. My vision of the proper content of multigenre research papers came from Michael Ondaatje, who had investigated a historical person and created from that knowledge.

Problems, Issues, Dilemmas of the Multigenre Research Paper

Since then, although some of my students continue to find fulfilling research and writing by focusing on a historical figure, other students have followed their passions down different roads. They have written multigenre papers about music, travel, running, truck driving, children, fathers, mothers, distant ancestors. They have written about teaching, generation X, racism, athletic teams, places, and critical personal experiences. Research is still a significant part of the project, although sometimes that research is of the interior rather than the exterior.

Teachers with whom I have shared the multigenre paper idea have adapted it to their own needs and visions. One teacher in New York State requires students to include the genres her curriculum guide mandates. An elementary teacher has her students research animals of their choice and create multigenre papers about them. A teacher of college freshman composition has students write multigenre papers out of their research of an era: Vietnam, the Great Depression, World War II, the 1960s. Other teachers have had students collaborate on multigenre research papers. One English teacher near Cincinnati is passionate about the theater, so a significant part of her students' multigenre research projects centers on dramatic performance. Students in other classes have created graphic art, played music, written reflective essays about their multigenre work. I fully expect some day to access a multigenre project in hypertext.

Our passions might limit us, but they also empower us.

❧
RELATIONSHIPS WITH LITERATURE

In junior high school I discovered the library, housed in a small room adjoining study hall. A shelf by the entrance held books about dogs and the Far North: Sled Dog of Alaska, Moog, The Call of the Wild, *and more. When I read these books, my adolescent mind left small-town Ohio and mushed a team of faithful dogs down a snow-packed trail by a frozen river. The math teacher called me "Yukon Tom."*

In junior high school I usually did my homework, got B's, occasional A's, C's in science. I kept my Far North novels with me throughout the day. In study hall, in classes when the teachers ran out of gas, at home after my favorite television shows, I hit the trail, fed frozen fish to the dogs, was careful not to get my feet wet—a sure way in the Far North to suffer frostbite, maybe amputation, possibly death.

Each morning before I left our apartment for school I lived literature as I sat alone at the kitchen table, drinking sugared tea, just as the characters I read about did in their cold morning camps on the tundra.

When I was seventeen, I saw The Sea Wolf *on television. It starred Edward G. Robinson and John Garfield, and I loved it. The sea, the adventure, the tension. I figured the 1941 film* must be based on a book, so I asked my mother to look for that title the next time she went to the city.

One night when she got home late from bridge club, she left the novel on the kitchen table. In the morning—to my delight—I saw the book was written by Jack London, my old Yukon friend from junior high school. The Sea Wolf, I determined, would be the topic of my next oral book report.

I was primarily drawn to the book because of Wolf Larsen, London's philosophizing, brutal sea captain, who inflicted calculated suffering and offhanded death. And I—who had lost my father two years earlier—grew tense and thoughtful as I read Captain Larsen's position that life was meaningless, observed his disdain for those sniveling souls who feared death and clung to life at any cost.

The deeper I read into the novel the more engaged I became in imaginative thinking of a different sort. Not only did I envision scenes of illegal seal hunting, random violence, and rugged life aboard The Ghost, I also constructed arguments that opposed Wolf Larsen's ruthless stance. Through this dialectic with a literary character, I further shaped my own philosophy of living and dying.

For a British literature survey course my sophomore year of college I read poetry and fiction, attended class regularly, and listened to a professor who seemed bored and distracted as he carried on conversations with himself for fifty minutes. To each class I arrived initially confident, quaked at arcane questions, soon grew baffled, and sometimes wondered if I'd read the right literature.

The professor gave a test six weeks into the semester. Our first grade. I brightened when I saw the question on John Keats. I wrote my heart out, filled one bluebook and began another, then waited . . . and waited . . . and waited. Seven weeks later, the thirteenth week of the semester, I got the test back: D+.

My only grade in the course with two weeks left in the term.

And English my major!

And John Keats, god bless him, the poet who just two years earlier had seen me through my own adolescent brand of coming through slaughter.

I was nineteen years old when we read "The Minister's Black Veil" in American Literature. I remember the story's being hard reading for me. I *couldn't grasp the import of Hawthorne's weird preacher who wore a black veil over his face. I was conscientious, though, read closely, and tried hard to understand. I paid attention to class discussion from where I sat in the back row of a classroom packed with fifty students.*

The discussion turned to the minister's love interest—Elizabeth. His fiancée, the professor called her. Fiancée? I'd thought they were married. I debated this in my head a few minutes while discussion moved on. Finally, I raised my hand.

"Mr. Romano?"

"Weren't Elizabeth and the minister married?"

Forty-nine students, each amazed at my obtuseness, turned to look at me.

"No, Mr. Romano," said the professor, "they were not *married."*

I persisted. "I'm sure the story said that Elizabeth was his wife."

"They were, Mr. Romano, decidedly not married."

I swallowed and needed a black veil myself.

Next to me my roommate whispered, "I can't believe you asked such an asinine question! And then you wouldn't keep your mouth shut after he corrected you!"

When class was over, I read through the story until I found the passage that proved the Reverend Mr. Hooper and Elizabeth were married: "As his plighted wife," wrote Hawthorne, "it should be her privilege to know what the black veil concealed."

Plighted wife, I thought, damn right! If I were married to someone who wore a black veil twenty-four hours a day, I'd be in a fix too!

In a course called British Novels of the Nineteenth Century I learned what it was like to enter a fictional dream of massive proportions. One book—Dickens's Bleak House—*contained sixty-nine characters, excluding walk-ons, of course. Twenty-three of us were enrolled in that class, which met at 8:00 A.M. Monday, Wednesday, and Friday. Twenty-one of us were young women.*

One of the novels we read was Tess of the D'Urbervilles. *The more I read, the more I resisted. I was taking a fiction writing course at the time, where I was asked to write honestly, say it simply, and suspend the reader's disbelief. So what was all this cloaking Thomas Hardy was doing? Tess is seduced and returns home disgraced. She's learned a hard lesson, I'm thinking. Then one day when she takes a break from sheathing corn in the field, her sister brings her an infant to suckle. Huh? my 1969 twenty-year-old self asked. She was pregnant all this time? No* swelling stomach? No enlarged breasts? No halted period? I'd read nothing about that.

So one day in class, before discussion began in earnest, I raised my hand.

"How come Hardy didn't mention that Tess was pregnant? It's her story. Things happen to women when they're pregnant."

At the podium Dr. H. (who hadn't missed the Victorian Age by much) frowned regretfully.

I cleared my throat and continued, "There are physical things that happen to women when they're pregnant. How come she didn't know?"

The quiet classroom continued. No one turned to look at me where I sat in the back. Dr. H. kept frowning; the young women gazed at their desks. Suddenly, I realized that someone was sitting in a British literature class at a great university with dog shit on his shoes.

When I taught in high school, my friend and fellow English teacher John Gaughan stopped by the house one evening. We were drinking beer and talking about teaching, writing, reading, and school politics when Mariana, then a teenager, arrived home from her long day: swim practice at 6:00 A.M., school from 7:30 until 2:30, swim practice again after school until 5:30. She dumped her books on the dining room table, walked into the family room, and sank into a chair. John greeted her and began chatting about school, particularly, of course, her English class.

"We had a test today," said Mariana.

"You did?" John asked. "Over what?"

"The isms of literature."

"The what?"

"You know," said Mariana, "realism, naturalism, modernism, postmodernism."

"Pedanticism?" I asked.

She sighed. "We haven't got that far yet."

In doing some work a few years ago at a wealthy suburban school, I was given a copy of an in-house publication filled with articles by teachers and administrators. I came upon an article by the head of the high school English department, a driving argument detailing the reasons classic literature must be taught in secondary school. The article was well written and readable. It began with an anecdote:

As the author stood in the checkout line at the grocery store, the mother of one of his former students approached him and said, "Mr. Thebes, I want to thank you for making Charles read Silas Marner. If he hadn't gotten that experience in high school, he never would have had it."

This was the author's point. If students don't "get" the classics in high school, they may never come to know them. His opening anecdote, however, didn't end there.

The mother continued talking about her son. "That boy's been out of school four years now, and he hasn't read a book since!"

Hamlet made me squirm in college.

A father dead, foul and unnaturally.

A mother remarried. . . . My own mother had remarried after four years of loneliness and those terrible first months of intense grief, precipitous weight loss, and excessive, drug-induced sleep. Her role as wan ghost of the apartment was over.

The prince's prolonged, melancholy funk. . . . Just what I experienced when my thoughts turned asudden to my father—the arguments I'd had with him, the unreasonable animosity I'd sometimes felt toward him that spewed from a volatile teenager struggling for independence but still in need of parenting.

The dramatic moment of death—poison poured in the actor's ear in The Murder of Gonzago. . . . That horrid, forever killing night on the highway I'd imagined a thousand times: hurtling steel crushing flesh and bone and love.

The ghost of old King Hamlet appearing on the ramparts to Horatio, Bernardo, and Marcellus, wearing "a countenance more in sorrow than in anger." . . .

My father had appeared to me in a dream when I finally found sleep near dawn after hours of stunned grief on the night he was killed. In my dream my father sat leaning forward on a cot, his elbows on his knees, wringing his hands, saying again and again, "If there was only more time. If there was only more time." And I knew as I watched his anguish, unable to speak to him, that there was no escape. The cot he sat on was in a prison cell.

Yorick's skull and Hamlet saying to Horatio: "I knew him well. . . . He hath borne me on his back a thousand times." I was touched to tears *with that image of boy Hamlet piggyback on the jester, laughing, delighted, a time forever gone.*

And the ghost of Hamlet's father in words more eloquent than my father ever used, telling his son of sulphurous days and nights doomed to walking the ramparts and then the sticking line: "If thou didst ever thy dear father love—Revenge his foul and most unnatural murder. . . ."

I wouldn't go to the trial of the men who drove the drag-racing cars that collided with my father's. I didn't want to see their faces, didn't want to know facts about their lives or facts about that night. My imagination had enough to work with.

But my mother went to the trial. She lived with grief and burned with hatred. The trial lasted weeks and she looked those men in the eyes each day they walked into the courtroom. The jury convicted them of second-degree murder for their disdain of others that irrevocable night on the highway. They went to prison for eleven months before the verdict was overturned.

And for years after reading the play, the image flashed into my mind of Hamlet recklessly stabbing Polonious and later killing the king. I thought of the two men who killed my father, saw my mother staring into their eyes every day of the trial, imagined a rapier in my hand and more reckless stabbing. I shuddered, righteous, repulsed, and terribly frightened.

Chapter Nine

READING FOR THE REAL WORLD

I SEND YOU MY POEMS THAT YOU BEHOLD IN
THEM WHAT YOU WANTED.

Walt Whitman

*T*he way we approach reading and literature helps determine how hospitable our classrooms are for risk taking, alternate styles of writing, expression in multiple genres, writing with passion, and voicing necessarily idiosyncratic readings. For years my classroom was filled with personality, passion, and unique ways of knowing—mine. A substantial dose of those qualities still fills my classes, but now I've made more room for students.

SYSTEMATIC DESKILLING

When I became a high school teacher in 1971, I stumbled into the same pernicious bog that elementary teachers often do. In *Broken Promises* Patrick Shannon describes how elementary school teachers become "deskilled" of their ability to teach reading by basal reading programs that lay out skills to be learned, lessons to be administered, questions to be asked, work to be managed. Exit teacher. Enter clerk (DeLawter 1992).

A similar deskilling awaited me as a high school English teacher. My teaching skills had just begun to evolve when I encountered the great corrupter of secondary school literature study that twisted, skewed, and further elited my teaching style. Accompanying the massive literature anthology was the "teacher's manual," a Iago-like companion that whispered foul notions in my ear: brief critical analyses dictating how each piece of literature must be read; essential vocabulary words; ten-point, nit-picking, supposedly objective (who are we kidding?) comprehension quizzes; and lists of discussion questions complete with answers that were, of course, *the* questions to ask about works of the human imagination. This information—which students did not have—enabled me to conduct class like most literature professors I watched in the late 1960s.

My self-confidence was tenuous, my experience next to nil. I had little chance of resisting the authority and insider information of the teacher's manual—my swarthy companion who showed me a dozen ways to one-up students' thinking. I became addicted to the teacher's manual (and to the occasional special literature units that featured fifty-question multiple-choice tests, expository writing prompts, and creative writing suggestions sent free from publishers keen to sell copies of *To Kill a Mockingbird*, *A Separate Peace*, *Twelve Angry Men*, et al.).

There I was, dependent on the man, so to speak—

I, whom literature had uplifted,

> empowered,

> carried away;

I, who had glimpsed possibilities in literature

> for living that seemed instantly right;

I, who knew firsthand what mattered in literature

> beyond its revered titles,

>> momentous dates,

>> recurring themes,

>> and renowned practitioners;

I, who knew what it was like to

> live imaginatively through language,

> reflect profoundly on my own life,

> encounter ideas and images that struck

> chords in me that reverberated beyond

> the immediate experience of turning pages.

The heaviest thing in my briefcase was the teacher's manual, more valuable to me than the literature it pertained to. With the teacher's manual to stand on, I could prattle at length about a four-line poem, invoke literary terms of use only to PhDs, undermine every student's response as "almost perfect, but not quite." If I read and studied only the literature, questions arose in my mind (which is, of course, as it should be), but I was embarrassed that I didn't have unassailable answers to those questions. I didn't want students to know I didn't know.

That problem, however, was academic. I needed only to flip open my briefcase, and the teacher's manual ensured fraud. I was the least authentic reader in the classroom. I tried not to let that enter my mind, though it often did, particularly when I thought something about the literature that wasn't mentioned in the manual. When that happened, I sighed and wished I were smarter and a better reader. Instead of valuing and nurturing my insight, I capitulated to the manual.

Class periods were lectures that passed as pseudodiscussions, just the way most of my professorial models had conducted their classes, just the way the teacher's manual assumed I would conduct mine, since it provided questions to ask and explicit interpretive information that surely I was meant to deliver to students, else why was it in the teacher's manual that accompanied the literature anthology requisitioned by the English department, adopted by the school board, sanctified by the state office of education?

Recently, one of my Utah State University students made me shudder when she thought back on her experience in literature classes in secondary school. Melinda wrote,

> I would devour a book and make my own impressions but then we would talk it to death in class, ruining any enthusiasm I felt, and making me feel that my own impressions were wrong. It seemed to me that my teachers went out of their way to make me distrust my own impressions.

That very thing had been done to me, and I had continued the cycle of abuse by doing it to my students. The authority of the teacher's manual, the models of teachers I emulated, the abeyance of my own urgent reasons for reading literature, the insecurity I felt as a young teacher—all these conspired to make my classroom a place that admitted little that wasn't expected by me or sanctioned by the curriculum. No alternate styles, no multiple genres, no risky reading, little authentic writing. Surprise and spontaneity—so delightful in class, so vital in life—were rare.

Taking a Look Around

When I teach literature these days, I am no longer concerned with making sure students learn accepted readings of texts. I am no longer concerned with covering a portion of some publisher's marketing department's idea of a country's literary heritage. Corpses are properly *covered*, not literature.

What I *am* concerned about is that students experience literature, transform written symbols to images, ideas, and emotions. This means I devote some class time to actual reading just as I devote some class time to actual writing. Experiencing literature means arranging for students—all students, even those with dog shit on their shoes—to voice their responses. Small peer groups afford the best chance that this will happen. Engaging students with literature means getting them to write expressively about their reading. It means encouraging students to use all they have in the way of world experience, linguistic ability, knowledge of genre, and cultural awareness to collaborate with their classmates and teacher in evolving an understanding of literature. Judith Langer calls such meaning making "building an envisionment" (39). In short, making sure students actively engage with literature means asking them to do all the things in their reading that I ask them to do in their writing.

In *The Call of Stories*, Robert Coles has written that "the task of those who teach literature . . . [is] to engage a student's growing intelligence and any number of tempestuous emotions with the line of a story in such a way that the reader's imagination gets absorbed into the novelist's" (63).

That's akin to my tundra tea drinking as a twelve-year-old; my impassioned, twenty-six-minute oral report on *The Sea Wolf* that wrecked the English teacher's weekly lesson plan; my deep introspection after reading *Hamlet*, acknowledging my anguish and urge to strike out at those who caused my father's death.

Coles writes about a young man whose life had turned a corner after he read a Tillie Olson short story and reflected on his own life with his father, a heavy drinker: ". . . an intense classroom experience, as it connected to his everyday home life," writes Coles, "had most definitely touched him, prompted him to take a look around" (54).

That articulates an important reason why I teach literature. I want the stories, ideas, and characters of literature to enter the developing moral core of students. I want literature to prompt them to take a look around.

As it did Cindy. She was a senior Intensive Office Education student, none too thrilled about coming to my classroom during the afternoons of her final semester (when she otherwise could have left school early) to take modern American literature in order to pick up the one remaining English credit she needed to escape high school. I had asked students to find three effective passages from the novels they were reading and, after one of them, to tell why they had responded to it. Cindy had read Richard Wright's *Black Boy*, the story of the author's oppressed life and quickening awareness as a child in the South. Cindy chose this quotation from late in the book after pages of repression and degradation:

> And no word that I had ever heard fall from the lips of the Southern white man had ever made me really doubt the worth of my own humanity. (283)

Cindy wrote this about the quotation:

> This last quote really hit me hard. It's hard for me to believe that a person can go through all the criticism and abuse and still have faith in themselves as a person. I can't imagine what it was like for black people back then. This book has really affected my feelings towards blacks.

Cindy was wrong. Not only *could* she imagine what it was like for African Americans in the South during the early decades of the twentieth century, she *did* imagine it. Her growing intelligence, tempestuous emotions, and knowledge of racial stereotypes had engaged with the story line of *Black Boy*. Richard Wright's imagination had absorbed hers. She had marked that transaction with her own values by creating a visual collage of the book and by further writing her interpretations and amazements:

> Richard Wright explained how blacks were treated in the South. I think that you will find no better book than this one if you really want to know what it was like. The white people called them niggers and bastards and anything they wanted because the black people could not rebel against them.
>
> The whites had total control over the blacks. The blacks worked for less money, had worse jobs, got treated like dirt and had to take it. They did not have the courage to stand up for their rights.
>
> All during Richard's life he was taught that he was inferior to whites. He was taught this by everyone; society, community, employers, friends, and even family.
>
> All through the book Richard was beat by his family. Everything that he did wrong, even if he thought it was right, he was beat for. He even got beat for things he didn't do.
>
> His family was obsessed with religion and thus thought Richard was doing the devil's work when he wrote a story for the local newspaper. They thought this because he used the word "hell" in it. I don't know about you, but my parents would not think anything of it if I used the word "hell." Certainly they wouldn't think I was

possessed or that I worshipped the devil. I don't think it's any cause for a beating.

Richard was moved around from place to place all through his early years. His father left them when he was young. After his father had gone they were sent to an orphanage, then with an uncle, back to grandmother's and so on. Finally, he got sick of the religion and the beatings and the lectures and left for Memphis to make a life of his own, in which, obviously, he succeeded.

Cindy Lawson Hall, Senior, Edgewood High School

Cindy's transaction with *Black Boy* had caused her to take a look around. The experience had touched her developing moral core and, as she said, "really affected" her "feeling towards blacks," this teenage girl who lived in a largely segregated community and attended a school system in which ethnic minority students accounted for less than one percent.

Now, did Cindy really "take the book to heart," the phrase so many of Coles's students used to describe their reaction to literature that affected them deeply? Did she change the way she spoke about and interacted with African Americans? I don't know. But I do know this: because Cindy was encouraged— even prodded—to speak the rude truth in her particular, full-voiced way, I learned that a book about an alien time and culture and people had seized her mind. That's an auspicious start.

SALVATION

If there is salvation in teaching literature, especially to those students not destined to teach English or become professional writers—the bulk of them, in other words—it is by way of Louise Rosenblatt's transactional theory of reader response (1938, 1978). When I learned of her theory (not until the mid-1980s, for god's sake!), it held immediate appeal for me. I vividly remembered my earnest, deeply felt responses to literature that had so often been summarily dismissed.

The transactional theory of reader response, I learned, not only validated my students' readings, but also my own. The theory offered me deliverance from pedagogical fraud I felt when I touted readings of canonical literature I had gleaned from teacher's manuals and critical sources, readings I'm sure students thought I had arrived at alone.

The idea of accepting readers' responses to literature, of sanctioning them, in fact, changed the atmosphere of my literature classroom. Oh, I probed students' readings, brought up aspects of a text I wanted students to think about if they had ignored them, asked students to extend and revise their envisionments through dialog and writing. But the notion of right answers and who knew them shifted in my classroom when I relinquished a large chunk of my traditional lit-teacher agenda and asked students to be aggressive, risk-taking readers, reading as though they were cavorting in the park—playing tag, cartwheeling, diving for a Frisbee and sliding in the grass, sometimes, alas, ending their literate frolic with dog shit on their shoes.

To solicit students' honest transactional responses to literature, to get them, in fact, to think things on their own terms about literature they haven't thought before, I often ask students to write expressively: no-holds-barred, damn-the-torpedoes, full-speed-ahead, near-reckless use of language—all in the name of hotly pursuing thought. "Romping on the page," one student described such writing.

The priority of expressive writing (whether in a reading log, journal, or first draft) is for students to arrive at meaning. Our attention to errors of spelling, misapplied punctuation, grammatical infelicities, or usage faux pas is nil. Our only concern is for students to get at their puzzlement and understanding.

In Figure 9–1 Aimee, a high school sophomore, grapples in her reading journal with Saki's "The Open Window."

I included Aimee's original journal page so you can see my marginal comments. Aimee, who was repeating the second semester of sophomore English, had worked hard to make meaning of Saki's widely anthologized short story. She dumped a synopsis of the story's plot, a meaningful act that often disappoints teachers because they want students to move quickly to interpretation, analysis, and evaluation. But dumping the plot is necessary for many of us. Such narrative acts allow us to live through the experience of literature and learn or reacquaint ourselves with what is significant, just as Uncle Gigi (see Chapter 1) relearned his reason for leaving Italy by repeating the story of an important time when he was asked why he had come to America.

"The Open Window" contains alien elements for Aimee, like "daily shooting," "letting" rooms in the country to calm one's nerves, possibly "large French window." So hard does she bear down in describing the climactic scene in which Frampton Nuttel dashes from the house without apology or goodbye that Aimee uses an approximation of Saki's language—awkward for this late-twentieth-century teenage girl—to describe Vera's uncle and two companions as they returned home: "they saw 3 objects coming towards the house. One even had additionally burdened with a white coat hung over his shoulders."

Aimee can't quite figure out a meaning for the study. She concludes with this sentence: "Then toward the end of the story it ended as if the guy visited

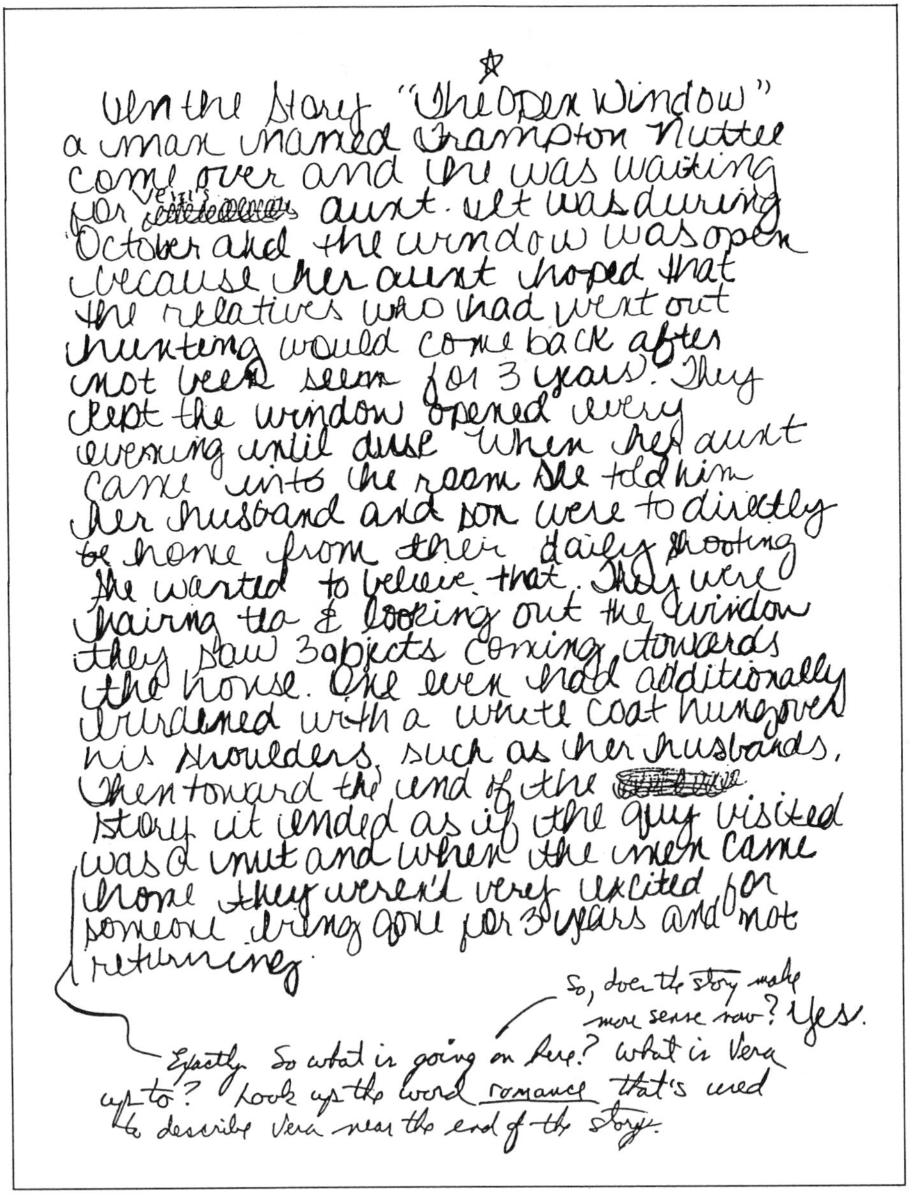

In the story "The Open Window" a man named Framptom Nuttel came over and he was waiting for Vera's aunt. It was during October and the window was open because her aunt hoped that the relatives who had went out hunting would come back after (not been seen for 3 years). They kept the window opened every evening until dusk. When her aunt came into the room she told him her husband and son were to directly be home from their daily shooting. He wanted to believe that. They were having tea & looking out the window they saw 3 objects coming towards the house. One even had additionally burdened with a white coat hung over his shoulders, such as her husbands. Then toward the end of the story it ended as if the guy visited was a nut and when the men came home they weren't very excited for someone being gone for 3 years and not returning.

So, does the story make more sense now? Yes.
Exactly. So what is going on here? What is Vera up to? Look up the word romance that's used to describe Vera near the end of the story.

FIGURE 9–1

was a nut and when the men came home they weren't very excited for someone being gone for 3 years and not returning."

And here, as a teacher, is where I blew it. I glimpsed but ultimately missed a teachable moment. I wanted to help Aimee become a feisty, aggressive reader, one who both trusts her impressions and remains open to new information. At the bottom of the page I drew a vertical line by the bit of resistance Aimee felt in the disparity between the men coming home yet not being "very excited for someone being gone for three years."

I wrote, "Exactly," and asked Aimee what, then, was going on in the story. I should have stopped there. That was all I needed to push Aimee to probe these two parts of her perception that didn't fit: Vera's revelation that the men had left three years earlier, never to return, and Aimee's real-world knowledge of how people react when reunited after long absences.

But instead of leaning on the promising dissonance in Aimee's mind, I went on to direct her to Saki's last sentence: "Romance at short notice was [Vera's] specialty" (Saki 116). Aimee dutifully looked up *romance* and in addition to learning that it meant what every teenager knows it does, she found that *romance* also meant *exaggeration* or *falsehood*.

On the back of the journal page Aimee wrote the new definition of *romance* she'd found and turned it in to me. In writing I asked if the story made more sense now. "Yes," Aimee wrote back. And we danced the old school dance. I led, of course, and directed her precisely where I wanted—to the correct answer—ignoring the possibilities she had for her own movement. When Aimee completed my prescribed choreography, I asked if she understood. She curtsied and said, in effect, "Yes, m'lord."

I didn't feel good that Aimee used the dictionary efficiently and finally understood Saki's little joke and "Aha" into characterization: Vera is a liar! That's peanuts. And that's what I went home with. I missed the entrée, the excellent opportunity Aimee's good-faith, struggling journal entry offered to empower her as a reader and thinker.

Aimee didn't need to look up *romance*. She understood the word, just as I understood it when I was sixteen years old. And it didn't mean *lying* or *fabricating*. Romance meant flushed cheeks, double-time heart rate, the sweet touch of flesh. In fact, I think Saki's last sentence is condescending and elitist. "If, dear reader, you haven't gotten the story by this point," the presence of the sentence implies, "then an educated understanding of *romance* will enlighten you." That final sentence belabors what Saki has already masterfully shown. It is the one unartful move in an otherwise wonderful story.

Sheila—another tenth grader—read the same story, didn't know the specialized meaning of *romance* either, but trusted her own lights:

> But still, I'm a little confused. Maybe the Aunt was really waiting on them to come back someday, but then she probably would've reacted more excited to see them. This was good.
> *Sheila Puckett Robinson, Sophomore, Edgewood High School*

To grow as a reader Aimee didn't need further work with the dictionary. She needed an opportunity to work with a more experienced other—me, in this case, her mentor in reading. She needed support and guidance, encouragement to grapple with the meaning she made from the text, to rub her dissonant thinking together to see what sparks flew so she might light a fire of understanding from them. But I blew it. I doused the spark instead of moving the kindling closer. I gave Aimee a vocabulary lesson and reinforced the notion that teachers had the answers to literature and she did not. That's surely a romantic notion. And I won't do it again.

ANY RESPONSE?

Teachers often bristle at the idea of accepting *any* reader response. Some reader responses, they argue, are wrong. Wouldn't it have been wrong, for instance, if Aimee had believed that Vera was the character who dashed from the house when the men returned? Wouldn't it have been wrong if Cindy had believed that Richard Wright was Caucasian?

I don't think so. I know—that sounds risky, doesn't it, maybe even absurd? But let me explain: readers don't formulate impressions from nothing. I thought the black-veiled Reverend Mr. Hooper was *married* to Elizabeth because Hawthorne described her once as his "plighted wife." I knew *plight* as jams and fixes and tough situations. I didn't know *plight* as betrothal. There is intentionality in what readers do. Even the rare student who baits the teacher by making preposterous assertions about literature has a reason for doing so. He wants attention? Needs to provoke authority? Seeks to mask some inadequacy he feels, some fear that the literature has raised?

"The important issue," John Mayher explains in *Uncommon Sense*, "is to find out what meaning the student has made, and to help her reflect on why she has made the meaning she has, not to weigh in with our superior response, which usually has the effect of further alienating precisely those readers who most need encouragement and support if they are to continue to engage in the [reading] process" (1990, 222).

One afternoon a group of three seniors—Mike, Bryan, and Traci—discussed Ondaatje's *The Collected Works of Billy the Kid*, particularly the thumbnail character sketch of Pat Garret, the man appointed sheriff of Lincoln County, New Mexico, who eventually killed the Kid. The students talked of Garret's two-year program to learn how to drink alcohol without getting drunk or sick; his subsequent alcoholism, how Juanita Martinez found him unconscious in her house (he had been robbing it), cared for him, and "un-iced his addiction" (29). Garret and Martinez married; two weeks later she died.

When I walked by Mike, Bryan, and Traci, they were trying to figure out the cause of Juanita's death. Mike didn't have a clue, wouldn't even speculate. Bryan was mum, playing his interpretive cards close to the vest. Traci, god bless her, had an idea and was speaking it.

"I think she drank herself to death."

"What?" said Mike. "Why would she help Garret beat alcoholism, then turn around and drink herself to death?"

"I know that doesn't make sense," said Traci, "but I still think she drank herself to death."

Mike rolled his eyes; Bryan stayed mum.

"Why do you think so, Traci?" I asked.

"Right here," she said, pointing to the text. "Right here it says, 'They married and two weeks later she died of a consumption she had hidden from him.'" (29).

I was astonished, informed, delighted. Traci was precisely the kind of reader I wanted students to become, one who uses cues from the text (alcohol abuse *was* a crucial part of the sketch), knowledge of vocabulary (just as I'd known *plight*, Traci knew *consume*), a mind driven to connect, and bravery in articulating her thinking. The students talked more. Bryan revealed his cards: from health class he remembered that *consumption* was an old term to describe tuberculosis. Even though Bryan revealed his knowledge gently, Traci was embarrassed about her ignorance of the word. I made sure to tell her that she'd exercised excellent reading skills.

I want the Aimees and Tracis, the Mikes and Marianas to understand what Charlene Dunn, a fourth-grade teacher at Beacon Heights Elementary in Salt Lake City, came to understand only after years of teaching and schooling: "I'm glad to finally realize that as a reader and writer I have not only the right but the obligation to think for myself and to form my own interpretations based on my background and knowledge."

It takes courage to voice tentative beliefs, to explore puzzling tensions, to examine dissonance, and to inquire into open questions. Faith and fearlessness again. Faith in the validity of your own impressions and fearlessness to entertain opposites, consider the unthinkable, conjecture the improbable.

COLD READING

As a way of inviting students into engagements with literature in which they feel safe to inquire, examine, voice, explore, and conjecture, I sometimes come to a reading cold, just as students do. The first or second meeting of a new class I bring copies of a short story I've never laid eyes on before. The story is usually provided to me by my wife, Kathy, a registered nurse who likes to read and is uncluttered by literary theories.

After distributing copies, I read the story aloud. My purpose is for students to see a real reader at work, one encountering a text for the first time, mispronouncing words, misinterpreting sentence rhythms, backtracking occasionally to make sense of a passage. After the read-aloud, in which students sometimes take part, we write expressively for ten minutes, trying to make sense of our reading experience. When I read what I've written, I want students to see me discuss my puzzlements and grope for meaning, perhaps—I hope—even share my delight when I come up with interesting observations and surprising connections that I became aware of only as I wrote.

We who teach English demonstrate the writing process pretty well. We model brainstorming, drafting, revising, and editing. We lay bare for students the process of writing, but the process of reading remains a mystery to many students. They have too often read texts only to come to a class in which a teacher reveals a reading of the literature so detailed, polished, and logical that the performance leaves many students nonplussed and feeling inadequate of ever being able to understand literature.

Students don't see, of course, how the oh-so-convincing reading was created. They don't see the many rereadings of the text, the searching for answers to puzzlements, the marginal notations, the notes taken, the teacher's manual or literary criticism consulted. In short, students don't see the gloriously messy process of reading.

I want to remove the mystery of reading for students; I want to "unmask" the reading process, as Tom Newkirk puts it (1990b). I want students to see a college-educated adult stumbling with words during a first-draft reading, just as students often do. I want them to see the process of reading, not merely the finished product neatly encapsulated in a lecture, study guide, or list of leading questions.

After we finish writing expressively for ten minutes about our cold reading, some of us read our responses to reveal our idiosyncratic meaning making and to spur talk about our understandings. We collaboratively build envisionments. Since I, the teacher, am unmasked and wearing an earnest, accepting expression, the students more readily share their thinking. I'm hoping our cold reading, good-faith writing, and subsequent discussion toll a proclamation throughout the classroom: this is how we will approach reading; this is how real readers read.

CHASING THE RASPBERRY SEED—
RESOLVING RESISTANCE

Forty miles north of Utah State University, half in Idaho, half in Utah, lies Bear Lake, a visual bit of the Caribbean. My first time driving to Logan from the Midwest, rounding a curve in the road, I was startled by a splash of turquoise amid the light brown and sparse green of the surrounding mountains. Not only is this Bear Lake region pleasing to the eye, it is also pleasing to the tongue. The high altitude, sandy soil, warm summer days and cool, often cold, nights, are perfect for raspberries, particularly the plump variety of raspberry at Bear Lake grown for sweet eating, not long-distance shipping. My wife, a raspberry aficionado and confirmed midwesterner, says that Bear Lake raspberries are the best thing about Utah.

Every once in a while after eating Bear Lake raspberries, I feel a seed in my mouth. With the tip of my tongue I'll chase it around my teeth, over my palette, and down along my gums. Sometimes the seed lodges in a dental crevice. It doesn't hurt, but the unaccustomed pressure demands attention. My raspberry-eating experience isn't complete until I dislodge that blasted seed and crush it between my teeth. When I do, I feel so satisfied. The resistance that drove me to pursue the seed is over, resolved, and I remember again how good the raspberries tasted.

I encourage students to track down and deal with raspberry seeds in their reading, too: the character action that confounds, the word combination that doesn't make sense, the information that raises a question, the image only partially seen, maybe simply an unarticulated, vague emotion—any resistance to something in the text. It's a raspberry seed, for sure, stuck somewhere, causing discomfort, demanding attention.

I push students to acknowledge their resistances when discussing or writing about their reading. Don't shy away from puzzlements; delve into them. Speak your resistances. Face them, reread, talk. Don't retrench and set your mind stubbornly to defend your interpretive turf. Step forward with good faith and acknowledge what you wonder. Speculate about it. The world often opens.

One recent summer I observed a small group of adults in a reading and writing workshop I taught in Rochester, New York. They were discussing David Allan Evans's poem "Bullfrogs":

BULLFROGS
—For Ernie, Larry, and Bob

sipping a Schlitz
we cut off the legs,

packed them in ice, then
shucked the rest back into
the pond for turtles

ready to go home
we looked down and saw
what we had thrown back in:
quiet-bulging eyes nudging along
the moss's edge, looking up at us,

asking for their legs

The group talked about the shivery imagery and nonchalance of the act. Revolting, they agreed. There didn't seem to be any tension present in their reading or discussion. Indeed, there didn't seem to be any tension needed save the tension in their stomachs. But then, Bob, the only man in the group, uttered a resistance he felt.

"The thing that bothers me," he said, "is that I don't see any remorse on the part of the narrator."

Kathleen and Cheryl thought otherwise. Bob's resistance introduced a valuable tad of productive tension to the discussion, just enough to push Cheryl and Kathleen to articulate why they thought there was, indeed, remorse present in the poem: the very fact that the narrator was writing about the incident, they said, indicated that he was uneasy with what had occurred. And the final image of the dismembered frogs nudging along the moss's edge, their bulging, accusing eyes asking for their legs, had driven home to them that the narrator— by using the word *asking*—felt guilty about what he had done.

Exploring our resistances in reading—our qualms, puzzlements, wonderings, and tensions—however foolish or inconsequential they may seem, can drive forward our thinking, broaden our interpretations. And that holds true for writing texts as well as for reading them. I think of the most declaimed speech in Western literature: Hamlet's "To be or not to be" soliloquy.

For nine lines the prince thinks aloud about his plight: a sea of troubles, heartache, the thousand natural shocks that flesh is heir to. Hamlet builds his cognitive momentum into thinking about how death ends the slings and arrows of outrageous fortune, when suddenly a seed of resistance enters: "To sleep, perchance to dream. Aye, there's the rub." Hamlet doesn't shy away from that distressing thought. He doesn't dismiss his resistance. He follows it, worries it, hounds it, speculating and conjecturing about the "undiscovered country from whose bourn/No traveler returns." Shakespeare takes us—and himself as a writer when he composed this soliloquy—ever more deeply into the psychology of a tortured, irresolute spirit.

CLASSROOM PRAGMATICS

My bottom line in a literature class: I want students to engage in the act of reading, eye decoding symbols on the page, mind creating images, formulating ideas, following extended discourse. In my classroom, engagement takes precedence over identifying grand themes, writing analytical essays, and covering someone's canon. Consequently, we do a lot of reading and responding in class.

We also, though, read longer works that cannot be completed within a single class period. If we are reading a novel together, for example, I often begin by reading a few pages aloud, letting students see me enjoy the pleasure of saying language, letting them taste the rhythms of the author's sentences through a spoken voice. We talk then about the sense we make and conjecture about what may come. The students read silently for the remainder of the period. By the next class meeting, I'll expect students to have read to a certain point.

But what happens when they don't? You've been there and you know. Small-group discussions founder. Prepared students sometimes resent having to bear the burden of talk. Large-group discussion lumbers along amid that broadening, tension-filled feeling that some students—maybe many students—are unengaged, uninterested, waiting out the period. I'm reminded of classes I both sat in and conducted in which actual engagement with words on the page was unnecessary for success. If you took good notes—or even if you didn't—you could pass. You really didn't have to negotiate extended reading experiences.

Literature study is a sham if students do not experience the unfolding of stories, the gestalt of poems, the progression and development of thought in essays. The idea of successfully completing a literature class without engagement in reading is as absurd to me as successfully completing a writing class without writing. I want students to gain facility as readers, to become adept at dealing firsthand with texts. I want students to engage in the process of reading as Aimee, Sheila, and Traci did, not merely memorize the "isms of literature."

Because I value engagement in literature so much, I take students' unengagement personally. Are some students trying to pass my class without experiencing the literature? I begin to wonder if they are abusing my openness to reading responses and my listening mode of teaching. Are they blithely and deceitfully sailing along, four-flushing their way to credit? I feel used, buffaloed, duped. I become indignant.

So I find myself urged to check students now and then to see if they have engaged with a text we're reading, especially when the bulk of the reading is to be completed independently. But my decision to test students occasionally to see whether they've read poses a philosophical dilemma: how do I gauge their good-faith participation in reading without abandoning my commitment to the transactional theory of reader response? I don't want to send the message that the reading of literature is a game of trivial pursuit in which students must pass ten-point, nit-picking, supposedly objective (who are we kidding?) comprehension quizzes.

Reading logs are an answer for many teachers. In them students write what they need to about their reading. Aimee's important thinking in her log entry about "The Open Window," for example, showed clearly that she had engaged with the story. Whether she'd read the work was not an issue. I must admit, though, that sometimes when I read log entries, I wonder if some students have read the text. And when I taught 148 students in Ohio or when I observe Utah English teachers contending with 200 and more students each day, I realize that reading so many students' reading logs can become stressful and quickly impractical.

So what to do?

Part of Rosenblatt's transactional theory of reader response is the distinction she makes between efferent and aesthetic reading (1978). In pure efferent reading, we read to carry away information. From the label on a bottle of medicine I want to learn the correct dosage. From the telephone bill, I want to find out the dollar amount of my daughter's long-distance calls. I'm reading efferently, and I don't care if the prose sings; I'm not looking for a lived-through experience with a text.

But I don't read novelist Barbara Kingsolver efferently. I read her aesthetically. With *Pigs in Heaven* I entered a fictional dream in which a clear-minded, feisty young woman, Taylor Greer, raises an abandoned Cherokee child with love, concern, and care. I also meet a formidable, intelligent, doggedly committed Cherokee attorney named Annawake Fourkiller who is determined to see that Cherokee children are raised within the tribe so the Cherokee culture survives. As I travel deeper into Kingsolver's imaginative world, I grow to respect and care about both women. And when Taylor and Annawake collide, my gut churns at the dilemma. I'm sympathetic to both characters' sides of the story, and I'm driven through the novel to learn how the tension will be resolved and to see if the characters I've come to care about will be all right. The novel is a lived-through experience for me, an altered state of consciousness. That's how I read *Pigs in Heaven*. Aesthetically.

My purpose in reading the novel was not to find out how an intelligent, unmarried, high school–educated young woman raising a child might struggle with poverty and hunger when she loses her system of love and support. I didn't read the novel to find out how leaders of the Cherokee nation are genuinely concerned about making sure that Cherokee children are not adopted out of the nation into white families, where they are raised with little or no knowledge of their cultural heritage. My purpose in reading *Pigs in Heaven* was not efferent. Nevertheless, I carried away from my reading knowledge about Native American cultural concerns and insight into how decent people can become snared by poverty.

Efferent and aesthetic are knotted together, just like analysis and synthesis, just like emotion and intellect. Unless I get so obsessed with hunting facts that I lose the story, efferent information enhances my aesthetic response. And a deepening aesthetic response increases my attention to efferent detail. Facts become meaningful when my emotional investment is heightened, when the damp of night has been driven into my soul.

Consider a book near the opposite end of the efferent-aesthetic continuum from a novel: the book you are holding. I am writing *Writing with Passion* for efferent purposes: that you will carry away ideas about the irreplaceable motivating force of passion, the importance of story to cognition, the absurdity of splitting analysis and synthesis, the effectiveness of alternate styles of writing, the possibilities of multigenre research papers, the reliability of process, the need for harmonious others in sustaining faith and fearlessness, the appropriateness of reader-response methods in teaching students to read and write.

But I have aesthetic interests in writing this book too. I want readers to experience my book in some ways like a novel, be touched emotionally here and there, live through with me the influence on my life of my daughter, my father, my relatives, see how my own reading, writing, and teaching experiences have shaped my philosophy of literacy. I'm hoping *Writing with Passion* will be an aesthetic experience for readers as well as an efferent one.

In much reading, especially the kind we often do in English classes, efferent and aesthetic overlap. I can tap into students' efferent understandings of literature to enhance their aesthetic responses and, as a byproduct, satisfy my shameful pedagogical suspicions about whether students have, in fact, engaged with the texts we're reading.

Recently, I asked students to finish reading Octavia Butler's historical/sci-fi/realistic novel *Kindred* for the following weekly class. A past reading assignment had aroused my suspicions that some students in this class of twenty-nine were not participating in good faith. I often have students write one-page responses or log entries about their reading. But this time, because of the hefty amount of reading they were required to complete, I didn't want to burden students with a writing assignment. Reading the book would take time enough.

I decided I could find out what I needed to know about students' engagement with the book in ten or twelve minutes of writing at the beginning of class. The activity would set students to thinking specifically about the book and serve as a cognitive jump-start to our discussion. I gave students a writing prompt and was out-front about why:

I'm seeking to discover two things:

1. If you've finished *Kindred*.
2. What kind of meaning you make of the novel.

Describe how you felt about the evolving relationship between Dana—the narrator—and Rufus—her distant ancestor.

As you discuss your feelings, refer specifically to events and characters' actions in the novel that illustrate why you feel as you do.

In your discussion, be sure to write about the end of the relationship between Dana and Rufus.

The kind of prompt I created for *Kindred*—asking students to show how they feel but also to discuss specific details of the book—demands that students have engaged with the literature and tells me about their good-faith participation. The emphasis of the question is on how students feel, think, and connect, not on how well they remember picayune facts. The prompt does not send the message that literary understanding means accumulating "massive amounts of trivial information" (Probst, 61). I didn't administer a strictly efferent quiz with discrete questions like

When Dana time travels where does she end up?
What triggers Dana's time travel to the past?
What triggers Dana's time travel to 1976?
Who is Kevin?
What physical punishment does Dana suffer twice?
Who hangs him/herself near the end of the novel?
What is the fate of Rufus?
Which character likes being read to?

or for easier grading, multiple-choice efferent questions like

At one point in the story Rufus suffers (a) a broken hand (b) a broken leg (c) a broken arm (d) cracked ribs (e) all of the above.

I also sometimes give writing prompts that supply students with specific information from the reading and ask them to connect or discuss it. Instead of quizzing students efferently, I *give* them the kind of discrete information that might be asked on a purely efferent quiz. I want students to use the information to make larger meanings in their writing and not be hampered if actions or the names of characters and places don't come to mind. An example: students in Beginning Fiction Writing were to finish the last half of Tim O'Brien's *The Things They Carried* for our weekly class. I asked them:

> Discuss these parts of the book; tie them together and make sense of them:
> Kiowa's death.
> Norman Bowker's endless driving around the lake in his hometown in Iowa after the war.
> O'Brien's return to Vietnam with his ten-year-old daughter, Kathleen, years after the war.

I didn't ask students which character drowned one terrifying night in the shitfield where the platoon had ill-advisedly bivouacked. I didn't ask what action Norman Bowker had repeated after he returned to the states. I didn't ask who accompanied O'Brien when he returned to Vietnam and the place where Kiowa had drowned in excrement.

Details can slip the mind. Characters' names might blank out on you. Engagement and meaning making are what I'm concerned about.

CONCLUSION

The world of literature is large and contains multitudes. We jointly explore a portion of it with students, directing them to good reading, accompanying them into occasional difficult texts. We launch students on exploratory odysseys of their own when they choose literature themselves, reading individually or in groups. The way we manage our classes can show students that reading texts involves risk, surprise, conjecture, and multiple meaning, just as writing our own texts do. In fact, in both situations—reading someone else's writing and creating their own—students build meaning. I need to hold students accountable for engaging with literature, but I want to do this in such a way that my classroom remains a place that values approximation, encourages students to speak the rude truth, nudges them to look closely at their resistances and to scratch persistent itches. I want my literature classes to get students both to trust their subjective impressions and to consider the subjective impressions of others, including mine. I want them to examine why they think what they think. I want them to use reading and writing to take a look around.

An *I* Only with Others

I am not writing this alone. All through this book the writing of students has provoked and illustrated my thinking. In the works cited section is a list of writers—living and dead—who have informed my words. Without all these people to build upon, I'd have no book to write. For forty-six years now I've explored the world and learned language with others in social settings—at home, in classrooms, in my dad's barroom and bowling alley, at professional meetings. Interacting with people has taught me the language I think with. During the last two years, I have talked with friends and strangers about my book. They have listened, asked questions, made suggestions, and contributed ideas.

But now—as I write—no one sits beside me. I am alone. No one acts as my other self, prompting words, spurring ideas. The words come from within me, from the language I've developed during my transaction with my culture.

"It can never be the case," writes Jerome Bruner, "that there is a 'self' independent of one's cultural-historical existence" (1986, 67). I am made of much, composed of many. And like poet Walt Whitman—the quintessential nineteenth-century representative of the romantic, self-made individual voice—I celebrate myself and sing myself. But I don't sing alone. I sing amid many. Every note celebrates that indispensable, collaborative chorus.

Chapter Ten

AN ALLY
IN OTHERS

I STOP SOMEWHERE WAITING FOR YOU.

Walt Whitman

*A*s I discuss in Chapter 3, faith and fearlessness are essential traits for writers. Allies of those traits are process and development. We have yet another ally to nurture our faith and fearlessness, and, as a bonus, to deepen our thinking and sharpen the quality of our writing. That ally is the minds of others. Admitting people into the process of our writing, however, is a greater act of faith and fearlessness than writing about what we feel strongly but cannot yet envision. When and who we ask to respond to our writing is not a decision to be made casually. The very one we thought might be an ally could prove a saboteur.

During the summer of 1987 Don Murray, Ruth Hubbard, Linda Rief, Bob Yagelski, and I taught a writing course for teachers at the University of New Hampshire. Don headed our teaching team and delivered one-hour talks on Tuesdays and Thursdays, after which Ruth, Linda, Bob, and I met with our grade-level groups. The Wednesday one-hour presentation slot rotated among Ruth, Linda, Bob, and me. I presented on the first Wednesday.

My topic was Winston Weathers's Grammar B. I had been working with Grammar B in my high school classes just over a year and had brought along an article-in-process of the experience that I planned to work on at UNH, then send to *English Journal*. I referred to the article in my presentation, which the audience found appealing. Afterward, one of the participants—a stranger—asked if she and her friend could read my article. I beamed. Flush with the success of the presentation, I handed over the manuscript, my ego a bit out of control.

The next week the manuscript appeared in my mailbox. I was flabbergasted to find that the duo had gone through it meticulously with a red pen, correcting usage infelicities, casting aspersions on my exuberant style, chastising me for purposeful rule-breaking of standard English in my article about purposeful rule-breaking of standard English. I had given them the manuscript because I thought they were interested in the topic, not because I sought their editorial input. Theirs was a presumptuous, superior, imperious response, unconcerned with helping, all concerned with correcting, criticizing, and categorizing. It was unexpected, one-upmanship feedback, an intellectual sucker punch. I was astonished and indignant for days, showing my ruler-slapped manuscript to colleagues, railing about the temerity of the two.

And guess what?

A month later when I was tightening and sharpening the article for the last time, I incorporated one of the myriad comments the Grammar A crusaders had made on my paper.

My first year at Utah State University, anywhere from four to eight of us met each month in a writing group. One month I submitted a review I was writing of Linda Rief's *Seeking Diversity*, a book whose writing is fine and whose pedagogy is sensible, informed, and humane.

The talk about my review that evening was sniping and dissatisfied. There were painful, undeveloped spots in the review, some complained. I wasn't critical enough. Rief's program can't be this successful. My heart beat a little faster; the hair on my neck prickled. By the time the group was through with my review, I wondered whether *Seeking Diversity* was as good as I'd thought. During the raking, one group member looked positively angry with me. Her eyes were unforgiving, her brows troubled. She frowned severely. My voice and what I had written had apparently damaged the tradition of book reviewing.

After the session, I wasn't sure I wanted to work further with the review, even though my deadline was approaching. But an ally, a group member who hadn't said much during the workshop, undid the work of the saboteurs. He had responded to my review in writing, marking pluses in the margins next to parts that worked for him, offering alternative ways to say something, suggesting how I might rework gnarled passages. After reading his comments the following morning, my faltering faith revived.

And as I revised, guess what?

One of the disparager's sarcastic comments stuck with me: "This reads like an advertisement for Heinemann." That drove me to add an important final paragraph to the review.

Am I too sensitive? My skin not thick enough if I am going submit my writing for publication? Can't take it? No balls, as I've heard a person described who wouldn't publish in workshop? I don't doubt all that. Delicate sensibilities, thin skin, low testosterone. I need companions for my words, not adversaries; allies, not saboteurs. Companions and allies are straight with you, can be most critical because you know they genuinely care that you write well and that, most important, you keep writing.

"Putting your heart on paper is scary even if you're brave," wrote Jennifer, a Beginning Fiction Writing student. I put my heart on paper every time I write. That's not hard to believe, I suppose, about my journal entry describing my father's death and the excerpt from *Blindside* about Nick's father's funeral that I include in Chapter 3. But is my heart really on paper in a book review? That's a report, for god's sake!

Yes, I must answer. My heart *is* on the paper then, and so, too, are my intellect, ability, and taste. I write reviews for books I become passionate about. Otherwise I wouldn't write them. The words of a review reflect what I have synthesized from my analysis. And my analysis emerges from my very being— what I've learned, what I've experienced, what I already know and believe.

I have trouble being dispassionate, do not easily separate the dancer from the dance. Because I write about things I care about deeply, I become invested in my topic—whatever it is. Because I care about writing—the sounds of words, the rhythms of sentences, the progression of ideas—I care about the way I craft writing, the way I shape my voice on the page to sound like the me I've come to be in forty-six years of living.

I think of this statement from a Don Murray essay in *To Compose*:

> The deeper we get into the writing process the more we may discover how affective concerns govern the cognitive, for writing is an intellectual activity carried on in an emotional environment, a precisely engineered sailboat trying to hold course in a vast and stormy Atlantic. The captain has to deal with fears as well as compass readings. (Murray 1990a, 116)

I'll go even further: in me the intellectual and emotional are knotted. Intellect enables emotion; emotion intensifies intellect.

That's why I am repulsed by some of the metaphors routinely used to describe responding to writing. A graduate student hands me her thesis proposal and says, "Rip it to shreds." I give a colleague back his personal essay on which I've asked questions and indicated how various passages struck me. Two days later he says, "Just what I needed—an old-fashioned, bare-knuckled response." You've heard, no doubt, such metaphors, too: tear it apart, make it bleed, lay waste to it, reduce it to rubble, destroy it, flay it, nuke it. Some of my friends see such metaphors as macho, war-like, red in tooth and claw—the John Rambo school of writing response.

When writers use such metaphors are they protecting themselves against the worst? If I've told you to tear my poem apart, and you do, then I appear steeled to take the worst. I, in fact, invite it. Hit me with your best shot. Punish me. Hurt me. All the pain will make me tough.

Does low self-esteem make writers use such combative language to describe the meeting of two minds through writing? The battered writer who feels she deserves what she gets? If she were only smarter, more self-sacrificing, more efficient, then she wouldn't earn such deserved abuse. Is it a power thing learned from teachers, so often have students and their writing been dominated, overpowered, intellectually pistol-whipped?

I have friends and colleagues, of course, who have written well within the pedagogy of ripping, tearing, and bloodletting. Not me, despite the carping comment about Heinemann advertising that drove me to write an important paragraph in my review of *Seeking Diversity*, despite the one piece of sound, trivial advice I used from the denigrating duo in my alternate style article. I've found combative writing conferences stressful, regardless of whether I've been the bludgeoner or the bludgeonee.

As a writer, I prefer to confer with people with whom I am harmonious, "someone who responds to the pace and degree that seems congruent" to me (Stafford 1986, 65). They are interested in me—what I see, what I think, how I write. They want me to see clearly, think deeply, and write well. They delight in a well-turned phrase I have created. They give me good advice about language and sentences. They are more concerned with seeing me stretch and discover than with making sure I adhere to traditional essay structure or regulated, well-mannered sentences or an "appropriate" academic voice.

With harmonious people I not only get good, specific response to my writing, I also experience *resonance*. Karen Burke LeFevre (1987) explains this concept as it relates to the act of invention:

> Resonance comes about when an individual act—a 'vibration'—is intensified and prolonged by sympathetic vibrations. It may occur when someone acts as a facilitator to assist or extend what is regarded as primarily another's invention, or when people are mutual collaborators at work on a task. Resonance also occurs indirectly when people provide a supportive social and intellectual environment

that nurtures thought and enables ideas to be received, thus completing the inventive act. (65)

Linda Cunningham, a teacher at Salt Lake Community College and recent graduate student at Utah State University, experienced this resonance with harmonious others during a course I taught. Linda was writing a multigenre research paper about Sioux Indian Mary Crow Dog and the American Indian movement of the 1970s. In her research Linda was appalled to discover that rapes and murders on the Pine Ridge Sioux reservation were seldom investigated. During our weekly conference, Linda told me what she was learning. The information was abominable, grim, political, and disgraceful. "There are a lot of opportunities for you to be graphic," I told her. This set her to writing. Our class met once a week in Logan, eighty-five miles from Linda's home in Salt Lake City. In preparation for our weekly conference, Linda mailed me the following poem:

A drunk Indian girl
Thirteen, fourteen years old
Can't be left lying in alleys or
On sidewalks—public places.

Officers
Cuff her, jail her for the night.
Lead her stumbling to a cell
In the back
Where most won't see them
Pull dirty denim pants down her wobbling legs
Then mount her, one hand over her mouth
To muffle her weak crying.

"They love this. They're always asking for it.
Did you see how she wiggled her ass at me?"

This was tough stuff to write about. But I was glad to see it. Linda, "a fifty-one-year-old Mormon woman," as she described herself, was investigating native Americans after reading Mary Crow Dog's *Lakota Woman*. During her first reading of the book several months earlier, Linda had grown angry at the author's assault on the white race. Linda hadn't constructed intricate defenses, however, or turned from the book in scorn as so many of us do when confronted with something alien and adversarial. If the book bothered her so much, Linda reasoned, she'd better read it again. As she extended her research and gained empathy for the plight of Native Americans, the above poem emerged.

I found the poem stark, bold, and hard-hitting. I asked Linda if she could create particular images to let readers get to know the girl more intimately, to make her human and real. This question led Linda to make a "series of visualizations," she explained, "mental pictures to help me see the young Indian woman, her location, the officers involved, etc. The mental pictures I conjured up were fairly sharp, and I was able to extract detail from the scenes I saw in my imagination."

Linda engaged in a satisfying dialectic between verbal and visual thinking. Her research had provided unsettling, surprising information. Her conference with me had resonated her growing authority and directed her to the graphic possibilities of what she knew. The language Linda generated to establish drama sparked images; those images evoked further language that fully realized her vision. The interaction of verbal and visual thought upped the cognitive ante.

Linda shaped a longer version of the poem, which she brought to her peer group. They reviewed it "very enthusiastically," Linda said. They made plenty of suggestions and these suggestions "set off a rush of ideas in my head about how I might revise." Linda was in harmony with these two other graduate students. They resonated her thinking, validated her experience, became so involved in imagining the horrid scene she had created that they made suggestions for what more might be seen. Some of these suggestions Linda took; some she didn't. Her faith and interest in her material soared.

Here is the final draft of the poem as it appeared in her multigenre paper (Cunningham 1994):

BUSINESS AS USUAL

She sat slumped in the alley
Like a half-empty sack of Dakota grain.
One arm curved loosely around an empty bottle of Jim Beam.
Fourteen, maybe fifteen
A kid in blue jeans and black braids
Senseless of dark or danger.

Like deer hunters with telescopic sights
Officers on patrol spot her there in the alley
And close in on her.
She hears nothing: not the car, not their boots on asphalt,
Not the smash
Of glass
When they kick her empty bottle against the concrete wall.

"She's a goner, Bud. Won't wake up anytime soon.
Might's well take her to the tank
Before Ruby sees this Indian layin' around her laundromat."

Dumped half-conscious onto the back seat of the patrol car,

She tries to sit, falls back swearing
And slurring familiar syllables
"Goddam, Kanji—need five bucks, goddam."

The car moves through silent streets,
No lights or sirens; this business is routine.

At the jail the officers drag the boozy kid
Like a dressed venison out of the car
And into the cell at the back.
Her shoes drag along the painted concrete floor,
Rubber soles squeaking faintly.

They let her fall on the skimpy cot;
Big key clicks in the lock
And she cries weakly: "Kanji—need five bucks."
"Honey, I ain't your Kanji, and you don't need no five bucks.
But I do have somethin' here that you want.
Look at this, sweetheart; look at this!
Roll over now, honey; I like 'em to look at me."

Rough hands force open the snap on her jeans and yank them
Down, over young, muscled thighs and wobbly knees.
One small brown hand grabs at the air,
Reaching, finding nothing but the cold, hard metal
Of the sheriff's badge.
"Fucking Indian! Don't touch nothin' here!
You just lay still and take it—easy."

The tiny cot tips precariously.
His savage assault tears her body
And scars her soul
With rage
And shame
That will not fade.

Four violent thrusts and he shudders, satisfied.
"You want some, Bud?" he says,
Sliding off the back end of the cot.

"Nope, maybe next time. Get your pants up;
I gotta get home."
"Suit yourself." Big key clanks in the lock again.
Echoes of footsteps fade down the hall
And she's alone.
Blue jeans crumpled in careless folds at her ankles,
Blood smeared on bare, trembling thighs.
Silent, muffled sobs "Kanji, Kanji . . ."

Outside the lock-up, dark, cold night.

An Ally in Others

"They love this, ya know. They're always askin' for it.
We done her a big favor.
She could have froze to death out here."
Linda Cunningham, Teacher, Salt Lake Community College

It strikes me that what Linda has done is precisely one thing we want students to do when they conduct inquiry. Through her research, she has come to know a different culture so well that she writes convincingly and sympathetically about it. She has moved in close, is not merely caught up in statistics and theories. She has developed genuine empathy for the people involved in her research.

WRITING ON DRAFTS

Writing comments and making corrections on students' papers has been second nature for most writing teachers. Canadian teachers speak of "marking" papers. American teachers "grade" papers. Post–writing process teachers "respond" to papers.

I used to write a great deal on students' papers—drafts, final copies, it didn't matter. I wrote all over them, everything from nit-picking comments about grammar and usage to larger matters of development. I sprinkled "good" and "nice" and "great" on the pages when students wrote well, deftly turned a phrase, or riveted me with a stunning example.

I don't write on students' papers much anymore. In fact, for a couple of years I didn't write on students' papers at all. As I gained more and more respect for students' intentionality, I wrote less and less on their papers. I also began to understand that students couldn't possibly attend to the overload of comments I dumped on their essays, stories, and poems. Half the time I don't even suppose they could read my handwriting. I stopped writing on papers altogether, particularly final copies, since students weren't going to do anything further with them. After all, my mentors in graduate school—Don Murray and Don Graves—hadn't written on my papers. They conferred with me plenty about my writing, initiated discussion, asked a lot of questions, but never wrote on my papers.

Recently, however, I've had to step back and reconsider my "talk only, no writing" stance as a responder. One of the best responders to my writing here at Utah State University is Bill Strong, director of the Utah Writing Project and author of books about teaching writing. Bill is a spirit with whom I am harmonious. And he writes all over my manuscripts. He corrects errors, makes suggestions, asks questions, writes pluses in the margin.

When I ask Bill to respond to a draft, he walks right into my writing, takes his shoes off, and makes himself at home. He begins to wonder how I might clarify and extend my vision. Through his marks on my manuscript, Bill loans me his intellect and perceptions. I stand on his shoulders and glimpse possibilities. He nudges along my development as a writer. And maybe most important, when I finish reading Bill's response, I want to write more.

Let me illustrate. I asked Bill to respond to a review I was writing about *Authors' Insights*, edited by Don Gallo, eight articles, all by authors of young adult books, about teaching writing and literature, an eminently readable and provocative collection. The bulk of my reading, thinking, and writing was completed, but I didn't think the review was quite done. I felt imbalances, murkiness, jumps in logic. I needed an ally to confer with. A page of the manuscript is shown in Figure 10–1, along with his handwritten comments. Bill suggests cutting the first sentence and using the third sentence as the topic sentence. That would highlight Louise Rosenblatt and emphasize her transactional theory of reader response.

I had already included examples of a bent to reader response from Sandy Asher and Paul Janeczko. Bill suggests I find "one more summarizing example of the 'bent' toward reader response [that] would put the YA authors up front in the article." He suggests that I make a paragraph out of the final two sentences of the section.

In the right margin Bill also asks, "Don't you want present tense?" Which I do, after he's alerted me. He tentatively suggests I use *underlies* in place of "was present throughout." He recommends that in the final line that "may be lost amid the pedantry" be changed to "may be a casualty of such pedantry."

Figure 10–2 is that same copy, now with my revisions overlaid on Bill's response. Bill had noted little infelicities like wordiness and tense shift, things that nonetheless concern me. I accepted those suggestions/corrections readily, even his last recommendation to replace "lost amid the" with "a casualty of such," which strikes me now simply as his wording preference to mine. I accepted them, though, dispatched them, if you will, because something much bigger was at stake. Bill's interaction with my text had gotten me thinking about larger organizational concerns, an issue that struck to the heart of the imbalance I felt.

Bill's suggestion to make the Rosenblatt sentence the topic sentence seemed immediately right. Not only could I eliminate the opening Harry Mazer sentence then, as he suggested, but I could delete the second sentence. My meaning changes somewhat. Instead of emphasizing respect for students' responses, I hit the idea that the authors decry the teaching of literature in a way that students' responses take second place to teaching the technicalities

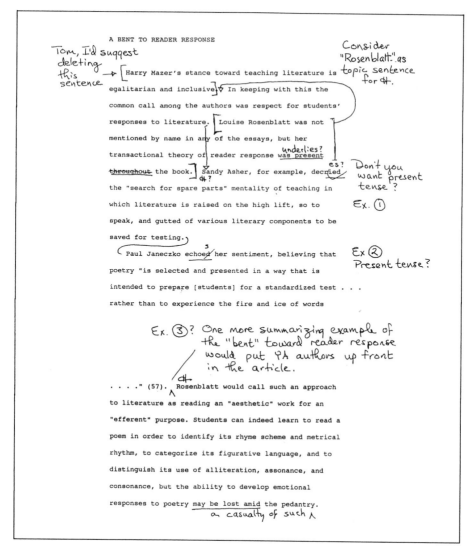

A BENT TO READER RESPONSE

Tom, I'd suggest deleting this sentence →

[Harry Mazer's stance toward teaching literature is *Consider "Rosenblatt" as topic sentence for ¶.* egalitarian and inclusive] ↓ In keeping with this the common call among the authors was respect for students' responses to literature. [Louise Rosenblatt was not mentioned by name in any of the essays, but her transactional theory of reader response *underlies?* was present throughout the book.] Sandy Asher, for example, decried *es? Don't you want present tense?* ¶? the "search for spare parts" mentality of teaching in which literature is raised on the high lift, so to *Ex. ①* speak, and gutted of various literary components to be saved for testing.

Paul Janeczko echoed her sentiment, believing that *Ex ② Present tense?* poetry "is selected and presented in a way that is intended to prepare [students] for a standardized test . . . rather than to experience the fire and ice of words

Ex. ③? One more summarizing example of the "bent" toward reader response would put YA authors up front in the article.
/¶

. . . ." (57). Rosenblatt would call such an approach to literature as reading an "aesthetic" work for an "efferent" purpose. Students can indeed learn to read a poem in order to identify its rhyme scheme and metrical rhythm, to categorize its figurative language, and to distinguish its use of alliteration, assonance, and consonance, but the ability to develop emotional responses to poetry may be lost amid the pedantry. *a casualty of such* ∧

FIGURE 10–1

of literature (Asher's "spare parts" mentality and Janeczko's "standardized test" complaint).

Bill recommends a third example of the authors' "bent toward reader response" that he feels "would put YA authors up front." In my notes I had such an example—a sterling one—from Norma Fox Mazer's essay. But try as I might I couldn't fit the example into the place Bill recommended. At this point in the writing I was ruled by "the grammar of meaning" (Murray 1993); I couldn't get Bill's suggestion to make sense. In working with the text,

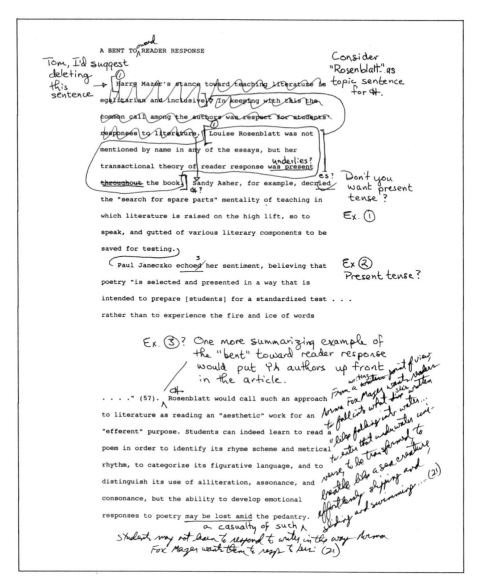

FIGURE 10—2

however, I saw that the Norma Fox Mazer quotation would perfectly illustrate Rosenblatt's idea of aesthetic response to literature. The quotation clarified that concept and enabled me to work into the review one of the best passages from *Authors' Insights*. My final change was to add an image of Professor Rosenblatt (I'd just seen her the week before at a convention). Figure 10—3 shows how the paragraphs appeared in *English Journal* (Romano 1992).

I was delighted with the revision. Bill had been very directive about what

FIGURE IO–3

I should do. In fact, he later told me that he was concerned that he'd gone too far. Although Bill's "Rosenblatt as topic sentence" dictum had untangled my thinking and although I'd heeded his suggestions about small matters of correctness and preference, in big matters of organization, emphasis, and clarity, I hadn't done what he'd suggested. I'd taken my own course. I was, I must admit, a bit smug.

I showed Bill my revision.

"Look at this," I said to him, laying the pages on his desk. "I didn't do what you said about adding a third example from a YA author, but I did something better, something neither you nor I had thought of."

Bill looked up at me. "Isn't that the way response is supposed to work?"

I blinked.

It certainly was. Not to adhere slavishly to every admonition the written responder makes (some suggestions might be outlandish and damaging), but to use the responder's marks to spark further transaction with the text. That's when collaboration of this sort is best—when writer and responder create something together neither could have created alone.

But I am an adult writer.

I've been seriously involved with my writing since I was twelve years old. My experience has provided me with reasonable amounts of faith and fearlessness. I am confident enough to look at Bill's directions, weigh the sense they make, then deviate from them if I must.

Would inexperienced, shakily confident writers—whether twelve, twenty, thirty, or fifty—be overwhelmed with such detailed, written responses to their writing? Would they look at such extensive commentary as ripping, tearing, and bloodletting because their own way of seeing and saying seems dismissed? Very possibly, I think. And for that reason alone, I am careful about how soon, how much, even if, I write on students' papers.

There is this, too: I *invited* Bill to take a direct role in the development of my review (in the development of myself, too). He wasn't a stranger or intruder who elbowed his way into my writing and began making demands. I wasn't disempowered by all his scribbling; I was interested in seeing the workings of his mind. I was excited to see how those workings would spur my own transaction with the text. I knew he could help me think. I was not territorial about my review, and I did most of what he suggested, but not what didn't seem feasible. And Jesus, he wasn't dour or condescending, severe or pedantic.

An *I* Only with Others

In the previous interchapter, I write about Walt Whitman, refer to him as "the quintessential nineteenth-century representative of the romantic, self-made individual voice." The Whitman *I* rose above all others, independent, atomistic, self-contained. Or so it seemed.

An Ally in Others

When *Leaves of Grass* was published in 1855, Whitman sent one of the 795 copies to Ralph Waldo Emerson, arbiter of American literary tastes and leading thinker of the day. Emerson wrote Whitman back, thanking him for the book that he thought "the most extraordinary piece of wit and wisdom that America has yet contributed" (quoted in Kaplan, 202). He went on to tell Whitman, "I greet you at the beginning of a great career, which yet must have had a long foreground somewhere, for such a start" (203).

Emerson was right on both counts. The poet did indeed have a long foreground, and it was America—as composed in the mind and spirit of Whitman—that produced *Leaves of Grass* and kept producing it through eight subsequent editions.

In *Walt Whitman: A Life* Justin Kaplan discusses influences on the poet: phrenology, the Long Island seashore, Italian opera, democracy, the expanse of America, Lincoln, abolitionism, transcendentalism, bad poets of the day, the bustle of Broadway, the New York World's Fair of 1853, periodicals from Victorian England, the slang of street roughs and the genteel locutions of cultivated travelers, *Sartor Resartus*, Pfaff's beer cellar, articles on history, law, geography, exploration, astronomy, archaeology, fine and applied arts, geology, life in foreign counties, oratory, religion, science ...

In "Song of Myself" Whitman sings and celebrates himself for fifty pages in a distinctive, eloquent barbaric yawp that eventually altered the style of writing poetry in America. In the final three lines of this poem, Whitman writes,

> Failing to fetch me at first keep encouraged,
> Missing me one place search another,
> I stop somewhere waiting for you.

The last image of the poem—inclusive and compassionate—is indelible to me: the poet patiently waiting for the reader. Of course, he had no other choice. The Whitman *I* was made of much, composed of many. It developed through a collaboration with others and the world they lived in, a collaboration at once intimate, profound, and democratic.

DIANE

A few years ago I received a letter from a former student—Diane Wooten Rowland. For two years in the early 1980s when Diane was a teenager, I'd delighted in her voice and sensibility. She'd been especially good at writing compelling narratives. Diane knew how to create and maintain tension by revealing information little by little through dialog. Her great strength, though, was her drive to be particular. No abstractions. No generalizations. Diane wrote in details. They built throughout her narratives, and then often, in the final lines, she used the most significant one, a detail you'd temporarily forgotten about, even though she'd been mentioning it here and there all along. The resulting echo in those final lines resulted in a startling, satisfying moment of recognition that usually left me—as a reader— on the seat of my pants.

For two years Diane's poems and stories were published in the high school newspaper and creative arts anthology. She was proud of that. She graduated and married the young man she'd fallen in love with her senior year. I lost track of her and so was happy to hear her voice in an unexpected letter eight years after I'd taught her. She was living in rural Indiana with her husband and three children.

With her brief letter Diane included the main reason she was writing: a six-page, handwritten personal essay. She asked me to respond to it.

Diane's essay was about not having time to write. She still loved to, she said, but at that time in her life, the chances to write were few: "I can think a whole story out in my head, but as soon as I sit down to get it on paper the phone rings, the kids start arguing, the baby starts crying or my husband can't find his socks."

With humor and insight Diane went on to detail life with her children that made mothering imperative and writing nearly impossible. In the final paragraph Diane wrote,

> I feel really good. For the first time in years I have written down my thoughts. I'm not a teenager anymore. I'm a grown-up, a wife and mother, but for a few hours I've felt like a teenager with a little bit of talent. I started out writing about me and ended up writing about my children, but maybe, at this phase of my life, that's what being me is all about.

Diane's essay was a classic example of writing leading to understanding, of synthesis making analysis possible.

In part, I wrote back to Diane:

> I still think you're a writer, Diane, even if you don't get time to write much anymore. For some of us there's no getting around the need to put words on paper, to make sense of experience with written language. That's part of who you are, Diane, as much as you are wife and mother now, too.

Along with my letter, I sent Diane a copy of Gail Godwin's essay "Becoming a Writer."

I knew it was going to be hard for Diane to keep writing. I hoped she could make time here and there. For many of us the act of writing is one of the great pleasures on earth. It makes living sweeter. Even amid the hectic busyness of her day, Diane knew this too. The first paragraph of her essay read,

> I used to be a writer, or at least I thought I was. I may not have been that good but I felt good doing it.

Chapter Eleven

BLISSFULLY LOST
IN LITERACY

GIVE ME THE SPLENDID SILENT SUN WITH ALL
HIS BEAMS FULL-DAZZLING.

Walt Whitman

After that first group of high school students finished their multigenre research papers, I asked them to assess their experience. One of the questions I asked them was, What did you learn about reading and writing from this project?

Mary Beth, who composed the sensitive paper about Marilyn Monroe, adapted her slang usage of sexual intercourse to fit a school publication, and wrote, as she said, with "no *pre* to it," responded:

> I got so caught up in books. It was amazing to feel that adventurous, to be there in the pages, to hear the words, and see, and feel the people and emotions.

Mary Beth had experienced *flow*, what psychologist Mihalyi Csikszentmihalyi calls "optimal psychological experience." Csikszentmihalyi describes flow as:

> a sense that one's skills are adequate to cope with the challenges at hand, in a goal-directed, rule-bound action system that provides clear clues as to how well one is performing. Concentration is so

intense that there is no attention left over to think about anything irrelevant, or to worry about problems. Self-consciousness disappears, and the sense of time becomes distorted. An activity that produces such experiences is so gratifying that people are willing to do it for its own sake, with little concern for what they will get out of it, even when it is difficult, or dangerous. (1990, 71)

Like Mary Beth, you too no doubt have experienced flow while reading a novel. You lived in the pages of a book, saw characters move, heard their talk, felt their emotions. Your behavior was rule governed as you read symbols and turned pages speeding toward the denouement, anxious to relieve the tension you felt. Clear indications about your performance arrived regularly as you gained more information and built an ever richer envisionment of the fictional dream. The world fell away until suddenly the telephone rang or someone knocked at the door, and you found you'd been reading for hours.

I believe that flow is what I experienced in junior high school when I read those adventure novels of the Far North, in senior high school when I passionately reported on *The Sea Wolf* and researched and wrote about the life of John Keats—that long-dead poet who understood young love and irrevocable loss. I experienced flow last winter when I wrote "The Silence That Widened" and countless other times when living in language became an altered state of consciousness, vivid, challenging, absorbing, and fulfilling.

Writer Donald Murray describes the optimal psychological experience he finds in his work:

> I come to writing depressed, worried, angry, confused, fearful, unhappy, in pain, and, most of the time, I start a sentence and by the time I get to the end I am lost in the task. I forget the clock, do not realize the CD has played to the end, am not aware of the snow falling outside my window.
>
> Writing brings one of the great gifts of life—a far greater gift than publication, applause, awards, even royalties—concentration. In the act of writing I experience a serene, quiet joy, a focus of all my energy and knowledge and craft on the task, losing myself in the job that strangely allows me to become myself. (1990, 189)

It is not only with reading and writing that we can achieve optimal psychological experience. Any activity has the potential for flow: swimming, jogging, racquetball, hunting, painting, teaching, quilt making, cooking, eating, gardening, making love, collecting coins, mowing the lawn ... The diversity of the list is as endless as the diversity of people. The most unlikely activities, in fact, may evolve into optimal psychological experiences.

As I wrote the comprehensive exam for my doctorate at the University of New Hampshire, for example, I slipped into a state of flow. This was in part because of the humane way the testing was done. Before Christmas break, I met with my committee to discuss areas I would be asked questions about. During the vacation, my adviser, Tom Newkirk, created thirteen essay questions from which I would answer eight. When I returned to UNH in January, I picked up the questions and took them back to my dormitory room, the place I'd been writing for months and where I felt strong, confident, and comfortable. I had four days to create my essays.

The thinking and writing were intense, and all the elements of flow fell into place. I was challenged. Although most of the questions dealt with theories and books I knew, Newkirk had written them to make me stretch. One of the areas I had agreed to write about, for example, was using writing as thinking or writing across the curriculum. I wasn't, however, simply asked to discuss the foundations and use of writing-across-the-curriculum pedagogy. Newkirk added a twist:

> Choose four authors who have influenced you most about how humans think and apply their philosophies and findings to the teaching of reading and writing across the curriculum.

Being asked to tie cognitive theorists to writing across the curriculum surprised me. I hadn't thought about them in that context. I believed fervently in using writing as thinking, though, and I felt strong loyalty to the authors who had influenced me about how people think (the personal tie that generated passion). Although the question was unexpected, it wasn't a curve ball. It was still a fat pitch, but with unexpected spin that challenged me to add a dimension to how I looked at the topic. I chose James Britton, Jerome Bruner, Janet Emig, and Lev Vygotsky and got to work.

Other elements of flow were present in this exam taking. Because my committee members—Newkirk, Jane Hansen, and Don Graves—knew how writers worked, they extended that understanding to graduate students: I was allowed to take the questions away and answer them in my own familiar place, in this case, my six-by-fourteen-foot dormitory room with a wooden chair padded with a pillow and my computer set up on a card table. I had choice about what I would write. I had an extended amount of time to involve myself in my writing processes—my greatest ally in enabling me to produce more than "rough drafts, only drafts." The act of writing provided me with clues about my performance as I formulated arguments, explained positions, showed examples. I wrote what I planned, but also surprised myself with new thinking *during* the writing. My essays were expositions, but in one of them I used a series of eight narrative crots to set up my persuasion. Further performance clues came when I reread my essays and discovered failures of word choice and garbled meaning. Following fast on the heels of these failures came alternate ways of wording and arranging. Four mornings, afternoons, and evenings I was absorbed in matters of reading, writing, and focused thinking. I was one with the work, and the time whizzed by.

Csikszentmihalyi's research shows that a flow activity provides

a sense of discovery, a creative feeling of transporting the person into a new reality. It pushed the person to higher levels of performance, and led to previously undreamed-of states of consciousness. In short, it transformed the self by making it more complex. In this growth of the self lies the key to flow activities. (74)

When I began swimming in 1976, forty lengths of the pool felt like the right distance. That was challenge enough. I emerged gasping from the pool after twenty-five minutes. In a matter of weeks, however, I became too comfortable with the one-thousand-meter distance. Gradually, I doubled it. After I learned to handle the new distance, technique became important. I learned flip turns, altered my stroke so my hands pushed water behind me instead of slicing through it. I began to vary my workout. Every other day I mixed fifty-meter sprints with distance swimming. I bought streamlined, nylon trunks and more expensive swimming goggles, ones with better seals and lenses that didn't fog. I concentrated on kicking and breathing until they were as natural as bringing my arms forward to stroke. I bought an inexpensive swimmer's watch, so I no longer had to count the lengths I'd swum. With the countdown set on the watch, I let my mind wander amid the bubbles, strokes, and breathing, flowing along in my best thinking of the day.

My swimming self was transforming and becoming more complex. My skills improved. My capacity for aerobic exercise expanded. Now, nearly two decades from the day I first eased into the pool, I am still swimming. It continues to challenge me and hasn't become drudgery. My time in the water is physically and psychologically fulfilling. I don't swim for points or a grade. I swim because of flow. I swim because I attain an altered state of consciousness, because my time here on this earth is enhanced by swimming, just as it is enhanced by writing, reading, talking, teaching, gardening, and loving.

Let me bring this discussion of flow back to literacy, to acts of reading and writing. It seems clear to me that if we want students of any age to become one with literacy, we must afford them chances to achieve optimal psychological experience through reading and writing.

About his multigenre work Jon wrote:

It is not a very earth-shattering discovery, but I was convinced that the words are more passionate and therefore interesting if the author is immersed, not dabbling.

Jon is not talking about moderation. He is talking about passion, obsession, complete surrender to an act of literacy one cares about. Jon is presently striving to become a playwright. As a high school senior he had read extensively about Tennessee Williams, then rendered that imaginative, intellectual experience in multiple genres. Writers can also achieve flow by meeting the challenge of alternate styles of writing, looking at personally important topics through the lenses of labyrinthine sentences or a series of crots, building a structure of writing they come to care about . . . or by capturing in precise language indelible memories from childhood or the way light appears on sidewalk ice one frosty night . . . or by writing in any genre about ideas, emotions, and learning that dwell strongly within them.

"It takes passion to teach well, doesn't it?" Bill Strong once said to me as I led a workshop for Utah Writing Project teachers.

No doubt.

And it takes passion to write and read well, too. Passion, immersion, and commitment. All the elements that make for flow: confidence in our skills, a clear task to accomplish (one that involves some choice on our part), clues about our performance, deep concentration, extended chunks of time that enable us to get blissfully lost in our work.

I don't have to write about my father or daughter to immerse myself in writing. I can develop flow about most topics and genres: a letter to a friend, a memo to colleagues, a book review, an article.

I told a technical writing colleague of mine that I didn't think much that was good got written unless the writer began to feel some passion toward the topic.

"Like writing specs for the army," he said, wryly.

He had me, I thought. I couldn't imagine growing passionate about writing specs for the army.

But my colleague went on: "I actually get a charge out of translating the mass of abstractions that are the regulations into a clean, understandable spec."

My colleague is talking about intellectual engagement. Matters of mind offer challenges and fulfillment just as physical matters do. In fact, thinking is the physical act of the mind. Imagining, feeling, analyzing, using language, happen because of electrochemical activities and blood flow.

But what about the quality of intellectual engagement achieved through reading and writing? What happens when students' acts of literacy don't meet our standards? "Face it," writes Peter Elbow, "if our goal is to get students to exercise their own judgment, that means exercising an immature and undeveloped judgment and making choices that are obviously wrong to us" (1993, 197).

When this happens—as it is bound to in learning—teachers must exercise their understanding of approximation and development. We value the experience of the five-year-old who fearlessly uses invented spelling to make words, the student teacher who stutters and stumbles as she learns to confer with adolescents about their writing, the forty-five-year-old graduate student who makes hasty judgments in her first foray into qualitative research. Then we nudge and teach and move students to reflect on their experience.

Csikszentmihalyi laments an unfortunate inclination in our society: "Increasingly the emphasis has been to value behavior over subjective states; what is admired is success, achievement, the quality of performance rather than the quality of experience" (140).

Make no mistake: I value quality performance. In previous chapters I've included some of the best student writing I've encountered in my classrooms. And you can bet that the language on the pages of this book has been revised and polished considerably. But although I value the quality of performance, I also value the quality of experience: Mark's spending hours as a seventeen-year-old scholarly detective hunting laboriously through periodicals from the 1940s to find early stories by J. D. Salinger. Linda Cunningham's dogged obsession to use language to create the image of what it might have been like for a fifteen-year-old Sioux girl to be raped by police officers. Mariana's discovering Ellis Island and 1914 and writing prose that brought to life a grandfather she never knew.

What matters most in our classrooms, despite what test designers might advocate, is the quality of subjective experiences students achieve with reading and writing. Memorizing definitions of parts of speech, reading classic works of literature, understanding the difference between simile and metaphor, are not crucial to literacy development. But it is crucial that students involve themselves in acts of reading and writing that evolve into optimal psychological experiences. They will seek such experiences again, just as Diane did when she wrote her thoughts for the first time in years. We need to look at what we compel students to do in our classes. We need to look at how we approach literacy to see what messages we send.

Louise Rosenblatt writes about an aspect of reading that cuts to the heart of students' engaging in quality subjective experiences with literature.

My concern is simply with the social and intellectual atmosphere that set up 'good literature' as almost by definition works accessible only to the elitist critic or literary historian, and that leads the average reader to assume that he simply is not capable of participating in them. Our whole literary culture tends to produce this defeatist attitude. Critics, professional and academic, have reinforced it. (1978, 142)

What Rosenblatt advocates is a social and intellectual literacy atmosphere in which everyone can find a place, in which my subjective experience with literature (or with my own writing) is not diminished because someone else doesn't think it is deep enough or sophisticated enough and thus disparages the quality of the literature I've read and the way I've read it.

We want all students to have quality subjective experiences with literacy, whether they are reading Sweet Valley High novels or Raymond Carver, whether they are writing literary exegeses or limericks. The "lived-through experience" is what Rosenblatt is after in reading literature, a subjective experience of quality. That's an egalitarian view of literacy, not an elitist one. Flow, too, is egalitarian. It is available to all. And it enables us to live deeply, keep growing, and suck the very marrow from life. Flow makes life meaningful, fulfilling, exhilarating. It enables us to live each detail and moment well.

Recently, I reviewed for *English Journal* (Romano, 1993) Rebecca Rule and Susan Wheeler's *Creating the Story*, a wonderful text for engaging secondary school and college students in the process of writing fiction. In fifty short chapters Rule and Wheeler suggest ways of generating fiction and discuss various aspects of the genre from a writer's point of view. I've used the book with Fiction Writing students at USU; I would have used it with high school students.

I have only one complaint with *Creating the Story*. In the chapter on publishing, the authors write,

If you've had about fifteen stories rejected fifteen times each, then perhaps it is time for you to climb a mountain by yourself. Ask yourself: Do I want to continue to write fiction? Is my work good? Do I still believe in what I'm doing? This is a long, lonely, soul-searching climb. If your answers are yes, don't give up. (249)

Fifteen stories, fifteen rejections each. Most of my students won't get to that point. Most of them are not seeking to make their way in the world as fiction writers. But I resist the implication that it is professional publication that validates the fiction writing experience, that the act of creation with language is not of itself worthwhile, that any intrinsic pleasure taken from writing stories, from becoming completely absorbed in a fictional dream is not worth the time if the story is not published.

The young adult novel I wrote a few years ago that I excerpt a passage from in Chapter 3 has been rejected by publishers and agents twenty-three times. I've stopped sending it out. Still I long for its publication. As an English teacher, I make my living in language. I talk with students and colleagues. I read language every day. I exist amid language and know that through writing my own language—revising it and polishing it—I find I can be my very best as a thinker, a teacher, a person. And when someone wants to publish my language—usually someone my ego has driven me to seek out—well ... I'm flattered, fulfilled, self-actualized. I know my students feel the same way when their language is published. Publication is something I strive for, something I make part of my classes.

But publication, I must remember, is not the only reason—and certainly not *the* reason—to write. Publication is not what made creating *Blindside* so valuable to me. The work made the experience gold, the two or three hours of daily writing, the feeling of being challenged and meeting those challenges, the sense of accomplishment as I saw myself getting better at creating tension, using dialog to deepen character and advance plot, rendering—not ideas—but the "experience of ideas" (Burroway 1992, 297), ending chapters definitively, the total concentration of becoming blissfully lost in language, image, and the lived-through experience of story. I never lived better.

The value of subjective experience was driven home to me by Mariana. She spent one semester in Italy studying at Loyola University's Rome Center. A Romano had made it back to the old country. For her two-week spring break Mariana took a whirlwind Eurail visit of seven countries. Here is the beginning of a letter she wrote to me during that spring break:

Dear Papa,

I'm on a train to Spain—we're about an hour away. For the past day or so I've been into Tim O'Brien's *The Things They Carried*. I feel heavy after reading that last chapter. O'Brien is so hip to so many things. I saw so many lessons in this book, not only about Vietnam, but how important it is to *write* and to tell your stories and to *listen* to other people's stories. So many times this book brought tears to my eyes. For some reason this book reminded me of you—the relationship with his daughter and the importance of his need to just *tell* this story. And here's where one lesson lies ... about your story—it brewed for twenty-five years—you never really *told* it until you wrote the novel. The death of Grandpa was a personal torture for so long—I know it's frustrating when you get rejections, but some people just don't want to *listen* to other people's stories. It doesn't mean they aren't *good*, and sometimes they have to be told to be dealt with. You told it and so many people in your family read your book and understand—me and Mom understand; Grandma Mae and Aunt Nancy can sigh with relief because they can relate. Maybe your story can help them tell their stories. . . . I felt O'Brien was trying to get all these messages across. Stories have to be told to keep people *alive* in a sense—even the person who is living has to be kept alive through stories. . . ."

Writing is a worthy human experience—whether you're writing fiction, dramatic encounters, journal entries, poetry, songs, articles, letters, or reviews, whether you're experimenting with Grammar B or developing a topic through multiple genres. We grow and become more complicated as our literacy evolves. Our lives are enriched by the doing. Never forget that.

EPILOG

ALL GOES ONWARD AND OUTWARD, NOTHING
    COLLAPSES

Walt Whitman

*M*y mom is eighty years old, quite frail now compared to her forty-year-old vigor when I was a child. "I feel young," she tells me, "but I look in the mirror after a shower and I think, I can't be that old!"

Mom has had triple-bypass open-heart surgery, carotid artery surgery, cataract surgery on both eyes. She's fallen and badly broken her right hand, suffered flare-ups of diverticulitis, wears two hearing aids, and takes a daily thyroid pill. She can't hold her great-grand babies unless she's sitting down. "I feel good," she says, "but one thing after another needs doctoring."

In 1929, one month shy of promotion, she quit ninth grade in Salinesville, Ohio, ending forever her formal education. That's about the same time she started to smoke unfiltered cigarettes. After heart surgery fifty-two years later, she quit smoking. Six weeks after that, during her six-week checkup, the doctor asked her a question that astonished me: "You aren't smoking more than a pack a day, are you?"

Mom's eyes lit up as she happily confessed, "No." That afternoon she began smoking again.

She's been married four times, divorced twice, and widowed twice. Mom's last husband died in 1979; she's lived alone since then. She stays up until four or five each morning reading thick romances, mysteries, and gothic horrors. She doesn't usually like the books I recommend to her. When she calls me on the telephone, she laughs and says my name, so delighted and surprised is she to hear my voice. Her ingenuous laugh is one of the great sounds in the world.

Last spring I sent her some of my poems. She called a week later with her response.

"I read your poems, Tommy. I had to read that one about your old baseball glove three times. And, you know, it made me sad at the end."

Three weeks after I finished the first draft of *Writing with Passion* I received permission from Diane to print excerpts from her letter in the final interchapter. Her new letter exhilarated and humbled me.

April 11, 1994

Dear Mr. Romano,

WOW!

This is great. You definitely have my permission and Thanks! Wow! What are you doing in Utah? I've thought about you often over the years, and if I ever get my first book written I'd planned to dedicate it to you. I don't know if I ever told you this but you really saved me. By the time I got to Edgewood from Talawanda I was really on a downward spiral. I didn't want to go to a new school in my junior year, and I didn't care about anything or anyone and I felt as if no one cared for me. I don't know if you remember but I was expelled from school when you called me and told me you wanted to put my story "An Army Jacket" in *Menagerie*. You were the first person to tell me I had talent as a writer and I'll always be grateful. From the time I was eight I'd pecked away on my dad's manual Royal typewriter and it was great to realize that my writing might somehow touch someone else.

I would like my name as Diane Wooten Rowland. I'm still married to Lester and he's still wonderful. He's excited as I am about this. He came and picked me up from work (I work part-time at a department store) and told me he had something that was going to make my day and gave me your letter. And he was right, it made my day! There is one thing that was wrong, we only have three children (thank the Good Lord!) and not four.

I'm really happy that you are having a book published. I still have every single paper I ever wrote in your classes, and most of your words written in red I've memorized. Your words help, they criticize, they praise, they make you want to learn more and do better. I'm glad more people may benefit from your love of writing. You're the best teacher Mr. Romano because you care about what you teach and who you teach it to.

As for me and writing: You told me once that to people like us writing was as much a part of us as breathing. I'm still breathing therefore I'm still writing, as much as I can because I love it so much.

> Thanks again Mr Romano
> Good Luck!
> Diane

I wasn't going to use this letter in the book—too self-serving, I feared. My friends Bill and Carol Strong, both professors at Utah State University, however, believed otherwise. When I read the letter to them, tears rose to Carol's eyes, so powerfully did she respond to Diane's situation: three children to care for, a part-time job, a husband who understood her passion for words.

"She gives everything she's got to her family," said Carol, "but writing lets her hold on to another part of who she is."

"Don't be embarrassed," Bill said to me. "We all need to remember that we make a difference in countless students' lives, even though we never hear about it. Think of all those unwritten letters out there."

A love of writing and mutual respect caused Mark and me to continue our friendship after he graduated from high school in 1975. He immediately got a job at Armco Steel and made more money than I did as a teacher with four years of experience. He took classes sporadically at Miami University's Middletown campus and grew to hate his job at the steel mill though he became accustomed to the income. He continued to party.

In the summer of 1990 Mark hit bottom. A relationship with a woman he loved was failing. Nearly twenty years of drug and alcohol abuse had taken their toll. He wasn't convinced he needed treatment, but he checked himself into the Ligonier Valley Treatment Center in Pennsylvania anyway, for six weeks of intense therapy, analysis, and discussion. I was teaching in the summer writing program at the University of New Hampshire. I wrote Mark letters from Durham and sent him a copy of Mike Rose's *Lives on the Boundary*, the best book I'd read in years.

When Mark returned to Ohio near the end of the summer, he was changed, somewhat subdued. He had taken to reading the Bible. Always thoughtful, he now reflected on his past, present, and future through a new lens: he realized he had an addictive personality.

Mark resumed his job at Armco Steel and enrolled full-time in an associate degree program at Miami University. After three semesters, he transferred his work to the Union Institute, a nationwide college program for nontraditional students seeking higher education. He majored in psychology, focusing on substance-abuse counseling. He would be one of the walking wounded, he told me. We spoke on the phone and saw each other infrequently, Mark busy with work and college, I busy writing my dissertation. Kathy and I invited him for Thanksgiving, but he couldn't come.

In February of that year, Mark and I went to dinner. I told him about the job I had accepted at Utah State University. Mark told me things too. He questioned the authenticity of my friendship. He believed I hadn't supported him during the two most important relationships he'd had with women. He further felt I had excluded him from social gatherings because he labored in a steel mill and wasn't college educated. He had many things to work through, Mark said, and one of them was coming to grips with people and events of the past so he could step into the future. "I know this is not about you as much as it's about me," he told me, "but I have to say these things to you." Because Mark believed what he did, he ended our friendship.

I denied his allegations. Mark wouldn't be swayed. We parted that night, two stoical men. No handshake. No embrace. No "I'll see you . . . ." And I began to wonder: by my past actions and inactions had I been unsupportive of Mark in the two pivotal relationships with women he loved? Had I subconsciously excluded him from social gatherings for the very reasons he believed? I didn't think so, but the raspberry seed was lodged and I worried it plenty. Just as I believed in reader response and knew that students didn't think things about their reading for no reason, so too did I respect Mark enough to understand that the reasons he felt as he did were real.

I wrote him twice that spring and received no response. Late that summer Kathy and I moved to Utah. I knew I'd never see Mark again, one of the best friends I'd ever made.

In September of 1991 Miles Davis died. Mariana was a senior at Indiana University. Miles's death shocked her. She linked him with Mark and her own childhood. When Mariana was a little girl and our friendship with Mark was just beginning, he introduced me to jazz: Rahsaan Roland Kirk, Charles Mingus, Eddie "Cleanhead" Vinson, Cannonball Adderly, Paul Desmond, Chick Corea, John Coltrane, Thelonius Monk, and Miles Davis—a model for Mark, who had played trumpet in the high school band. One night Mark and I went to Cincinnati's Music Hall to see Miles in concert. Miles wore a jumpsuit and beret, both pink. He wandered about stage, playing his muted trumpet at select moments with the young musicians in his band. I came home with a jazz rhythm in my head that I hummed to Mariana, who wrote out the notes and played the piece on her clarinet.

Mariana's childhood was filled with bebop, blues, and electrified jazz. Every month or so Mark came to the house for supper, music, talk, and, I'm afraid, too much drink. Some of Mariana's childhood was lost forever when Miles Davis died. And his death made her think of Mark, another part of her childhood she'd lost. She wrote to him. Although I don't know what she said, I have no doubt the letter was like her usual ones: impassioned, full-voiced, and urgent.

Eight months after my February dinner with Mark, Mariana's letter reopened the lines of communication, though neither Mark nor I used them. Mariana had reminded us of elemental things: love and friendship, the sacred past and impermanence, and the development that weaves through it all.

One evening a year after Mariana's letter to Mark, I came into the house from walking our schnauzer to find Kathy talking on the telephone. Mark had called. She talked awhile longer, then handed me the phone. Mark's voice— so damn fine to hear.

Mark graduated from the Union Institute with a bachelor's degree in the summer of 1993. He was thirty-five. The previous winter he had applied to Wright State University's prestigious doctor of psychology program. He was not accepted. He had, however, been named an alternate and placed on a waiting list. If anyone deserved a little luck, Kathy and I thought, it was Mark. In late August Mark called to tell me that an opening had come available. He would begin classes in a couple weeks. I wept.

Mark quit his job of eighteen years at Armco Steel, moved to Dayton, and rented an apartment. After he'd settled some, he wrote me a letter:

When I told you about this, I was numb, unable to feel much of anything—mechanically going through the steps I knew I had to take—move, apply for funds, etc. Your reaction helped me to experience the joy vicariously, strangely. But Wednesday last was convocation. During the reading of the oath your boy broke down and sobbed tears of joy, disbelief, relief. I was overwhelmed, overjoyed, happy.

Mark began the most intense study and stimulating experience of his life:

Midterms are over, and I'm passing by the skin of my teeth, as they say. A, C, B, B and P. The C is not passing but it was almost a B and with another project in, it averages to the B range. The B's were both just lovely. Three more weeks of class and the finals. I have three papers due before then. I guess I'll make it. Beginning to feel a bit overwhelmed and yet, OK with being constantly behind. I am not used to struggling to keep up while others get A's. The realization that I am in a very different place than many of them hit me today. That helps; just feel I'll have to approach it a little differently.

As the semester progressed, the pressure and intense study increased:

Classes are tough now. I've spent about seven hours in two nights conceptualizing a case that was presented to us in psychopathology on Tuesday (diagnosing, backing up, relating, cross-checking symptoms and the length and severity of the disorder). It's very interesting stuff and I'm learning more from this exercise, trying to find the right diagnosis in the *Diagnostic and Statistical Manual of Mental Disorder*, than I have yet, elsewhere. But, the fun leaks out of it as I realize I need all 50 points available on this to help cushion potential finals week atrophy. For the first time, this past week, I've wondered what am I doing here. Or, more like, How will I ever keep this up for three years? Then I feel guilty for even having those thoughts. All of this second-guess stuff wastes energy. Energy I'm finding more and more advantageous to conserve.

I hope you both are well. And thanks for listening. It always feels better to write.

It's going to take passion, commitment, and hard, sustained work for Mark to complete the doctor of psychology program at Wright State. I think of the teenage boy who manipulated the school system so he could spend his time as he wanted, who read Salinger's books and as many of his uncollected stories as he could find. I remember the boy who tried writing like Hemingway and who articulated an understanding of literature that startled me and made me aware that students could perceive things beyond the teacher and his manual. Now I know the man. I have complete faith in Mark, in his intellect, his integrity, his courage. He has come so far. He needs now to keep faith in the small steps of workmanlike progress.

One Friday morning in late April 1992, Mariana called me from Italy. "I'm going to try to find Madonna de Grazia tomorrow," she said.

I was relieved. I feared that during her semester at Loyola's Rome Center, she would miss the opportunity to find the birthplace of my father.

"Remember me telling you about my friend here—Jen Ferone? Her grandfather was born in Accera. That's near Naples, too, so we're going to travel together."

"That's great, Mariana."

"Only one problem," she said. "There are four Madonna de Grazias in Italy."

"Pick the one near Naples," I said.

"None of them is near Naples."

My heart sank.

"What should I do, Papa?"

"This makes me think, Mariana. One time I asked Uncle Tony about Madonna de Grazia. He got angry and said that the family wasn't from there. They came from Nola, he said. Go to Nola. I know that's near Naples."

Mariana called Saturday night.

"I found Nola, Papa! Jen and I took the train to Naples, then another one into the country. It's a holiday here, Liberation Day, I think. Everything's closed. But there was a wedding at the church in Accera, so Jen was able to get a photocopy of her grandfather's birth certificate. Then we went to Nola. It was the next stop after Accera."

My heart beat fast. "What was it like?"

"Just how I pictured southern Italy: dusty, hot, and sunny. And you'll never guess what happened, Papa! We were walking around and ran into this street named Madonna delle Grazia."

"So it was a street, not a town?"

"Yeah. And it's Madonna *delle* Grazia."

"The name just got changed a little in the family stories."

"But here's the best part, Papa. We walked down Madonna delle Grazia and we found a church with the same name!"

"This all makes sense now," I said. "Mom said that Daddy talked about all the festivals when he was a child. The church held a festival for everything."

"There were two churches," said Mariana. "There was a more modern one that looked like it was built in the nineteen-fifties. And down the street was this old, decrepit church. It was made of stone, real boxy and simple."

"That's where Grandpa went."

"It had this massive padlocked door. Above it, behind glass or something, was a picture of the Madonna, kind of cracked and faded. She looked down at people who walked through the doorway. I went right up to it."

Mariana told me more about their trip. I listened with tears in my eyes. I pictured my twenty-one-year-old daughter standing on that dusty street in sunny Nola, the same street my father, Uncle Joe, Uncle Tony, and Aunt Filimon had stood on eighty years earlier.

After I hung up the telephone, I was still keyed. I had to talk to somebody, somebody who knew. I called Mom and my cousin Billy, Uncle Joe's son, and told them about Mariana's discovery. Then I called Aunt Filimon, my father's oldest sister. She was eighty-three then and had lived alone for the last five years since Uncle Gigi's death.

"Tommy," she said, "where are you?"

"I'm in Utah, Aunt Filimon."

"Oh, Utah. I thought you were calling to come visit."

"Maybe this summer when I drive through Ohio," I said. "But, Aunt Filimon, the reason I called is because of Mariana."

"Mariana? How is she? She still in college?"

"Yes, still in college. But she's studying in Italy this semester, in Rome."

"In Rome?" said Aunt Filimon. "She like it?"

"She loves it. She's coming home in a few weeks, but today she took a trip."

"Where'd she go, Tommy?"

"She went to the place you were born, Aunt Filimon. She went to Nola."

"Nola? That's a long time ago."

"She found the church where you must have gone—Madonna delle Grazia. The street it's on has the same name."

"That's nice, Tommy. That's nice. I don't remember much. I was a little girl."

"I know one thing you remember."

"No, that's a long time ago. I don't remember anything."

"You remember about coming to America and landing in New York. You remember that man who wanted to buy you."

"Oh, yeah, I remember that. He never saw such curly red hair on a little girl. He told Mom he wanted to buy me. But that happened over here, Tommy—after we come 'cross. I don't remember Nola."

"Tell me the story you do remember, Aunt Filimon. Tell it to me again."

Appendix A

*R*obin Back Fakes *wrote this alternate style personal essay during the* *last month of her senior year of high school.*

DECISION

WHAT

         AM

             I

               GONNA

                   DO?

What place do I have in life?
Didn't someone say to dream your dreams and follow them?
Aren't there pots of gold at the end of the rainbow?

               buildup?
Why does everyone try to   what I'm trying to
        tear down

Decision?

Yes, I'll be this   No, I'll be that

But Mom says . . .   Who cares

More money . . .   in exchange for less happiness

Do what you want   SURE!

You have to make a . . .   Decision

Decision

What a little word with a gigantic question mark

Confusion

Another big question mark

lots of confusion

severe confusion

By whom

Come on you know

No I don't

I'm just— — —confused.

MOM

Don't be a teacher. You'll ruin your whole life. You could make more money ringing up groceries at Kroger. You'll spend your whole life paying for college when you could work about anywhere else for more money.

MONEY   MONEY   MONEY

I'd rather be poor   Watch it, Jill,
                                             you're crying again.

I can remember a time   You were a stone face

when you never cried.   Look at you now!

You're disgusting   I hate you

I don't like you anymore   I want to stay home

LEAVE ME ALONE

MOM

Look at your sister. She went into nursing & in a few years she'll be making more than your dad.

    Look at your brother. He has a good paying job.

Look   at   You

               disgusting you

You won't be anything great.

Just scraping money from paycheck to paycheck
You'll never be of any count.

         COUNT?

   another one of those words with a question mark

     Count on who?   Not her.

       Who can you count on?

DAD

Go ahead & do what you want, Jill. I think you'd make a good teacher. Your mom is a little old-fashioned. Don't let her force you into anything you don't want to do.

   I'm going to bed
   Give me a kiss
      SLURP

   Alone at last

       Freedom

MOM

Jill, you shouldn't be a teacher because they don't make much money & you'll be poor all your life. You need to do

      something that pays   MORE
        so you can have   MORE
       & give your kids   MORE

I guess you're right, Mom.   No, you're not.
                                   Who cares about
                                   money as long as
                                   I have enough to
                                   live on. I'll make
                                   it. If I have kids
                                   I'll give them extra

love because it's
better than

MONEY

There's that word again

I'm not trying to force
you into anything,
but the lady from
Mercy Hospital
called & wants you
to come in for an
interview for the
radiology program.

Do what you want.

Sure. Do what I
want. (More or
less do what YOU
want ME to do)

OK, Mom. I'll call this
week & go in for the
interview. Maybe I
should be an X-ray
technician. It pays
MORE and takes
less time.

SMACK YOURSELF

What happened to your dreams
your gold
your esteem?

YOUR—that means mine

I like that

Tuesday morning. Get up. Get dressed. Hair curled. Suit pressed. Panty hose.
No runners. Smile. Be Impressive. Fake it.

CONFUSION?

INTERVIEW

Questions asked.

Make sure you smile.

Sell yourself

Make them like you.

DO YOU REALLY WANT TO BE HERE?

"How do you feel about having to X-ray
DEAD BODIES?"

OH - - - - - - MYYYY - - - - - - GOD!

Uh-h-h. Well, I think
if I made it through
the first time I'd
be all right.

Sure, Jill, you know
you'd be as stiff as
those dead bodies
you're working with.

"Does the sight of BLOOD scare you?"

Well, I really haven't
been exposed to that
much. I think I'd do OK.

LIAR

"Jill, help me."
"What do you want, Sue?"
"My toe. I slammed it into
the register. Oh God, it hurts so
bad. It's slit down to the middle
of my toenail."
"Uh, uh. I'll get you a
washrag."
"No, come & look at it, Jill,
come & help me."
"Mom, hurry, come fix Sue's
toe."
"Jill!"

"Do you think you'll like our program?"

"Yes." I nodded my head.
"I think I'll like it."

You know you won't
like their program
but your mom will.
That's all that
matters.

Maybe you will.   YOU WON'T

Maybe?
another question mark.

"We'll let you know by April."

Relief
postponed decision

Miami University of Hamilton
another decision (question mark)

What now? expectations
WHAT WOULD YOUR MOTHER THINK?

YOU gotta do what YOU want!

"Who says?"

"Your, MOM, dummy."

"What if you & Jim get married?"
"You just want to teach because he is."

"I'm too young for such seriousness."

Decision?
Question mark

X-ray technician
Teacher
X-ray technician
Teacher
X-ray technician

teacher?

Decision

who knows?

Robin Back Fakes, Senior, Edgewood High School

Note: Robin is now a first-grade teacher at Heritage Elementary School in West Chester, Ohio.

APPENDIX B

The following short story, "Masquerade," by Jennifer Steele Christensen—a college sophomore, is written in a series of present tense crots.

MASQUERADE

Rebecca laughs and sends a stuffed animal flying across the room. "Look at these bruises! Shoot, my poor legs look like yours. What do you do, beat me in my sleep so we'll match? I'm telling my mother!"

We compare battle scars. My wounds are hard-earned on a soccer field, but Rebecca's just appear. "How on earth do your legs get pounded like that?" Neither of us can explain it, so Rebecca cracks jokes.

"They say leukemia causes bruising. Maybe I'm chronic."

"That's not funny," I say.

"Chill out," she orders. Rebecca's grin is wicked. "Hey, the 'Sinead look' is in! A little chemo, and this mop on my head would finally be no problemo!"

"I said it isn't funny, Rebecca. Something could really be wrong."

"Nothing is wrong, you worry wart. Hurry up or we'll be late for school."

It's early evening, and I'm making spaghetti when Rebecca gets home. "I don't like pasta," she says.

"If you're hungry, I can fix something else."

"I'm not."

"You're never hungry anymore. Are you okay? When do you eat?"

"Get off it, Jane," she says. She flips on the television and talks to the screen, "I'm fine."

Rebecca plays racquetball with Amber, our neighbor. Amber calls to chat, and she mentions her P.E. class. "Jane, you really oughta come play with us sometime. Beck and I, we'll kill ya!"

"Maybe I will," I reply, "if you'll go easy on me. I'm a total beginner."

Amber fidgets with small talk for awhile until I finally corner her. "Get to the point, Amber. What's on your mind?"

"I've been wondering about Rebecca. What's up with her and losing so much weight?"

I'm strangely defensive. "Huh? I have no idea what you're talking about."

"Don't tell me you haven't noticed how skinny she is, Jane. I was watching her change clothes today. You can count every damn one of her ribs."

February becomes March, and one day, Rebecca can't move. She collapses while trying to get out of bed, and I skip class to stay with her. Her lips are chalky, her face gray. She looks frail and frightened lying beneath rumpled covers, and I'm afraid she'll break.

I call her mother, and she sighs, "My goodness, you're dramatic. Becky's probably tired, and she needs some rest. Have her soak in the tub awhile, and put her to bed early. As for you, calm down. Don't make such a big deal out of nothing."

"It isn't nothing! Rebecca's been weak and sick and exhausted for three weeks. Can't you see?" I start shaking, and my voice cracks. "She's starving herself, and her body can't take this anymore. Please, listen to me!"

The woman's voice is hard-edged and cold. "Goodbye, Jane."

At midnight, Rebecca is still moaning. I call my mom this time. I'm scared, I don't know what to do, and I panic. "You've got to help me, Mom! Rebecca looks like she's dying!" My mom listens, and I compose myself. "What should I do?"

I make a decision and feign calm confidence as I help Rebecca to my car. She stretches painfully across the back seat and tries to untangle her matted hair. As she rolls over, she gasps and holds her stomach. Neither of us says anything, and I drive carefully. I wish I could suffer for her. I'm stronger than she is, and I wish I could bear the pain so she doesn't have to.

Rebecca stays in Emergency for two hours. An anxious nurse hooks up an IV, and I watch the doctor scratch his chin as he muses, "Dehydration, for sure. Let's get some liquid into this girl . . . Could be appendicitis." He creases his brow, then shakes his head. "No, it's got to be the kidneys." Soon, we move upstairs, and they deaden the pain with Percodan. I stay with Rebecca until she finally falls asleep. At four A.M. I stumble through the parking lot, exhausted.

The next time we see Amber, we're at the grocery store. She glares at us and turns sharply the other way. "What's with her?" I ask.

"We don't talk anymore," Rebecca answers. "She made me mad, and, yes, I'm holding a grudge." Rebecca looks defiant, like a teenager throwing attitude at her mother. I raise an eyebrow, puzzled.

"You won't believe this," Rebecca says. "She accused me of—"

She's interrupted by a husky, sarcastic voice behind us. "Believe it, ladies. I was there, I saw it with my own eyes, and I accused her of throwing up."

We whirl around to face Amber, who looks ready to pounce. I try to ease the tension. "Where'd you come from? Decided you're not too good for us after all?"

Amber laughs dryly. "You're real funny, Jane." She dismisses me and turns to Rebecca, fire in her eyes. "Don't tell me you're fine. Look at how freakin' bony you are! And you think I'll buy, 'I'm fine'? No way!"

"Please," I say, "can we discuss this some place besides Smith's?" I grab Rebecca by the arm. "Come on, let's go home."

Rebecca is preparing for a beauty pageant. I help her practice her talent, and we go shopping for a swimming suit.

"Green," she asks, "or this wild hot pink?"

"Try both," I say.

Rebecca tries the pink. I gasp when she steps from the dressing room. I want to look away, to pretend that nothing's wrong. Instead, I stare.

"What?" she asks. "Why are you looking at me like that?"

I can't answer. I just stare. Rebecca's body is bruised, and her skin is blue-gray. She looks like the starving children in those gut-wrenching Ethiopia videos. I feel sick.

Within a few weeks, Rebecca's kidney infection clears up, and her blood tests come back. The doctor calls. I leave the room.

Later, I ask about their conversation.

"I have some weird protein deficiency," she answers. "He asked about how and what I eat."

"Did you tell him the truth?"

Rebecca's jaw tightens. "What truth?"

"Did you tell him that you don't eat?"

"Jane, I can't eat." She spits the words at me, and I bristle.

"That's baloney. You just won't." The words are cruel, but I keep talking. "Does the attention you get make being sick all the time worth it? Is that why you starve yourself?"

She spins to face me and glares. "You think I like this?" It's an accusation, not a question, and raw fury clouds her eyes. Let me tell you how much I like it," she says, "I love feeling like shit every day. Please, let me feel worse. Let me spend more time in the bathroom. Make my stomach hurt worse. Damn. Give me another laxative!"

"Beck, it's just that I care. I—"

Rebecca grabs the knob and yanks the door open. "Why don't you take your 'just that I care' and leave me the hell alone?"

The door slams behind her. She doesn't hear me say, "Because I'm a coward, Rebecca. Sometimes saving a person means losing a friend, and I can't risk it right now."

"In every damn swim suit competition, I come in last!" Rebecca slams the brush on the dresser. "Last year, I was too fat. I came in eleventh." She yanks her hair into an elastic and glares at the mirror. "This year, I was too thin. And did you hear what that gray-haired bitch said to me? 'Sometimes, girls just work themselves to the literal bone. Are you anorexic, dear?' Hell yes. Just call me Becky Binge-and-Purge."

"Well, look at you, Beck. You've dropped thirty pounds in what, three months?"

Rebecca pulls her shirt over her head and tosses it on her bed. "You sound just like the rest of them," she says. Whose side are you on?"

"Yours."

Jennifer Steele Christensen, Sophomore, Utah State University

APPENDIX C

*T*his is the full text of "The Wooden Pony," the short story that Mariana wrote her senior year of high school out of family stories and her research of Ellis Island and 1914.

THE WOODEN PONY

Felice looked up to find the sun that had just disappeared. He searched the cloud-spotted sky and squinted as the sun slowly peeked back out. He lowered his head and put his *berretto* back on his curly dark red hair.

The mob started to move, inching its way from the ship. Felice tightened his grip on his mama's skirt. Giuseppe led the way, but he held on to mama too. Antonio held on with both hands and whimpered. Felice patted Antonio reassuringly and gazed up at his sleeping sister, Filomena. Her dark red curls bobbed and brushed against Mama's broad shoulders as they moved.

They stopped again. Felice felt he was drowning in the ocean of people. The thick smell engulfed him and he raised his head towards the sky again. He closed his eyes and tried to breathe. He could feel the small wooden pony against his heart and remembered Luca. Tears welled in his eyes but he swallowed them this time. Giuseppe would call him *bambino* again and hit him. Felice wanted to be strong too, and he wanted to be able to stand up to Papa like Giuseppe said he was going to.

Felice remembered how hard Papa hit and how loud he yelled, and he flinched at the thought. He'd stand up to Papa too.

Felice still thought of Luca. As he ran his fingers over the wooden pony Luca had carved for him, he could see his tanned brown face and disheveled thick black hair. Felice could hear his laugh, could see the way his nose wrinkled and eyes squint. Luca had a brown pony with a white splotch over its back. It looked like someone had hung a rug on him. Felice and Luca used to ride the pony all over the pasture that belonged to Luca's father. They rode for hours and Luca's parents laughed and told them that they would break the pony's back from riding him so much. Luca always told them that he didn't seem to mind because he never complained.

He didn't either; he didn't even mind when Felice's dog, Pasquali, chased him and barked incessantly. The pony just kept trotting.

Sometimes Pasquali followed Felice and Luca down to the creek. He swam while they collected clay, and then shook his wetness all over them. They laughed and yelled.

On really hot days in the summer Felice and Luca swam too. They swung on the vines and plunged into the cool refreshing water. They splashed and screamed and then they lay on a big smooth rock and fell asleep in the hypnotizing warmth of the sun.

Felice remembered one Sunday they brought Luca's father to their hidden fort in the wild bushes after church. He had crawled in and sat with them and examined all the things that Felice and Luca had made from the clay they got in the creek. Felice looked intently into his soft, kind, sun-worn face. After Papa left for America, Felice sometimes pretended that Luca's father was his father too.

Felice was yanked out of his thoughts by a violent tug, "Pay attention, *stupido*!"

Felice looked at Giuseppe's red-cheeked face.

"We don't want to lose you, *capisce*?"

Felice shook his head and looked away from Giuseppe. He felt childish; his heart felt heavy and he wanted to go home.

He had watched Luca carve the pony, every stroke and detail. On the bottom he had carved "Luca" and then handed it to Felice, and smiled.

Pangs of hunger awoke Felice. He shifted himself to relieve some of the stiffness. It seemed like it had been forever since someone announced to them in Italian that they would be given sandwiches.

Mama held one of Filomena's hands as she twirled slowly, picking up one black-booted foot at a time. She looked over at Felice, smiled and stuck her tongue in the new gap that made her look like a vampire. Felice smiled. Filomena looked at all her brothers, squealed and buried her head in Mama's stomach.

They all laughed and Mama ran her fingers through Filomena's mass of dark red curls.

Felice had the urge to run up and down the aisles of benches filled with people, shoulder to shoulder, knee to knee. He peered down the aisle of endless bodies. He shifted again, closed his eyes and wondered why they all had come to America.

A silence brought Felice out of his thoughts. He opened his eyes and looked around. He yawned sleepily and glanced at Giuseppe. Felice followed his wide-eyed stare down the aisle. A man with dark skin, dark like chocolate, dipped his hand into a bag and pulled out tiny white squares. He slowly made his way down the row of awestruck people. Felice was frightened by his looks. He studied the man's face and stared wide-eyed at him. He shrank back as the man handed him a white square. Giuseppe took it for him and set it on his lap. The chocolate man passed and systematically pulled the white squares from his bag.

Giuseppe nudged Felice and motioned him to open his white paper square. Felice stared blankly at his lap, then at the chocolate man and then at his brother. Bewildered, he carefully began to open the paper. He couldn't understand why Giuseppe was so calm. Everyone else had resumed their talking, and most people were eating the sandwiches that were inside the white paper squares.

Felice was confused and scared. Did everyone in America look like the chocolate man? He didn't feel hungry anymore. He opened his paper anyway and studied the sandwich.

The bread was as white and as square as the paper that had been wrapped around it. A neat light brown crust trimmed the edges. Felice opened the sandwich; there was an orange-colored thin slice of what he guessed was cheese. He thought it was about as strange as the chocolate man.

"*Formaggio?*" Felice asked Giuseppe.

Giuseppe shook his head and looked at his own sandwich disdainfully.

Felice shrugged his shoulders, placed the top piece of bread on the sandwich and took a bite. The bread stuck to the roof of his mouth like dough. Felice missed home even more. The smell of Mama's home-baked bread, the rough texture of the thick crust surrounding it and the strong smell of Roman cheese. Felice could taste every individual flavor. His mouth watered and he looked longingly at his pitiful American sandwich.

Felice looked over at the chuckling Giuseppe. He held his sandwich up to Felice. "*Benvenuto all' America, eh?*"

Felice laughed, stuffed the rest of the sandwich into his mouth, wiped his hands on his knickers, and grinned at his older brother who did the same.

Felice's whole body ached as he shuffled on to the ferry that went to New York Harbor, holding Mama's skirt tight again. He wanted to run, like he used to on the last day of school. He and Luca would race the whole way home. There was no where to run and his muscles were probably too stiff anyway.

Mama held Antonio. His sleepy angel face hung over her shoulder and watched Felice with closed eyes. Felice looked over at Giuseppe who cradled Filomena in his arms and stared lovingly into her plump face lost in sleep.

Felice squinted at the glare of the sun sinking into the city and plopped himself on to the wood bench. He stared blankly into the dark water. He felt Mama squeeze his hand reassuringly. Felice turned and looked into Mama's kind, tired brown eyes and smiled weakly. He turned back to the water, knowing she understood.

He tried to feel the wooden pony with his chest, but slipped his hand into his pocket to make sure he hadn't lost it during the examinations. Carefully, he took out the little pony and fingered the soft ridges. He ran his finger along its bottom and felt the L-U-C-A. Without looking at it, he placed it gently back in his pocket.

The ferry chugged away from Ellis Island and Felice sighed. He could feel the tears again. He wanted to cry this time; he didn't care what Giuseppe said. Quickly he turned and faced the blue lady with her torch held high, lighting his way in the early dusk. Felice thought of home, Luca, Pasquali, seeing Papa again, the chocolate man, the sandwich and the pony. Felice took a deep breath and looked up again at "*la statua di libertá.*" The tears streamed silently down his face.

Felice looked past Mama and met the gaze of Giuseppe. He watched two tears roll out of his older brother's eyes and make their varied path down his face.

The two brothers stared at each other expressionless.

Felice grinned. "*Bambino,*" he whispered.

They laughed silently together. Felice patted his heart and thought about the future.

Mariana Romano, Senior, Talawanda High School, Oxford, Ohio

APPENDIX D

*S*ix years after Mariana wrote "The Wooden Pony" she was a graduate student at Sarah Lawrence College in the Women's History program. In a course titled Women's Literary Culture her teacher, Lyde Sizer, asked students to write about their passions—to write about something that really mattered to them in their lives. Professor Sizer wanted students to bring voice to their writing, all their writing. This assignment would be a start. The students' essays were photocopied and used as a text in the classroom, along with thirteen other pieces of writing by women.

"My Quest" makes me think about my father's life story through the eyes of my daughter. I think of determination, loss, and triumph. I think of understanding. And, of course, at the bottom of it all, I think of passion, of the topic that has consumed my daughter's interest amid the years she spent writing reports, essay exams, literary exegeses, and term papers. At eighteen Mariana wrote a short story about Felice coming to America as a boy. At twenty-four she wrote an essay—part narrative, part reflection—about that same topic. Through these pieces of writing composed six years apart, you see the evolution of a young woman's mind, her growing self-awareness, her *need to meld analysis and synthesis, emotion and intellect, story and exposition.*

MY QUEST

My grandfather died in a car accident six years before I was born. Although I never knew him, I grew up feeling robbed. I remember crying once when I was seven after Papa and I had talked about his father. Papa told me how he had answered the phone one night when he was fifteen and a nurse from the hospital told him that his father was dead. Papa threw the phone and ran to Grandma's room. My grandfather had been stolen from this world by two young men, drag-racers on a back country road. Red Romano's death, as family legend has it, was a self-sacrifice. My grandfather swerved, saving the lives of his nephew and three friends also in the car. He was crushed by the impact that was concentrated on the driver's side. The boys were convicted of second-degree murder, but they served only eleven months. In one fateful chain of events, I lost a grandfather. I never held my grandfather's hand or listened to his stories or told him that I loved him. Surely, I would have loved him. Everyone loved Red Romano.

I do love my grandfather—the memory of him—constructed by stories and photographs. Grandma, Papa, aunts and uncles made Grandpa Red real for me through their memories. Aunt Filimon still chokes back tears—he was her favorite brother. As a child, I could never listen to enough stories about Grandpa. He was a part of me that was lost. A link of my history that made me Mariana Annette Romano. The uniqueness of my name intricately connected my Italian half with my identity and I wanted to discover its origins.

No one knew all the answers to the questions I asked. Grandpa had been born in Nola, Italy in 1905. In 1914, his mother; his brother, Giuseppe, 11; his brother, Antonio, 7; his sister, Filomena, 5; and he immigrated to the United States to meet their father who had been working there for two years. What had it been like in Italy? What did they do? What did their house look like? What was the passage from Italy like? What happened on Ellis Island? How did they know where to go? What did they bring with them? Why did they come to America? Uncle Joe died when I was two, and no one else could remember nor had anyone ever asked.

I consoled myself with the answers I did have. Grandpa had gone to school in the United States until he was in the fourth grade, all the while helping his father at a brickyard in northeastern Ohio. During the late 1920s and early 1930s, he owned a gas station. In 1935 he met and fell in love with my grandma, ten years his junior. They were married in October. He already owned a beer and wine tavern. By 1941 he had made enough money to buy the remaining liquor license in town and take out a loan to build a bar and two bowling alleys with an apartment above. The business, Red's Nite Club, was his life, and with his official citizenship papers, he was fully American. This had been his dream.

He wanted to be American, not Italian. His children would be American. Grandpa refused to eat polenta or drink red wine—to him it was the staple of peasants. His children did not learn to speak Italian. Papa had never asked why. Grandpa Red never mentioned his past, and no one asked. But the question, "why?" burned inside of me.

My obsession with my Italian heritage was apparent as early as the fourth grade. The class did "country reports" and I chose Italy. I constantly interviewed my relatives and relished any new information I could gather from their stories. I constructed my own memory of Grandpa Red. He was a good man, who was proud to be an American. He worked hard, liked to gamble, and enjoyed vacationing in Florida. Red was a man who lived in the present, he did not talk of the past. He lived in the world of his bar, friends, and family from 1941–1964. When he died, his history died with him. Mine died, too.

This void—the loss and sadness—drove me to attempt to discover my history. Although I was not aware of the origins of this motivation, it was a continuous process. Again the desire to capture my identity resurfaced, inspiring me as a senior in high school to write a short story that recreated my grandfather's immigration experience. For three months I researched, recalled stories, and imagined what life would have been like for a nine year-old in Italy. Grandpa Red became Felice, his Italian birth name. I tried to imagine Felice leaving his home, grandparents, and friends. He and his family left Italy for America to join his drunken father who abused them all. The more I wrote, the more questions I had.

I never consciously thought that in the attempt to answer those questions I sought to realize my own identity. I went to Indiana University and majored in journalism and English without a thought. I studied Italian and during my sophomore year I decided that I would go to Rome the second semester of my junior year—never realizing that I was on a quest.

Sophomore year ended and I stayed in Bloomington to take summer classes. "Introduction to Biology" and "English Literature Before 1600" filled my summer. Unconscious of my ideas and interests, I reveled in the time of knights and monsters. Stories intrigued me. I argued everything from an historical point of view. When my best friend, Ellen, and I talked about God, I historicized religion. When we discussed Marx, I countered the possibility of true-Marxism with the long history of competing nationalism. Finally in exasperation Ellen suggested that I change my major to history. I had never thought about it. So I dropped English and added history. But I still did not connect my insatiable appetite for the past with my own agenda. I threw myself into European history and prepared to study in Italy.

Italy opened my eyes. Being Mariana Annette Romano had more meaning. I saw frescoes that had been painted in the thirteenth century, and buildings built before the age of Christianity and Illuminations dedicated to God from the height of the Renaissance. Everything around me was intricately connected to history and the modern world—a part of the foundation. My roots were there, too.

One day in April I took a train to Naples and then another to Nola, a few miles east. It was exactly how I imagined southern Italy—hot, dirty, and old. On the train station map, I located my grandfather's parish, Madonna Delle Grazia. I meandered through the streets until I came upon an old locked up church with a cracked painting of the Madonna gazing down at those below. This place had been the beginning for my grandfather. Felice's eyes had scanned the countryside, had taken in the monastery on the hill, the vineyard and the church that I was seeing. Weeping, I sat on the church steps and imagined Felice grudgingly going to church on a Sunday he would rather have played. Felice, Grandpa Red, had never been, so I was told, very religious.

Although not many questions were answered on that trip, I came to an historical self-consciousness. I had taken Italian, gone to Italy, and changed my major to history to connect myself with my lost past. Tears still come whenever I discover a link to my heritage. It is why I study history and immigration and immigrants. It is who I am and a way to solve the mystery that died with my grandfather. Sometimes I think he is with me—looking over my shoulder as I write—at those moments I feel complete.

APPENDIX E

COMUNE DI NOLA

CERTIFICATO DI *Nascita*

L'Uffiziale dello Stato Civile del Comune suddetto certifica che riscontrati i registri di *Nascita* dell'anno *1905* all'atto segnato col numero d'ordine *51* risulta che *nel giorno ventitre Gennaio millenove centocinque nacque in Nola Romano Felice da Raffaele e da Basile Dulcixia, legittimi coniugi*

A richiesta del _____

si rilascia il presente gratis ed in carta libera per uso *d'Savaleo*

Nola li *26 gennaio* 192*8* (Anno VI). *E.F.)*

L'Ufficiale dello Stato Civile

Works Cited

An American Time Capsule. 1969. Directed by Charles Braverman. Santa Monica, CA: Pyramid Film & Video.

Berthoff, Ann E. 1987. "Dialectical Notebooks and the Audit of Meaning." In *The Journal Book*, edited by Toby Fulwiler. Portsmouth, NH: Boynton/ Cook.

Braverman's Condensed Cream of Beatles. 1973. Directed by Charles Braverman. Santa Monica, CA: Pyramid Film & Video.

Britton, James. 1993. *Language and Learning*. 2d ed. Portsmouth, NH: Boynton/Cook. 1970. Original edition, London: Allen Lane, The Penguin Press.

Bruner, Jerome. 1986. *Actual Minds, Possible Worlds*. Cambridge, MA: Harvard University Press.

Burroway, Janet. 1992. *Writing Fiction: A Guide to Narrative Craft*, 3d ed., p. 297. New York: HarperCollins.

Butler, Octavia. 1979. *Kindred*. Boston: Beacon Press.

Calkins, Lucy McCormick. 1986. *The Art of Teaching Writing*. Portsmouth, NH: Heinemann.

Coles, Robert. 1989. *The Call of Stories: Teaching and the Moral Imagination*. Boston: Houghton Mifflin.

Collier, James Lincoln. 1978. *The Making of Jazz: A Comprehensive History*. Boston: Houghton Mifflin.

Crow Dog, Mary, with Richard Erdoes. 1990. *Lakota Woman*. New York: HarperCollins.

Csikszentmihalyi, Mihaly. 1990. *Flow: The Psychology of Optimal Experience*. New York: Harper & Row.

Cunningham, Linda. 1994. "Dakota Grain: Writing a Multi-Genre Paper." In *Workshop 6,* edited by Maureen Barbieri and Linda Rief. Portsmouth, NH: Heinemann.

DeLawter, Jayne. 1992. "Teaching Literature: From Clerk To Explorer." In *Literature Instruction: A Focus on Student Response*, edited by Judith Langer. Urbana, IL: NCTE.

Dillard, Annie. 1989. *The Writing Life*. New York: Harper & Row.

Dos Passos, John. [1937] 1961. *The Big Money*. New York: Washington Square Press.

Dunning, Stephen, and William Stafford. 1992. *Getting the Knack*. Urbana, IL: NCTE.

Elbow, Peter. 1993. "Ranking, Evaluating, and Liking: Sorting Out Three Forms of Judgment." *College English* 55 (February): 187-206.

———. 1990. *What Is English?* Urbana, IL: NCTE.

Emerson, Ralph Waldo [1834] 1966. "Self-Reliance." In *The Literature of the United States*, edited by Walter Blair et al. 3d ed, vol. 1, pp. 1094-1112, Chicago: Scott, Foresman.

Evans, David Allan. 1983. "Bullfrogs." In *Poetspeak*, edited by Paul Janeczko, p. 45. New York: Collier Books.

Fader, Daniel N., and Elton B. McNeil. 1966. *Hooked on Books: Program and Proof*. New York: Berkley Medallion.

Fletcher, Ralph. 1991. *Walking Trees: Teaching Teachers in the New York City Schools*. Portsmouth, NH: Heinemann.

Gallo, Don, ed. 1992. *Authors' Insights: Turning Teenagers into Readers and Writers*. Portsmouth, NH: Boynton/Cook.

The Godfather, Part II. 1974. Directed by Francis Ford Coppola. Paramount.

Godwin, Gail. "Becoming a Writer." 1980. In *The Writer and Her Work*, edited by Janet Sternburg. New York: W. W. Norton.

Goldberg, Natalie. 1993. *The Long Quiet Highway: Waking Up in America*. New York: Bantam.

Goodladd, Jonathon. 1984. *A Place Called School*. New York: McGraw-Hill.

Hageman, Elizabeth. 1990. Personal correspondence. May.

Heard, Georgia. 1989. *For the Good of the Earth and Sun: Teaching Poetry*. Portsmouth, NH: Heinemann.

Hemingway, Ernest. 1972. *The Nick Adams Stories*. New York: Charles Scribner's Sons.

———. 1938. *The Short Stories of Ernest Hemingway*. New York: Charles Scribner's Sons.

———. 1929. *A Farewell To Arms*. New York: Charles Scribner's Sons.

Henderson, David. 1983. *The Life of Jimi Hendrix: 'Scuse Me While I Kiss the Sky*. New York: Bantam.

Jaeger, Lowell. 1988. *War on War*. Logan, UT: Utah State University Press.

Janeczko, Paul, ed. 1983. *Poetspeak*. New York: Collier.

John-Steiner, Vera. 1985. *Notebooks of the Mind: Explorations of Thinking*. New York: Harper & Row.

Johnson, David. 1990. *Word Weaving*. Urbana, IL: NCTE.

Kaplan, Justin. 1980. *Walt Whitman: A Life*. New York: Bantam.

Kingsolver, Barbara. 1993. *Pigs in Heaven*. New York: HarperCollins.

Langer, Judith A. 1992. "Rethinking Literature Instruction." In *Literature Instruction: A Focus on Student Response*, edited by Judith A. Langer. Urbana, IL: NCTE.

LeFevre, Karen Burke. 1987. *Invention as a Social Act*. Carbondale: Southern Illinois University Press.

Lueders, Edward. 1969. "Your Poem, Man." In *Some Haystacks Don't Even Have Any Needle*. Glenview, IL: Scott, Foresman.

Mayher, John. 1990. *Uncommon Sense*. Portsmouth, NH: Boynton/Cook.

Murray, Donald. 1993. "Surviving the Theology of Process." Individual presentation at the fall conference of the National Council of Teachers of English, November 21. Pittsburgh, PA.

———. 1990a. "Teaching the Other Self: The Writer's First Reader." In *To Compose*, 2d ed., edited by Thomas Newkirk. Portsmouth, NH: Heinemann.

———. 1990b. *Shoptalk: Learning to Write with Writers*. Portsmouth, NH: Heinemann.

———. 1985. *A Writer Teaches Writing*, 2d ed. Boston: Houghton Mifflin.

———. 1984. *Write To Learn*. New York: Holt, Rinehart & Winston.

Newkirk, Thomas. 1990a. "The Writing Process—Visions and Revisions."
Introduction to *To Compose*, edited by Thomas Newkirk. Portsmouth,
NH: Heinemann.

———. 1990b. "Looking For Trouble: A Way to Unmask Our Reading." In
To Compose, edited by Thomas Newkirk. Portsmouth, NH: Heinemann.

———. 1989. *More Than Stories: The Range of Children's Writing*. Portsmouth,
NH: Heinemann.

O'Brien, Tim. 1990. *The Things They Carried*. New York: Penguin Books.

Oliver, Mary. 1990. *House of Light*. Boston: Beacon Press.

Ondaatje, Michael. 1984. *The Collected Works of Billy the Kid*. New York:
Penguin. 1970. Original edition, Toronto: House of Anansi Press.

Piercy, Marge. 1969. *Hard Loving*. Middletown, CT: Wesleyan University
Press.

Probst, Robert E. 1992. "Five Kinds of Literacy Knowing." In *Literature
Instruction: A Focus on Student Response*, edited by Judith Langer.
Urbana, IL: NCTE.

Rief, Linda. 1991. *Seeking Diversity: Language Arts with Adolescents*.
Portsmouth, NH: Heinemann.

Romano, Tom. 1993. "Meeting Writers' Needs with Help from Two New
Guides." *English Journal* 82 (April): 93-95.

———. 1992a. "Don Gallo Presents *Authors' Insights* on Teaching
Literature." *English Journal* 81 (November): 96–97.

———. 1992b. "Multigenre Research: One College Senior." In *Portfolio
Portraits*, edited by Donald Graves and Bonnie Sunstein. Portsmouth, NH:
Heinemann.

———. 1978. "Censorship and the Student Voice." *English Journal* 67
(May): 40-42.

———. 1987. *Clearing the Way: Working with Teenage Writers*.
Portsmouth, NH: Heinemann.

Rose, Mike. 1989. *Lives on the Boundary: The Struggle and Achievement
of America's Underprepared*. New York: The Free Press.

Rosenblatt, Louise. 1978. *The Reader, the Text, the Poem: The Transactional
Theory of Reader Response*. Carbondale, IL: Southern Illinois
University Press.

———. 1938. *Literature as Exploration*. New York: Appleton-Century.

Rule, Rebecca, and Susan Wheeler. 1993. *Creating the Story: Guides for Writers*. Portsmouth, NH: Heinemann.

Saki (H. H. Munro). [1930] 1984. "The Open Window." In *Literature: Blue Level*, edited by David W. Foote and Brenda Pierce Perkins. Evanston, IL: McDougal, Littel.

Salinger, J. D. 1964. *Nine Stories*. New York: Bantam.

Shannon, Patrick. 1989. *Broken Promises: Reading Instruction in Twentieth-Century America*. Granby, MA: Bergin & Garvey.

Stafford, William. 1986. *You Must Revise Your Life*. Ann Arbor: University of Michigan Press.

Stafford, William, and Stephen Dunning. 1992. *Getting the Knack*. Urbana, IL: NCTE

Steinbeck, John. [1939] 1946. *The Grapes of Wrath*. New York: Bantam.

Tannenbaum, Philip G. 1984. "Poem." In *Literature: Blue Level*, edited by David W. Foote and Brenda Pierce Perkins. Evanston, IL: McDougal, Littel.

Thoreau, Henry David. [1849] 1962. "Civil Disobedience." In *Walden and Other Writings*, edited by Joseph Wood Krutch. New York: Bantam.

Vinson, Eddie "Cleanhead," [1969] 1993. *Kidney Stew Is Fine*. Delmark Records compact disk. Recorded March 28, 1969 at Studio Pathe Marconi, Paris.

Wainwright, Loudon III. 1993. *Career Moves*. Virgin Records LTD (compact disk). Issued under exclusive license in the United States by Charisma Records America. Recorded live at The Bottom Line, New York City, January 8, 1993.

Weathers, Winston. 1980. *An Alternate Style: Options in Composition*. Rochelle Park, NJ: Hayden Book Company. Distributed by Heinemann, Portsmouth, NH. OP.

Whitman, Walt. [1855] 1981. *Leaves of Grass*. Franklin Center, PA: The Franklin Library.

Why Man Creates. 1968. Directed by Saul Bass. Santa Monica, CA: Pyramid Film & Video.

Wolfe, Tom. [1979] 1980. *The Right Stuff*. New York: Bantam.

Wright, Richard. [1937] 1966. *Black Boy*. New York: Harper & Row.

ACKNOWLEDGMENTS

$\mathcal{B}$ook writing involves many. I am grateful to these people who were involved in the making of *Writing With Passion*:

Acquisitions editor Dawn Boyer was enthusiastic about this book when it was only a prospectus. Our last conferences together before she left Heinemann convinced me to write a prolog and helped me establish the final order of the chapters.

Production editor Renée Nicholls was precise, punctual, witty, and talented. Those qualities and her excellent communicative skills assured me that my book and I were in the hands of a professional.

Copy editor Alan Huisman helped me write more accurately and fluently than I can on my own, even though while proofreading I grew testy after the third fused participle.

Joni Doherty designed an elegant interior for the book and Judy Arisman, using a photograph, circa 1915, and my father's birth certificate, created a cover design that knocked me out.

Marketing manager Raymond Coutu got more information out of me than I knew I had.

Publishing director Toby Gordon: Had Hamlet known Toby he might very well have said, "Synergy, thy name is Gordon." Toby is a master of exploratory talk. Such talk over the telephone with her led me to think of using the cover photograph of my father and his brothers.

Ruth Hubbard of Lewis and Clark College and Steve Zemelman of National Louis University read my book prospectus and helped me see where to rearrange and where to omit tentative chapters. After I read their responses, I was eager to write, the bottom line, I think, for those who respond to the writing of others.

Pamela Sourelis responded to the entire manuscript with such detail that I thought about things from word choice to organization and made movement from that thinking.

These people from Utah State University were indispensable:

Bill Strong—incisive writer, expert English educator—responded to my writing with intelligence and sensitivity, sent me unfailing wishes of godspeed, and urged me just at the right time to "spend it all."

Will Pitkin, friend, wit, colleague, humanist, scholar, and gardener, is the best word-man I know.

My department head, Jeff Smitten, wise, flexible, and fearless, arranged a reduced teaching load for me so that I had time to write this book.

Christine Hult, my assistant department head, offered me encouragement and these words that caused me to step back and write a better prospectus: "Don't rush this, Tom. The reviewer first impressions are crucial."

Steve Siporin, friend and folklorist, helped me get the Italian right.

Anne Shifrer superbly combines intellect, good taste, and humor both outrageous and subtle. She sees to it that I know the latest about Mary Oliver.

Bobbie Stearman passes on to me good novels, tips about teaching fiction writing, and information about schnauzers.

Ken Brewer, poet, essayist, a writing teacher genuine and student-centered, reminds me to write about the "tough stuff."

My sometime poetry group—Alexa West, Veneta Nielsen, George Emert, and Ken Brewer: their reading and response—their very presence, in fact—caused me to write some poems that never would have existed and to revive dormant near-poems into completion.

English education student teachers winter and spring quarters of 1994 read my words and showed me home movies of their reading: Melanie Morris, Mary Sullivan, Shanna Jensen, Tanna Nixon, Chris Willis, Clel Robinson, Deanna Crask-Stone, Kristin Burt, Christie Hansen, and Julie Curran Hill.

Stacie Hansen, "the gal who reads on the sofa in the hallway," found "marinate."

Pam Bradshaw of Salt Lake City told me about "romping on the page."

Peggy Cooper and Ann Friedli, English department secretaries, photocopied the manuscript and helped me locate students.

I further thank these friends, mentors, and relatives (so glad am I they've been in my life):

Don Graves for his long influence on my thinking and for the Reading and Writing Seminar he taught in 1989/90 at the University of New Hampshire. In that course I pursued my literate passions . . . and it counted.

Bonnie Sunstein of the University of Iowa—my former UNH "academic sibling," as she puts it—for her expert editorial advice, keen ability to explain to me what I'm doing, and timely "You oughta" that spurred me to write the prospectus for this book.

Danling Fu of Towson State University for asking a simple question that led me to clarify Mark's passionate relationship with literature.

Lyde Sizer of Sarah Lawrence College for inspiring and mentoring Mariana.

John Gaughan of Lockland High School in Cincinnati for continued friendship, repsonse, and encouragement.

Nancie Atwell of the Center for Teaching and Learning at Edgecomb, Maine, for sound business council with a touch of chutzpa.

These important people for extending me repeated opportunities to work with teachers: Maura Eagle of Brockport, New York; Mike Ford of Wayne-Finger Lakes BOCES in New York; Carol Santa of School District Number 5 in Kalispell, Montana; Janet Ziegler, Mary Fuller, Max Morenberg, and Don Daiker of the Ohio Writing Project in Oxford, Ohio; and Tom Newkirk, director of the University of New Hampshire Summer Writing Program in Durham and *consigliére* of the first order.

Phyllis Neumann, former English department head at Edgewood High School in Trenton, Ohio, for helping me remember Mark and jogging my memory of the catastrophic fire in 1977 at the Beverly Hills Supper Club in Southgate, Kentucky.

Gene Smith, my former principal at Edgewood High School, for his specialty of clearing the way.

Mary Creekbaum, Rachel Gomia Koeller, Holly Schultheis, and Marcia Brown for helping me contact former Edgewood High School students.

Joe and Ruth Chiavari for information about Uncle Gigi and Aunt Filimon. My cousin, Bill Romano; my uncle, Tony Romano, my aunts, Filimon Romano Chiavari and Lucy Romano Cinson, for information about the cover photograph.

For their faith, fearlessness, and willingness to speak the rude truth: my former students at Edgewood High School in Trenton, Ohio, and at Utah State University in Logan, also teachers who wrote in my extension classes in Salt Lake City, and teachers from various parts of the United States and Canada who worked with me in workshops.

Mark Shadle of Eastern Oregon State University for pointing me toward the roots of blues and Diane Ackerman's *A Natural History of the Senses* and taking me to 10 Depot Street for food, drink, and good conversation.

Terry Moher of Exeter High School, friend from the New Hampshire Writing Program, for telling me that *passion* had to be in the title.

Teri and Will Pitkin and Carol and Bill Strong for superb dinners, sustaining laughter, and enough camaraderie to get anyone through a northern Utah winter.

John and Kathy Gaughan and their daughters, Amy and Kelly—"the mine-broke-off girls"—for steadfast friendship and unsurpassed hospitality.

Don and Minnie Mae Murray for their enduring friendship.

Mae G. Carnahan, my mother, for her love, honesty, and wonderful laugh.

Mariana Romano for insight and patience and the most passionate voice I know.

Kathy Romano, who—when we were both twenty-one years old in 1970—wrote to me on the inside of *The Short Stories of Ernest Hemingway*, "I hope you enjoy this book. May you write books of your own one day."

I did, Kath, and have. You cleared the way.

CREDITS

Credits